THE BEST PARTY GAMES

D1137305

JOSEPH EDMUNDSON

THE BEST PARTY GAMES

A PAN ORIGINAL

Illustrated by
JUDITH VALPY
and
PATRICIA MEARES

PAN BOOKS LTD : LONDON

The Pan Book of Party Games was first published
1958 by Pan Books Ltd.

The Second Pan Book of Party Games was first published
1963 by Pan Books Ltd.

This combined and revised edition published
1968 by Pan Books Ltd.,
33 Tothill Street, London, S.W.1

330 02188 5

2nd Printing 1969

*Printed in Great Britain by
Richard Clay (The Chaucer Press), Ltd.,
Bungay, Suffolk*

FOREWORD

In this *The Best Party Games* I have taken what I consider to be the best games and activities from *The Pan Book of Party Games* and *The Second Pan Book of Party Games* along with a few new additions so that they are all available in one compact volume.

Selection has not been easy; in general I have eliminated games which required considerable preparation, or which, after consideration, I felt had an unnecessary element of danger for children, e.g. games using sharp instruments such as needles or knives, or those in which naked lights were involved. I have also taken out some games which were simply variations of others.

J.E. 1968

CONTENTS

SECTION ONE
GIVING A PARTY

Generally speaking, the more spontaneous and carefree a party appears to a guest, the better it will be enjoyed. To achieve this spontaneity requires considerable and careful preparation beforehand – otherwise there will be awkward gaps when groups of children and adults will be left doing nothing at all. And the result might well be boredom – and your reputation as a party giver will be lost.

No hard-and-fast rules can be given on the way to run a party; much will depend upon the occasion, the age of those invited, and the amount of space available. Here, however, are some general rules which can be used for guidance.

CHILDREN'S PARTIES

With children up to the age of five there is no need to work out an elaborate programme at all. With very young children of three or four, all that is necessary is to provide them with your own children's toys and let them play among themselves for most of the time. At moments when they seem to be losing interest, or minor squabbles break out (as they will), gather them all together and play a simple game such as *Ring a ring o' Roses*, *Musical Bumps*, or *Oranges and Lemons*. Peace and enjoyment will quickly be restored – then allow them to play on their own again. At this young age, perhaps the most important things to them are the provision of a good tea with the inevitable jelly and ice-cream, plus a balloon and a small present to take home – even if it is only a small bag of sweets or a bar of chocolate.

It is also a good idea to present small prizes to the winners of the simple games, but the prizes should be trivial ones and the giving should not be overdone. (Even at this young age the born 'pot-hunter' will be discovered.)

Try also to ensure that when prizes are given it is not always the same child who gets them. This may need a little judicious cheating on your part in spotting winners but, in the interests of harmony and lots of peace and goodwill, it is well worth while.

Among the children invited there will always be the 'little horror' who wants to bounce on furniture or fight with the others, and the shy young boy or girl who shows the greatest reluctance to play anything at all.

With the first-named shocker one must exercise considerable tact and diplomacy and try to guide his high spirits (?) into the organized channels of some game or task which will stop him from breaking up your home. The shy child should be coaxed to take part in the games, but if coaxing is of little avail, let him (or her) enjoy himself in his own way. If too much pressure is put on such a child, tears will almost certainly flow.

With children from about six to nine years of age quite a number of games can and should be played, and included among these can be simple writing ones. These should be interspersed between the more active running or chasing games, not only as a simple disciplinary measure but also to avoid your own nerves becoming completely frayed.

These quieter games are also essential for a short period after the meal – otherwise someone is bound to be sick!

Between the ages of nine and fifteen, more and more general organization will become necessary, though many of the games will almost certainly be suggested and even organized by the children themselves; they will by this time have a fair repertoire of activities gained from previous parties and from school experience.

There will be a *slightly* lessened desire to rush madly about all the time and a greater willingness, particularly among the girls, to play 'brainy' games involving pencil and paper.

There will be, however, a growing tendency to self-consciousness and awkwardness among some of the children, due to the onset of adolescence; there will also be a growing desire for 'mixed' games in which boy partners girl. Games of this nature should therefore figure quite prominently in any programme you draw up: you must, however, use all your tact and diplomacy to prevent too much of the 'boy meets girl' atmosphere by including games which involve the mixing of partners.

TEENAGE PARTIES

In parties for young people of this often difficult age, one must accept the fact that boy has probably met girl, but at the same time the party must be planned so that boy meets other girl and girl meets other boy. In other words, there must be games which involve partners of the young people's own choice and games in which partners are changed. 'Pop' music also plays an important part in the lives of modern teenagers, and some attempt must be made to cater for it, even if only by the introduction of some musical games in which the latest type of music is played or sung.

Care must also be taken in the selection of games, particularly games which might involve some boy or girl looking foolish. Generally, it is advisable to avoid this type of game or to reduce the number to an absolute minimum. Pencil and paper games can be played to advantage as well as the more sophisticated type of games such as *Murder* (see page 131), *The Horror Game* (page 145), and games derived from popular radio or television programmes such as 'Twenty Questions' or 'University Challenge'.

Treasure hunts too, providing the clues match the general intelligence of the players, can be very popular, particularly if the players work with partners of their own choice.

The great danger in a teenage party is to allow any overemphasis of the 'boy *has* met girl' to develop. There are many young people at this age who are prepared to enjoy themselves at a party merely by sitting in a corner holding hands and looking into someone's eyes.

This must be stopped, otherwise some members of the party are liable to be embarrassed. Tact and diplomacy must be used to prevent it developing too much; perhaps the best way is publicly to ignore it but at the same time gently, light-heartedly, if needs be, involve the pair in some active game where it is impossible to hold the same person's hand or look into the same beautiful eyes all the time.

ADULT PARTIES

Much will depend upon the characters of the guests invited, but, in general, normal adults are quite prepared to enjoy the most foolish games.

It is essential, however, to start with a few 'mixers' (see pages 66–74), in order to thaw out the traditional reserve of so many adults. In most parties there will be the almost inevitable 'life and soul of the party'. This person, usually a male, can be a mixed blessing. If he is allowed a completely free hand he can well ruin all your carefully thought-out schemes, and before you know where you are it is *his* party and not yours, and sometimes (unfortunately) his party is quite a good one.

The only effective way to deal with this type is to enlist his aid in running your party and give him as much to do as possible. A tactful 'Will you help me with this game, Charlie?' or 'Charles, dear, will you run *Murder* for me, you do it *so* well?' and he will almost literally eat out of your hand.

As with teenagers, the games for adults must be mixed to include the more riotous and the quieter games. Where old people are present ('Grandma always likes to come, you know') care must be taken to see that they, too, are kept amused. Some old people are quite prepared to sit, watch, and laugh at the antics of their sons and daughters, but if there is room it is often advisable to arrange a quiet game of cards for those who can no longer rush about.

One word of warning about card games. There are many people who have strong and sincere objections to playing card games of any kind, and most particularly those where there is money (however small) at stake. Their objections must always be respected – in no circumstances try to press them into doing something they have no desire to do. This same rule, of course, must be applied to other games, particularly those where there is the possibility of someone either having to make a fool of themselves or being made to look a little foolish by others.

Try to persuade your guests to participate in the most excellent games you have arranged for their hilarious amusement – but in no circumstances try to batter, bully, or bludgeon a reluctant guest into doing something against his will.

If you have invited someone who won't do anything, the ultimate remedy is always in your hands. Don't invite him again. He probably wouldn't come, anyway – but don't take the risk.

In the following pages you will find a fairly wide selection of games suitable for all ages and also for special occasions, such as wet days at the seaside when the children are often bored and everyone is wishing they hadn't come, for the long car journey and for that one fine summer day when you go for a picnic or down to the beach.

There are, of course, many more games which you may know and which are not included here, but some of those that are in this book may well be new to you – and, perhaps, can be adapted, or may give you an idea for another game of your own invention which will be just the thing for Willie's birthday party.

SECTION TWO

ESSENTIAL PARTY EQUIPMENT

Certain small items of equipment should be available in every house where a party is to be held. Nothing can be more disruptive to the flow and continuity of a party than to find, at the crucial moment, that there is no scribbling paper, or there aren't enough pencils to go round. It is almost inevitable, too, that when such crises arrive it is either too late to go to the shop around the corner or (equally inevitable) it is early closing day.

By the invitations sent out and the replies received, you will have an approximate idea of the number of guests who should arrive. With children's parties, the numbers are liable to be slightly less than anticipated, as colds, mumps, chicken pox, and other illnesses are apt to play last-minute havoc with numbers.

With adult parties, the numbers may well be more than anticipated, as unexpected guests (and often unwilling ones) are apt to come along with the guests you hadn't really wanted to invite, anyway. ('Charlie popped in just as I was leaving, so I insisted he came; I said you'd be only too delighted.')

The following items of small equipment are therefore suggested as being indispensable, and should be obtained well beforehand.

FOR CHILDREN'S PARTIES

Balloons: one per child plus 100 per cent reserve for use in games and to replace the ones which burst just as the child is about to leave for home. With twenty guests, have not less than forty balloons.

Pencils: one per guest plus at least six spare ones. It is a

14

good plan to have a special box of party pencils. This can be started off by buying a dozen or so good pencils and cutting them in half. Most modern pencil manufacturers make pencils which are very difficult to break (the lead is bonded to the wood) and will stand any amount of rough usage.

The stock of pencils can be kept up by putting in the box all household or family pencils which are less than three to four inches in length.

Pencil Sharpeners: have at least two in the box. Buy two good ones; they will not only last longer but will also sharpen the pencils more efficiently and will thus save money by reducing sharpening breakages to the minimum.

Small Scribbling Pads: one per guest plus half a dozen spares. These can be obtained very cheaply at the local multiple stores, and will last for two or three parties at least.

A Supply of Paper Handkerchiefs: some child is almost certain to have forgotten or lost his or her handkerchief. They are also useful for certain games.

A Box of Drinking Straws (preferably plastic ones): these can be used in certain games (*Blow Football*, for example), as well as for their designed purpose.

Large Safety Pins: apart from their use in certain games, these are useful for immediately preserving the dignity of some young man who sheds a button during the excitement of a more boisterous game.

Table-Tennis Balls: indispensable for a number of games. Have at least half a dozen. Buy cheap ones, not the rather expensive balls used in first-class table-tennis circles.

Small Balls: old tennis balls will do admirably. If you wish, a small number of perforated plastic balls, which may be thrown about a room with no fear of damage to your guests or your best pictures, can be bought with advantage and used solely for parties.

Items of Spare Clothing: know where you can put your hands immediately on a pair of old knickers or underpants. Accidents will happen!

Packs of Cards: have two or three packs available. They can be used for a variety of games (see *Throwing Games*, pages 94–101). One or more packs of 'Happy Families' are also invaluable.

First Aid Equipment: this is a 'must' and should never be forgotten or neglected. Some child is almost certain to bump, bruise, or cut himself.

A Supply of Small Prizes: in no circumstances should these be expensive, or the inevitable pot-hunter will be disclosed. Bars of chocolate, small packets of sweets, pencils, thimbles, and such-like items are all that are necessary. It is also advisable not to distribute prizes too freely, certainly not for every competitive game, otherwise some children will soon be competing for the prize and not for the fun of the thing.

Individual Items: these may be needed for specific games you intend to introduce into your programme. Such items may include things like waste-paper baskets, bowls (for games such as *Duck Apple*), string, rope, clothes pegs, and so on. It is imperative that they should be immediately at hand when required and that you or someone else should not have to go hunting for them. It is a good idea to put all these items (and the others as well) into a clothes basket so that they are all together right from the beginning of the party.

ADULT PARTIES

Most of the items enumerated above (except spare clothing) will also be required for adult parties. Gramophone records may also be needed, particularly at parties catering for teen-agers. A greater stress is liable to be placed on the individual items for special games: newspapers, sheets of brown paper, and so on are almost certain to be required. To ensure that everything is available, *write down* the games you intend to introduce and by the side of them list the items of equipment which may be needed. Get these together not later than the day before the party (you will almost certainly be much too busy with food on the day itself) and, as with children's parties, have them immediately available for use when needed.

SECTION THREE
PARTIES FOR SPECIAL OCCASIONS

Most parties centre round special occasions such as birthdays, house warmings, wedding anniversaries, or are run on certain festival days such as Christmas, New Year's Eve, St Valentine's Day, Twelfth Night, and Guy Fawkes' Night. There are, of course, people who like giving parties just for the sheer fun of it and are even prepared to throw a party for the illogical reason that there is no excuse for having a party.

On all these occasions, the game content of the party can be much the same and a selection of suitable activities can be obtained from this book.

What these games cannot always give you is 'atmosphere' to suit the occasion. This 'atmosphere' can, however, often be obtained by paying special attention to such things as the nature of the invitation, by appropriate decorations, and even by the provision of special foods or dishes which are traditional for the occasion or time of year.

Below are given some notes for these occasions.

CHRISTMAS

The normal Christmas decorations, are, of course, holly and mistletoe with the added colour provided by Christmas cards. In the past it has been customary to arrange the cards as artistically as possible on the tops of sideboards and bookcases and on top of the fireplace.

As an alternative, however, why not try pinning some of them to the curtains or hanging them on the wall like streamers. The easiest way to do this is by means of lengths of Sellotape (Fig 1 (a)).

17

Another most effective decoration, using Christmas cards, can be made by covering a child's wooden hoop with ribbon or crêpe paper and then pinning the cards around it (Fig 1 (b)).

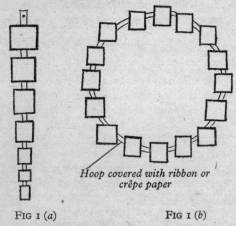

Hoop covered with ribbon or crêpe paper

FIG 1 (a)   FIG 1 (b)

Artistic and bright table decorations can be made with sprigs of holly and long taper-like candles stuck into a base of plasticine (Fig 2). If the plasticine base is brushed over with

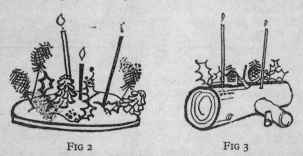

FIG 2   FIG 3

gum and then silver or gold glitter powder dusted over the gum, the result is very attractive.

Even a small log with small sprigs of holly gummed to it

and candles either stuck into plasticine or into small holes bored in the log can be made into a most attractive table decoration. Artificial 'frost' and 'glitter' can be added where necessary to enhance its appearance (Fig 3).

Another delightful table decoration can be made simply by sticking an interesting-looking branch into a colourful bowl and hanging from it a number of the coloured glass balls one usually hangs on Christmas trees (Fig 4).

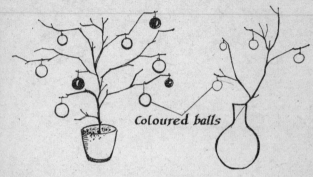

Coloured balls

FIG 4

The branches of the tree can be given added lustre by sprinkling on them artificial frost and glitter as was done with the log.

Even a large goblet filled with small, coloured glass balls will add brilliance to a table.

Tree branches (oak branches usually have interesting shapes) can also be used for wall decoration.

Coloured glass balls can be hung on the branches, or, alternatively, pipe-cleaner elves, pixies, or Father Christmases can be made (Figs 5 and 5 (*a*)) and perched at suitable places.

These pipe-cleaner figures can also be utilized for Hallowe'en decorations merely by changing their crêpe-paper clothing and making them into witches instead of pixies (Fig 5 (*b*)).

19

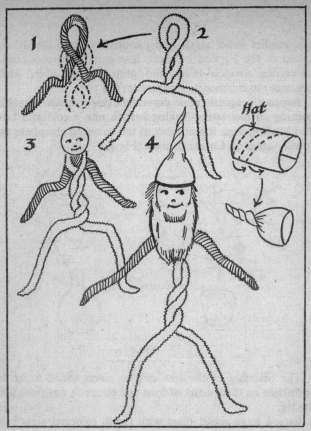

Hat

FIG 5

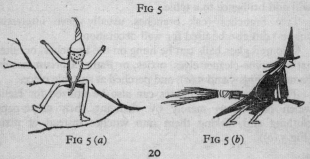

FIG 5 (a)

FIG 5 (b)

In the north of England, Scotland (Hogmanay) and in many countries on the Continent, this festival is perhaps even more important from a party point of view than Christmas. In southeastern England the reverse is more true.

As most of the Christmas decorations will still be up, all that need be added are cut-outs of Father Time to represent the Old Year and similar cut-outs of a bouncing baby to represent the New Year. Fig 6 shows a drawing of each which.

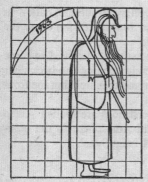 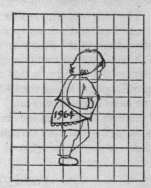

FIG 6

can be copied on to stiff cardboard, or if desired cut out of hardboard and painted with poster colours. The advantage of making the figures from hardboard is that they are sufficiently strong and durable to be kept from year to year; the only thing that will be necessary will be to change the date. Each square in the diagram is a quarter of an inch.

Traditional Customs

Certain traditional practices can be followed. (These are observed almost automatically in some parts of the country.) The ceremony of 'First Footing' demands, if luck is to be with the household during the year, that a dark man should be the first person to cross the threshold on January 1st. A careful host or hostess, bearing in mind the dire consequences of an error, will ensure that there is a dark man at the party and will see that he is put outside the door about one minute to midnight and that he will bar entry to all other people until he himself has stepped over the doorstep in the first few seconds of the New Year.

If the host is an absolute stickler for tradition, he will arm the 'First Footer' with a small lump of coal, a loaf of bread, and a Bible so that he brings with him symbolically, warmth, food, and spiritual well-being.

The host will, also traditionally, offer the obliging dark man a mince pie and a drink appropriate to the occasion – and the convictions of the person involved.

A less-involved tradition or superstition, observed in some parts of the country, is that of merely opening the back door of the house to let out the Old Year and then opening the front one to let in the New Year.

Perhaps these traditions or superstitions are foolish – who is to say? – but they certainly add atmosphere to the occasion – as does the singing of 'Auld Lang Syne'.

TWELFTH NIGHT

In olden times the eve of the Feast of Epiphany was one of the great Feast Days of the year. Now, along with St Valentine's Day, it is almost traditionally one of the great occasions for a teenage party.

Decorations

On this evening it is supposed to be lucky to take down the Christmas decorations – but before this is done, a further decoration representing The Three Wise Men can be added for the occasion. These can be 'cut-outs' or made from cardboard or even pipe-cleaners.

Traditions

At Twelfth Night parties it is traditional to tell stories sitting round the fire; these stories, however, should not dominate the party programme, but one or two should be interspersed as quieter interludes between the more active games. As it is also traditional *and* lucky to take down decorations (and unlucky not to), this can be made the culmination of the party. Providing the weather is suitable, any unwanted decorations can be taken out into the garden and burned with ceremony. If, before the party begins, some more balloons are added to the existing decorations, each member of the party could go joyfully home afterwards carrying some.

ST VALENTINE'S DAY

This is the traditional young lovers' day, and where are you likely to find love blossoming more than among teenagers – and therefore what better day for a party?

Decorations

Hearts, cupids, and posies are quite definitely the themes on which to base your decorations. These can be cut out of pink cardboard and festooned round the walls; heart-shaped paper doyleys can also be obtained for use on the table.

Small cakes can be made heart-shaped, and even the sandwiches can be cut to a similar shape by means of the cutters available at most stores.

Traditions and Games

Though the emphasis may be on young lovers, great care must be taken in the selection of games, otherwise a teenage party can become a complete flop, and even most embarrassing.

There should be games, of course, where the girl and her boy friend take part as partners, but there *must* be games in which the guests take part as a whole and where the young people are compelled to participate with partners other than those with whom they came, or those they were hoping to meet. Good-humoured tolerance, a little gentle chivvying and just a little leg-pulling will do much to keep the flow and continuity of the party.

EASTER

This is normally the time, particularly if Easter is late, when the hostess may hope that some of the games and activities might even be held out of doors.

Decorations

Easter eggs, lambs, chickens, young Teddy-Bears, in fact almost any form of young life can be used as decorations. In addition to the many and varied eggs which can be obtained from the shops, much can be done with ordinary eggs, hard-boiled and coloured with vegetable dyes or even painted. Names of individual guests can be written or painted on these eggs, and thus a most personal note can be added to the occasion.

Some suggestions for egg decoration and attractive and amusing figures made from eggs and egg-shells can be found in a leaflet, 'All About Egg Decoration', which can be obtained from The British Egg Information Service, Wingate House, 93–107 Shaftesbury Avenue, London W1.

Three delightful examples of the use of eggs for decoration, a simple Egg Man, the Egg Angel, and the Eggspress, are shown in Figs 7, 8, and 9. Before starting to make these decorations you will have to blow the egg. Do this as follows: At the broad end of the egg, make a hole – about $\frac{1}{16}$ inch – with a needle. In the narrow end, make a hole about $\frac{1}{8}$ inch. Hold the egg over a basin, and blow through the smaller hole until you have emptied it completely. Run cold water through the holes to clean the egg.

Simple Egg Man (Fig 7): a blown egg and some coloured pipe-cleaners are needed. The egg is painted and the hat (a plastic bottle cap is ideal) is stuck on. The arms and legs are fashioned

24

from pipe-cleaners and stuck on to the egg (the paint should be scraped away at the points where the pipe-cleaners are to be stuck). Glue the feet on to a wooden or cardboard base. His eyes can be made from beads and his nose from the head of a match.

Other decorations or features can be added at will.

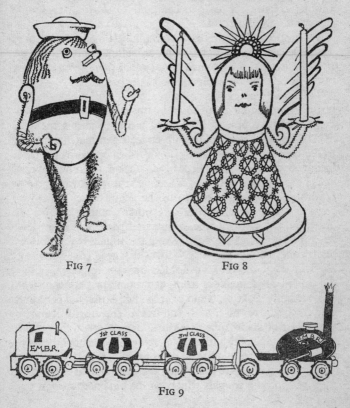

FIG 7

FIG 8

FIG 9

The Egg Angel (Fig 8): the body of the angel is made from coloured or painted cardboard, covered with a gold or silver cake mat. Cut the wings – together if possible – from paper,

25

and gum them to the cone. The angel's head is made from either a blown or hard-boiled egg. Use a silver or gold cake mat for the halo and glue it to the angel's head. The arms, as with the simple Egg Man, are made from pipe-cleaners stuck to the cardboard. The candles (which should be lit at the appropriate time) are the tiny candles which can be obtained in various colours for cake decoration. Stick the angel to a wooden or cardboard base.

The Eggspress (Fig 9): this delightful little model can be used as a table centre-piece at an Easter or birthday party. It can be, if so desired, also presented as a special prize to the winner of the most games or competitions at the party.

The bottom parts of each truck are made from open matchboxes. The engine is made from two matchboxes stuck together with a couple of protruding pieces to neaten the back of it. The last truck has one up-ended open matchbox stuck to the base. The wheels are made of crown corks (closed sides facing the carriages) with little beads stuck in the centre of each wheel for hubs. The carriages are made from blown, or hard-boiled, painted eggs; the egg in the engine truck should be painted black. Windows or any other embellishments are drawn on black sticky tape or gummed paper and then stuck on to both sides of each egg. Make the funnel from a roll of black paper with silver paper (cut with jagged edges), to look like smoke, at the top. To fashion the couplings which join the trucks, cut thin sticks from matchsticks or balsa wood, to equal lengths. Poke each end of each stick through a bead and glue the beads to the end of each truck. The engine cylinders should also be made from matchsticks or balsa wood, painted in a contrasting colour, and glued on to each side of the engine egg. Mount the train on to a strip of thick cardboard.

Another table centre-piece can be a farmyard thronged with the small, plastic animals which can be obtained in most toy shops.

The small prizes can also have an Easter theme: little chocolate eggs, or small bags of sugar eggs, can be most attractive for both young children and adults.

An idea which will appeal to small children is to make up one of the farmyard table centre-pieces suggested above. To the head or legs of each animal attach a long piece of white cotton and lead each piece of cotton either mazelike around the table to finish by each child's place (the end of the cotton should have a small tag on it bearing the name of the individual child) or draw them all together by passing them through a very small curtain ring and then fan them out so that the name tags are plainly visible.

Then, either towards the end of the meal or just before each child goes home, the children hold their name tags and pull gently to make one of the animals move. They then take home the one to which their own cotton is attached.

NATIONAL DAY PARTIES

People who run parties on national festivals such as St Patrick's, St David's, St Andrew's, and St George's Days need little advice on either traditions or decorations; national emblems such as the leek, shamrock, thistle, and rose, are obvious themes.

HALLOWE'EN

This is the night traditionally associated with witches, Black Magic, Jack o'Lanterns, hobgoblins, black cats, owls, spiders, and all the mysterious personages with which our superstitious ancestors peopled the dark nights.

Young and hopeful maidens, by the way, are said to be able to see the faces of their future husbands, if on this night they look into a mirror by candlelight!

Decorations

Black cats, witches, spiders, owls, and lanterns made from hollowed-out turnips are suitable decorations.

Small black cat silhouettes can be pinned to curtains or hung on tapes down the walls as was suggested for Christmas.

Small witches 'riding broomsticks' (Fig 5 (b), page 20) can be hung from electric light fixtures or suspended from thin black cotton fixed fairly high across the room.

Similarly, black spiders cut out of hardboard can be placed about the room hanging down on black cotton, or 'joke' spiders can be bought from shops catering for party occasions.

Lanterns made from hollowed-out turnips (Fig 10) can be

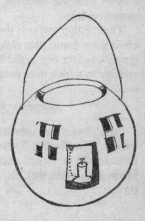

FIG 10

lit for the telling of Hallowe'en ghost stories. Even jam-jars decorated with black paper silhouettes can be utilized for effective candle lanterns.

Owls can be made in silhouette as suggested for the black cats; alternatively they can be made in the manner suggested below and as shown in Figs 11 and 12.

The top panel of Fig 11 shows the materials required. These are three pieces of white crêpe paper, one 7 inches × 5 inches, and two 8 inches × $\frac{3}{4}$ inch; a wad of cotton-wool approximately $2\frac{1}{2}$ inches × $1\frac{3}{4}$ inches × $\frac{3}{4}$ inch; two circles of plain paper each the size of a sixpence, and two small shoe buttons.

The method of construction is shown in the centre and bottom panels.

28

The cotton-wool is placed on the crêpe paper which is folded as shown: the bottom ends of the paper are folded over and gummed, and the neck is drawn in with thread and stitched in position.

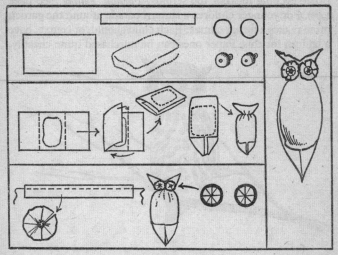

Fig 11

To make the eyes, run a gathering thread along the base of the eight-inch strips and draw tight to form circles.

Stitch the circles in place on the owl and trim the ears. The two circles of plain paper are divided into eight by lines and a thick circumference is drawn around them; a hole is pierced in the middle of each to insert the shanks of the shoe buttons. The eyes are then stitched into place and feathers painted on the crêpe paper with sepia ink or water colour.

The owls are then stitched or gummed to twigs to form the decoration (Fig 12).

Traditional foods for this evening are roasted chestnuts, walnut cakes (in fact, nuts in any shape or form) and fruit, particularly apples and apple dishes.

Traditional Games

Duck Apple (see page 137). and *Bob Apple* (page 137) are traditional games for parties on this day; it is also an appropriate evening for (not too serious) *Fortune Telling* (see page 243). For younger children a lantern parade around the garden often makes a fitting climax. Each child should, of course, have a lantern for this. Paper ones can be purchased quite cheaply,

FIG 12

but if someone in the family has the time and patience to produce a turnip lantern for each child (which they are allowed to take home with them) success is assured. To make a number of turnip lanterns will take some few days, and during those days the turnips tend to shrivel and go limp. To save all this work, it can be politely suggested on the invitations that 'Lanterns should be brought'.

GUY FAWKES' NIGHT

This is also so well known an occasion that little need be said about it. In addition to the fireworks, however, the evening can be made a fuller one by arranging for the children (and the adults) to roast potatoes and chestnuts in the embers. As it is frequently cold and frosty on this evening, it is also a good plan to provide refreshments by way of hot soup, hot cocoa, and other liquids often more favoured by adults. Home-made toffee is also customary on this evening in many parts of the country.

Make certain, too, that you have your first-aid box immediately at hand and that in it you have an ample supply of burn dressings and lotion or jelly. Someone is absolutely certain to need them.

SECTION FOUR

FANCY-DRESS PARTIES

Children (and many adults) love dressing up and an invitation to a fancy-dress party can cause a lot of excitement. At the same time it can cause a lot of headaches and perhaps considerable expense to the parents of the children concerned.

This must always be borne in mind when sending out the invitations. It can be suggested, for instance, that the fancy dresses should be improvised from crêpe paper and that not more than half a crown should be spent on materials. If it is also mentioned that a prize will be awarded for the most humorous costume made under the above conditions, this will prevent any child being embarrassed because some other child appears in an expensive creation.

With teenagers and adults the problem can be made much simpler. Themes can be suggested on which the fancy dresses can be based. For example, if you have a sportsman's and sportswoman's theme, the guests can turn up in tennis, netball, hockey, football, rugby, cricket, and skating clothes without incurring any expense whatsoever, as most of them will already have, or be able to borrow quite easily, the clothing appropriate to some well-known sport.

Similarly, a 'Tramps' Party' is one that saves expense for the guests, for old dresses and hats and old gardening jackets and flannels can form the basis of the costume to which can be added whatever additional trimmings the fancy suggests.

A 'Do-it-Yourself' fancy-dress party can serve a dual purpose by saving your guests a lot of trouble and money and providing them with an interesting and amusing test of their ingenuity on arrival at your party.

Provide each person with two or three sheets of different

coloured crêpe paper, some safety pins, and three or four elastic bands. The guests are then paired off, if they have arrived singly, or let them work with their wives or girl friends. Give them fifteen to twenty minutes for this and then hold a fancy-dress parade in which the men judge the girls' dresses and vice versa.

Another useful theme is that of 'The Good Old Days' where the guests arrive in Victorian dress which they may have been able to borrow from their grandparents or old people that they know. The men may have to content themselves by wearing side-whiskers and large moustaches.

Teenagers and young people would also enjoy a party on the theme of the 'Gay Twenties'.

Equally useful and inexpensive themes might well be 'Arabia' where miracles can be worked with old sheets and curtains, 'India' where sheets and curtains can be transformed into saris, and towels and scarves into turbans.

'Schooldays' will provide the opportunity for girls to dig out their old hats and gym-slips and for the men to appear in shorts and school or cricket-club caps.

Fancy-dress costumes can be hired, of course, but for the normal house party this involves an unnecessary expense. Much more pleasure and amusement will be obtained by the guests devising their own costumes which are appropriate to the particular occasion.

On the following pages are some suggestions and ideas for a number of inexpensive costumes which require little or no skill or trouble to make.

No suggestions are given on costumes or 'characters' which involve colouring or blacking any part of the body or the face. It is felt that for the ordinary party (as distinct, say, from a fancy-dress ball) the use of such make-up can become a very messy business indeed and could well mar the enjoyment both of the person concerned and others at the party.

Paper Parcel

Over normal dress, swathe the upper part of the body in large sheets of brown paper. Keep the paper in place by tying fairly thick string round the body. On the front, with black ink or poster colour, write in fairly large letters either your own or a mythical name and address. Stick on a number of old stamps cut from envelopes. Blobs of red sealing-wax and blue lines can be added, if desired, to indicate a registered parcel (Fig 13).

FIG 13   FIG 14   FIG 15

Sandwich-board Man

An extremely simple costume to make. Two large rectangular pieces of cardboard only are required. These are joined together by two fairly thick pieces of string which rest on the shoulders, one card hangs in front of the body of course, and the other down the back. The two cards can also be connected with each other by a string or rubber band under each armpit. On the two 'boards' can be put posters (a local printer or tradesman may help you with this) or two can be painted on white paper and posted on the boards. An old trilby or bowler

34

hat and a drooping moustache and old pipe will help to create 'character' (Fig 14).

A Zebra Crossing

This can basically be the same as for the Sandwich-board Man except that the 'boards' have black and white stripes across them. This can be done either with poster paint or by pasting black and white paper across the cardboard. An additional 'effect' can be a broomstick painted in black and white, or wrapped with strips of black and white paper, to the top of which is held an orange balloon (Fig 15).

A Draught or Chess Board

As with the Sandwich-board Man, two large sheets of cardboard are carried, but this time the boards are painted in black and white squares. Draughtsmen or chessmen are cut out of cardboard and stuck on appropriate squares.

Playing Cards

This is yet another variation of the Sandwich-board Man dress. The cardboard sheets in this case are painted to represent Kings and Jacks. Additional trimmings might be for the bearer to 'make up' his face to represent the face on the playing card which he is carrying.

The Scarecrow

This is such a well-known figure that little description is necessary. The oldest possible clothes are worn (those that you intended to throw away months ago). These should then either be torn at the elbows and knees and/or artificial patches sewn on in various places. Just inside the holes, pin or fasten small bunches of straw or grass so that the heads protrude from the holes. Straw can also protrude from the bottoms of the sleeves. An old, battered hat should also be worn with straw or grass hanging from real or made holes in the top and sides. The face can also be made up to exaggerate the size of the eyes. The nose and cheeks can also be reddened.

The House-decorator

Old clothes are again needed for this character; indeed the clothes you actually wear when decorating might suit the purpose admirably. An overall or apron should also be worn along with a cloth cap or beret. A paint-brush or distemper-brush and part of a roll of paper can also be carried for effect.

The Artist

An overall or buttoned coat liberally besprinkled with paint and a beret or floppy tam-o'-shanter-type hat are the basic ingredients for this costume. A real (borrowed) palette, or one cut from cardboard, plus one or two artist's brushes complete the ensemble, save perhaps for an artificial beard!

Father Time

A grey or white wig and beard are essential. These can be bought quite cheaply or improvised from wool or even the paper packings from chocolate boxes. A sheet draped toga fashion, bare feet, and sandals (the trousers can be turned up), plus a broomstick with a scythe-blade cut out of thick cardboard or thin balsa wood and painted silver or covered with silver paper, complete the costume.

Neptune

This can be basically the same as for Father Time except that a trident will be carried instead of a scythe. This again can be improvised from a broomstick and cardboard or balsa wood.

A Tinker

Old clothes, a battered hat, and a belt from which are suspended by string small items of kitchen ware such as saucepans, ladles, colanders, baking-tins, etc., make up the essentials of this costume.

Wee Willie Winkie

A night-cap (which can be run up very quickly from some cheap white material), a long nightie, bare feet, and slippers, plus a candlestick and candle are all the items required.

Flower Girl

This is an extremely simple and inexpensive costume which is nevertheless most effective. All that is required are a cloth cap, a shawl (a car rug can be used), and a small basket in which is arranged a selection of brightly-coloured plastic flowers.

Pirate

A brightly-coloured scarf tied round the head, an eye-patch plus a scar on the face (this can be drawn in with lipstick, rouge or grease-paint), a high-necked sweater, dark trousers tucked into Wellington boots, and you have a pirate's costume. If desired, a belt can be worn in which is tucked a dagger or a cutlass. These (made of plastic) can be bought quite cheaply from most toy shops or improvised from balsa wood and painted appropriately.

Cupid or Eros

This costume can be of two distinct characters. When worn by a small girl it should be essentially dainty. Light tights, a fairly tight bodice, and a short frilly skirt, plus an improvised bow and arrow, are required.

Alternatively, it can be a most humorous costume for a large man of the rugby-forward type or a tall, very thin man. A blond curly wig (improvised, if necessary), a white vest, and a frilly skirt made from crêpe paper (worn over rugby or football shorts), socks *and* suspenders, and sandals, plus a bow and arrow, and Cupid is (more or less) complete.

Witches and Magicians

Items required: A black conical hat (this can be made from thin cardboard), and a thin black dressing-gown. The hat and the dressing-gown should be decorated with magic symbols such as the signs of the Zodiac. These can be cut out of paper and stuck on the hat or tacked on to the dressing-gown. The magician can carry a wand, a thin stick painted in gay stripes; the witch should, if possible, carry a broomstick – a garden besom is ideal. If such is not available, a broom can be improvised from a broomstick to the bottom of which are bound thin twigs or rushes gathered from the garden or country-side.

Pick of the Pops

A contemporary costume (open to many variations) which can also be called *Juke Box Jury* or whatever similar type of radio or television programme is popular at the time of the party. To a light-coloured woolly, pin photographs (cut from magazines) of the popular recording stars along with strips of paper or thin card bearing the titles of the 'hits' of the moment. A belt can also be made by stringing together *old* small gramophone records. Alternatively, they can be suspended from a fairly wide belt.

An alternative idea under this heading is to devise a costume to represent a popular song of the moment. It is difficult to make concrete suggestions on this, as the songs of the future are obviously impossible to predict.

National Costumes

These can be many and varied; many of them can be improvised, but in other cases the genuine costumes may well be owned by the invited guests or borrowed by them from friends or neighbours. Obvious costumes are Welsh, Scottish, and Irish. Other popular ones which can be improvised without an undue amount of trouble or ingenuity are Dutch, Spanish, Hawaiian, Arab, Indian (an improvised sari can be made from

a sheet or cheap cotton material), Red Indian, Japanese, and
Egyptian (a long, loose nightgown-type smock and a fez).

An English Summer

An ordinary summer dress is worn, plus *half* an *old* plastic
mac. This will require pinning to the dress with small safety-
pins to prevent it slipping off the shoulder.

Chinaman (Coolie)

A hat made in the shape of a very shallow cone and either
coloured with crayons or water paints or decorated by pasting
on to it gaily patterned wallpaper (Fig 16). Alternatively, a

CUT OUT →

Fig 16

beach sun-hat can be used. A pigtail made from plaited old
nylon stockings dyed black can be pinned on the underside of
the rear of the hat. The two other items required are a self-
coloured pyjama jacket and tight-legged dark or black jeans
or trousers.

Nurse

A very simple costume to produce both for an adult or a
child. All that is required is a square of white material to be
pinned up as a head-dress and an apron with a bib attached.
This is pinned on to an ordinary dress, preferably a dark one.
In the centre of the bib should be sewn a red cross made from
any available material.

Cowboy

Most young boys possess so-called 'Cowboy Outfits' which can be used for fancy-dress parties.

Men need only wear a check open-necked shirt, a gay neckerchief, belt, and jeans to look like the popular television conception of a cowboy.

Red Indian

Again most young boys possess the trappings of a Red Indian Chief which can be used for parties.

Men need only wear a head-band to which a suitable feather has been pinned or sewn. The rest of the costume can be as suggested above for the Cowboy.

Television

There are many ways of suggesting television. Using the Sandwich-board costume, the 'boards' can be painted to represent a television screen. A picture of some well-known television personality can be pasted on to the screen to form a 'picture'. If a trilby or bowler hat is worn, a small 'aerial' fashioned out of thin wire can be fixed in the hat-band to stand vertically.

SECTION FIVE

CATERING FOR PARTIES

From a catering point of view, parties can be divided roughly into three main categories: (1) food for young children's parties; (2) food for young people between the ages of about ten and fifteen; and (3) food for teenagers and adult parties.

These are by no means hard-and-fast divisions for, in many cases, sandwiches, for example, different fillings can be used whatever the age of the guests. In a similar manner, most savouries used for adult parties will be appreciated by ten-year-olds if only because it makes them feel more 'grown up'.

When catering for parties every opportunity should be taken for using labour-saving devices such as paper plates and beakers which eliminate most of the washing-up after the party when one can be tired and irritable. Similarly, small wooden spoons can be used for ice-cream and ice-cream dishes, and cocktail sticks instead of forks for cating small savouries.

FOOD FOR YOUNG CHILDREN'S PARTIES

There are certain traditional foods which adults imagine young children favour, such as jellies, blancmanges, table creams, custards, and cream cakes. This does not always seem to be the case nowadays when even very young children develop more sophisticated tastes much earlier. So, for a young children's party, make sure there are plenty of savoury titbits available, such as sausages, flavoured crisps, salted nuts, hot dogs, and popcorn. They also like the conventional sandwiches, ice-cream, biscuits (chocolate-coated ones), and sweet cakes – but not usually the very 'gooey' or creamy variety.

Do not neglect jellies and table creams completely. Children like them served with fruit salad; this can be done attractively if the fruit and jelly are set in animal moulds. Jellies can also, without undue trouble, be layered in various colours.

Sandwiches are the mainstay of the party meal. These can be made most attractive if the crusts are cut off and the sandwiches cut in triangular or other shapes with metal cutters which can be bought quite cheaply at most hardware shops.

Time and labour is also saved if sliced loaves are used. Objections are sometimes raised that the slices in such loaves are too thick, but most bakeries producing such loaves make them in two slice-thicknesses, one for sandwiches, the other for toasting.

The various types of sandwiches should be kept on separate plates and labelled quite clearly by means either of special label sticks and flags or by improvised ones made from wooden cocktail sticks.

Various sandwich fillings can be devised; with very young children, however, it is wise to avoid highly-seasoned foods. The only possible exceptions to this general rule is the use of vegetable extracts such as Marmite, which should, when used, be spread sparingly.

Here, then, are twenty suggestions for sandwich fillings:
(1) Tomato; (2) egg (it is more economical if the eggs are hard-boiled and mashed or chopped up fine); (3) ham and tongue; (4) cheese; (5) sardine; (6) meat and fish pastes; (7) chocolate spreads; (8) banana; (9) egg and tomato; (10) egg and cress; (11) tomato and cress; (12) cheese and tomato; (13) Marmite and cress; (14) salmon (no vinegar); (15) ham and tomato; (16) sardine and tomato; (17) Marmite and tomato; (18) pastes and tomato; (19) Marmite, tomato, and cress; (20) sardine and lettuce.

Drinks

Most young children prefer fruit drinks, milk, or fizzy drinks, to tea. The fruit drinks can be made up beforehand and served in cardboard beakers (which can be bought quite cheaply) with plastic straws. Alternatively, bottles of orange juice can be obtained from most dairies. If the foil cap is kept on the small bottle and merely pierced to allow a drinking straw to be inserted, there will be less danger of drinks being knocked over or spilled all over the tablecloth or furniture. Cola drinks are always popular, also served in bottles with straws.

Milk shakes or flavoured milk may also be attractive for many of the young guests and you should be prepared for some child requesting a drink of this kind.

Cakes

Small cakes, chocolate, and sweet biscuits are always popular, as are filled sponge cakes. These can either be bought or made from the many varieties of cake mixes on sale today.

FOODS FOR THE TEN- TO FIFTEEN-YEAR-OLDS

Sandwiches will provide the main part of the meal. All the various sandwiches already mentioned will be found acceptable, but further variety can be added by introducing some more savoury fillings and small savoury titbits on biscuits, toast, or potato crisps. Children in this age group also like hot dogs, hamburgers with onions, savoury crisps, bacon, and sausages on sticks, popcorn, etc.

Drinks

At this age many of the young people, particularly in the winter months, may prefer hot drinks, but during the summer mild fruit cups, fizzy drinks such as lemonade, cream soda, Coca-cola, and ginger beer, or even milk drinks, may be preferred.

CATERING FOR OLDER TEENAGE AND ADULT PARTIES

For teenage and adult parties the basic requirements are almost the same as for children's parties except that whereas with children it might be advisable to seat the guests formally round a table (even if only to calm them down for a little while), with teenagers, particularly, and with adults, food is best served on the buffet principle and a perhaps more sophisticated approach is required in the presentation of the food. With children, the food at a party is almost if not equally as important as the games and amusements provided. With adults the food is still of interest, but the way in which it is presented is almost as important as the actual items.

During the cold weather you might well feel that an occasional hot snack or dish would be a very welcome addition to your party food. This, of course, will provide extra work and may take you away from your guests for a time – but the trouble may well be worth while, particularly if your party is a small one.

Toasted sandwiches, small portions of Welsh rarebit, hot sausage rolls, small portions of grilled bacon on attractively-shaped pieces of toast, and items such as black sausage, garlic sausages, etc., served similarly, will be found generally acceptable.

DRINKS FOR OLDER TEENAGERS

Teenagers nowadays expect to be treated as adults; but this certainly does not mean that you should provide them with 'hard liquor'. Ciders, beers, and perhaps a wine-based fruit punch can be provided in addition to soft drinks. It is imperative, however, that no guest should be pressed in any way whatsoever to have any alcoholic drink. This is most important at any party, but with the new drinking and driving regulations, it is absolutely vital to the teenagers who come either on scooters or in cars.

44

Make sure you have plenty of Cola drinks, tomato, pine-apple, and grapefruit juices, and fizzy drinks such as bitter lemon, ginger ale, and ginger beer. For the sixteen- to seventeen-year-old teenager you will be quite in order in offering them the soft drinks only.

DRINKS FOR ADULTS

In this particular section, I am assuming that at the party there are both those who are teetotal and those who are not.

I would suggest two general rules regarding the provision of alcoholic drinks. These are: (1) never press anyone to have such a drink who shows the slightest reluctance to do so; (2) if any of your guests have come in cars, never press them to drink. You and they may regret it.

It is also a good idea to pour out spirits in recognized measures and not just straight out of the bottle. By doing this your guests who have to drive will be able to keep a reasonably strict check on their consumption and will know when to stop.

SOURCES OF INFORMATION

Many commercial organizations and women's magazines can, and are more than willing to, provide information booklets, leaflets, and photographs on such things as special party recipes, hints on general catering and decorations, or to try to solve individual problems. When writing to them, try to be as brief and explicit as possible, and *do* enclose a fairly large stamped and addressed envelope.

Below are given some details of leaflets, booklets, etc., and the addresses from which they can be obtained.

British Egg Information Service, Wingate House, 93–107 Shaftesbury Avenue, London W1 (437 9200)
  Leaflets:
    (a) *Party Going Eggs*. Five recipes
    (b) *Soufflés*

(c) *Separated Eggs*
(d) *You Can Make an Omelette*
(e) *All about Egg Decoration*

Brand Services Dept., Smith's Food Group, Mortlake Road, Kew, Surrey
A leaflet showing methods of using crisps for meals, snacks, and parties

Kraft Kitchen, Kraft Foods Limited, Regina House, 259–69 Old Marylebone Road, London NW1
(a) Recipes for savouries, sandwiches, salads, cakes, etc.
(b) Information on cheese and wine parties
The Department will also be prepared to answer individual queries.

Woman, 189 High Holborn, London WC2
This magazine has an excellent series of leaflets dealing with many aspects of party giving.

H. J. Heinz Company Limited, Public Relations Department, Hayes Park, Hayes, Middlesex
The Busy Woman's Cookbook. A twenty-four page booklet for recipe suggestions and cookery ideas.
The Public Relations Department will also be pleased to deal with individual queries.

Schweppes Ltd, Public Relations, 26 Upper Brook Street, London, W1 Y 2DQ
Entertain Slimly by You Know Who. A leaflet on party-giving for weight-watchers. Contains exciting recipes, and exotic cocktails such as 'Orange Nectar Cup' and 'Lemon Blush Cup'.

Tanquerry, Gordon and Company Ltd, 260 Goswell Road, London EC1
A leaflet giving many recipes for cocktails and other mixed drinks

Most Wine Merchants and Off-Licences will provide both booklets of recipes for drinks, and, if desired, a full party service. They will not only provide beers, wines, and spirits on a sale or return basis but all the correct glasses as well.

GAMES FOR VERY YOUNG PEOPLE

Nursery Rhyme Mimes

As most young children live almost constantly in the land of make-believe, miming actions to Nursery Rhymes are always popular and can be used as quieter games between the more boisterous ones.

Let them all stand in a circle or sit on the floor, then you or they recite some well-known rhymes while they do the actions. Most of them will do it almost spontaneously, but if such is not the case you can suggest various actions which can be done. Two examples are given below:

'*Pat a cake, pat a cake, baker's man*' (Clap hands or pat knees)

'*Bake me a cake as quick as you can*' (Wave hands about quickly)

'*Pat it, and prick it, and mark it with "B"*' (Pat knees, pretend to make holes in it with a pin and draw a letter "B" in the air)

'*Put it in the oven for baby and me*' (Pretend to open the oven door, slide in the cake, and close the door)

'*Sing a song of sixpence*'

'*A pocket full of rye*' (Turn out pockets or put hands in them)

'*Four and twenty blackbirds*' (Flap arms or elbows about like wings)

'*Baked in a pie*' (Pretend to be mixing dough)

'*When the pie was opened*' (Pretend to cut open a pie and look in)

'*The birds began to sing*' (Whistle, chirrup, or sing)

'*Wasn't that a dainty dish*'

'*To set before a king?*' (Carry an imaginary dish and put it on the table)

'*The king was in his counting house*'
'*Counting out his money*' (Pretend to count – like a miser)
'*The Queen was in the Parlour*'
'*Eating bread and honey*' (Pretend to eat)
'*The maid was in the garden*'
'*Hanging out the clothes*' (Pretend to peg clothes on a line)
'*When down came a blackbird*' (A lot of wing flapping)
'*And pecked off her nose*' (Hold nose as if in obvious pain)

Other well-known rhymes suitable for miming are: Little Boy Blue, Humpty Dumpty, Little Miss Muffet, Ride a Cock Horse, Little Bo Peep, Goosey Goosey Gander, Little Jack Horner, The Queen of Hearts, Ding Dong Bell, There Was an Old Woman who Lived in a Shoe, Old Mother Hubbard, Simple Simon, Georgie Porgie, etc.

You will find that the children will almost certainly want to play three or four of them at least twice each – so that's a good ten minutes gone.

Oranges and Lemons (Indoors or outdoors)

This game is one of the most popular perennials ever. Two of the children make an arch by standing facing each other and holding hands above their heads. One agrees to be 'Oranges' and the other 'Lemons'.

The other children walk behind each other in a small circle, continually passing under the arch. As they walk, they sing:

'"Oranges and lemons," say the bells of St Clement's,
"You owe me five farthings," say the bells of St Martin's,
"When will you pay me?" say the bells of Old Bailey,
"When I grow rich," say the bells of Shoreditch,
"When will that be?" say the bells of Stepney,
"I'm sure I don't know," says the great bell of Bow.'

'Here comes a candle to light you to bed,
Here comes a chopper to chop off your head.'

As the last words are sung, the two children forming the arch move their arms up and down, finally bringing them well down to entrap one of the children walking through the arch. They then ask him or her which he chooses, oranges or lemons?

Having chosen, say oranges, he then stands behind the child in the arch who has previously agreed to be that.

The game goes on until all the children have been caught and chosen to be an orange or a lemon.

The oranges then have a tug-of-war with the lemons.

Looby Loo (Indoors or outdoors)

Most of the children will know the tune for this game, as it is almost certain they will have heard it on television.

As the actions are mentioned in the verses, the children do them. A circle is formed and the children sing:

'Here we go (or dance) looby loo,
 Here we go looby light
 Here we go looby loo
 All on a Saturday night.'

'Put all your right hands in
 And shake them all around
 Take all your right hands out
 And turn yourselves about.'

(Do the same with the left hand as well, then both hands.)

'Put all your right feet in
 And shake them all around
 Take all your right feet out
 And turn yourselves about.'

(Repeat this verse, saying 'left feet in'.)

'Put your both feet in
 And shake them all around
 Take your both feet out
 And turn yourselves about.'

Finish the game by singing:

'Put your whole self in
 And shake yourself about
 Take your whole self out
 And turn yourselves about.'

The children will almost certainly want to repeat it at least two or three times.

The Mulberry Bush (Indoors or outdoors)

This is a musical miming game in which the children mime the actions they are singing about. They form a circle and sing:

> 'Here we go round the mulberry bush
> The mulberry bush, the mulberry bush,
> Here we go round the mulberry bush,
> On a cold and frosty morning.'

(As they sing, they all walk round in a circle.)

> 'This is the way we wash our clothes
> Wash our clothes, wash our clothes,
> This is the way we wash our clothes,
> On a cold and frosty morning.'

(Each child pretends to be washing clothes.)

Each child in turn can then sing the first line of a new verse, and as it is sung the actions are mimed. Some suggested first lines might be:

> 'This is the way we iron our clothes,
> This is the way we darn our socks,
> This is the way we brush our teeth,
> This is the way we clean our shoes,
> This is the way we walk to school,
> This is the way we comb our hair,
> This is the way we scrub the floors,
> This is the way we dance at school,' etc.

Each child should have at least two or three turns at singing a fresh line. The moment they begin to run out of ideas, stop the game and start another one.

The Farmer in his Den (Indoors and outdoors)

There are several variations of this musical game, sometimes known as *Farmer in the Dell*. Here is a simple version:

All the children form a circle round one standing in the centre. They then walk round the centre child (the farmer) singing:

'The Farmer in his den,
The Farmer in his den,
Heigh-ho, heigh-ho,
The Farmer in his den.'

'The Farmer wants a wife
The Farmer wants a wife,
Heigh-ho, heigh-ho,
The Farmer wants a wife.'

(Here the farmer chooses a 'wife' to stand in the circle with him.)

'The wife wants a child,
The wife wants a child,
Heigh-ho, heigh-ho,
The wife wants a child.'

(The farmer's wife now chooses a 'child' to stand in the middle.)

'The child wants a nurse,
The child wants a nurse,
Heigh-ho, heigh-ho,
The child wants a nurse.'

(A 'nurse' is now chosen by the child and stands in the centre.)

'The nurse wants a dog,
The nurse wants a dog,
Heigh-ho, heigh-ho,
The nurse wants a dog.'

(A 'dog' takes his place in the centre, chosen by the nurse.)

'We all pat the dog,
We all pat the dog,
Heigh-ho, heigh-ho,
We all pat the dog.'

Everybody playing the game then proceeds to pat the dog (reasonably gently) on the head and back for a few minutes.

The game then starts all over again with the dog becoming the farmer.

Children will play this game without any signs of boredom at least four or five times.

The Little Clown

A singing game for the three- to six-year-olds. All the players except one join hands in a circle; the remaining player who is 'The Little Clown' stands in the centre of the circle. The players, still with hands joined, walk or skip round the little clown chanting or singing to the rhythm and tune of 'Here we go round the Mulberry Bush' the words:

> 'Oh look, here comes the Little Clown,
> The Little Clown, the Little Clown,
> Oh look, here comes the Little Clown,
> Let's copy whatever he does.'

On the word 'does' the players stop walking or skipping and give as loud a clap as they can.

The little clown then does some action such as running on the spot, flapping his arms like a bird, pumping his arms backwards and forwards and making train noises, jumping up and down, hopping on one leg, and so on.

The rest of the players copy little clown's actions.

Some other player is then chosen to be little clown and the game continues until all the players have had a turn in the centre. Each player should be encouraged to try to do a different action and preferably one that will make the other players laugh.

The Muffin Man (Children 5 to 8. Indoors or outdoors)

The players join hands in a circle in the centre of which is one player who is blindfolded and has a walking-stick or ruler.

The players skip or dance round singing:

'Have you seen the muffin man, the muffin man, the muffin man?
Have you seen the muffin man who lives in Drury Lane?'

At the words 'Drury Lane' they all stand still while the centre player points his stick or ruler at someone in the circle. Whoever is in line with the pointer moves forward and grasps the stick. The centre player then asks three questions – any questions will do, but they should require only one-word answers. 'Are you enjoying yourself?' or 'What kind of jelly do you like best?' The player answers the questions in a disguised voice, and the muffin man is then allowed three guesses as to the identity of the player holding the stick. If he guesses correctly, he joins the outside circle and the other player becomes the muffin man. If his guess is incorrect the game continues as before.

Ring a Ring o'Roses (Indoors or outdoors on a lawn)

The children join hands to make a circle and walk or dance round and round singing:

> 'Ring a ring o'Roses
> A pocketful of posies,
> Atishoo! atishoo!
> We all fall down.'

As the word 'down' is sung, still with hands joined, they all drop to sit cross-legged on the floor.

Even a simple game like this can be good fun for at least five minutes.

Three Blind Mice (Indoors or outdoors. Plenty of room needed)

The children join hands to form a circle round 'the farmer's wife', who can be a child or an adult.
They walk or skip round singing:

> 'Three blind mice, see how they run,' etc.

As the word 'mice' is sung in the last line they all dash for the sides of the room or lawn to avoid being tagged by the farmer's wife. The first one to be tagged becomes the farmer's wife in turn.

Squeak, Piggy, Squeak (4 plus to 7 plus. Indoors)

This is a great favourite with little girls from four to eight. Change the title to *Grunt, Piggy, Grunt* or *Roar, Lion, Roar*, and it becomes an equal favourite with boys of the same age.

All the players except one sit cross-legged in a circle on the carpet (or on the dry grass in summer).

The remaining player is blindfolded and placed in the centre of the circle, holding a cushion in front of her. (The cushion is for her protection.) She is led slowly round the circle and when she says 'stop' is turned to face the nearest sitting player to her. She then gently places the cushion on the knees of the sitting player, turns round, sits on it, and then demands 'Squeak, Piggy, Squeak', whereupon the player being sat on makes a little squeaking noise. The blindfolded player tries to guess who it is. If she is successful she changes places with the squeaker, but if unsuccessful she gets up and adopts a similar procedure until she finally succeeds in guessing right.

Find the Bellman

This variation of the old favourite, **Blind Man's Buff,** is suitable for young children up to the age of six or seven. It should only be played, however, where there is ample room for movement and where there is no danger of children running into obstacles such as furniture, radiators, windows, etc. Adults present at the party should act as guards to keep children away from potential harm.

All the children except one are blindfolded. The remaining child is given a bell or rattle (a marble in a tin will do). He or she then mingles among the blindfolded children, occasionally ringing the bell or rattling the tin. The blindfolded children try to tag the bellman. Any child so doing becomes the bellman until he in turn is tagged.

Pussy Wants a Corner (Indoors or outdoors)

All the children except one who is 'pussy' stand in corners of the room or at spots decided upon, if there are a large number of children.

Pussy goes from one child to another saying, 'Please let me come in your corner' or 'Pussy wants your corner'. They all refuse, but as pussy moves about or talks to a child in a corner, children in other corners try to change places with each other. Pussy (who must be very alert) tries to get into one of the empty corners as a change-over is being made. If she succeeds, the one left without a corner becomes pussy.

Are You Ready, Mr Wolf?

An indoor or outdoor chasing or tagging game for any number of children in the five to eight years age range.

One player is chosen to be Mr Wolf. All the rest of the children stand in a circle round Mr Wolf just out of touching distance.

Then, in unison, they call out, 'Are you ready, Mr Wolf?'

Mr Wolf then replies with statements such as, 'No, I've still to put my shirt on' or 'No, I've still got to put my trousers on'. Whatever items of clothing he mentions, he then goes through the pantomime of putting them on.

After being asked three or four times if he is ready he might suddenly shriek out 'Ready now.' The moment he says this all the children race for the sides of the room (or the edges of the lawn). The wolf rushes after them. Any child tagged before touching the wall is eliminated and sits down. The last player to be tagged becomes the wolf for the next round. Alternatively, the wolf can be changed the moment he tags one of the players; the person tagged becoming the wolf.

The Witch's Ring (girls or boys 6 to 8 plus. Outdoors or in a large room)

In the centre of the room or lawn is placed a mat or hoop, on or in which the 'witch' crouches down. All the other players walk round her in a circle singing nursery rhymes or popular songs.

Very slowly the witch begins to stand up. When she is at full height she suddenly shouts, 'Here I come,' and then chases the other players until she has tagged four or five. As each one is tagged, the witch turns her into some object which can be mimed, say a tree with its branches blowing about in a gale, a caterpillar, a windmill, and so on. The last person to be caught becomes the witch.

Suspense can be added if the witch varies her rate of rising or even sinks down again once or twice before reaching full height.

Squirrels in the Trees (6 to 9. Large room or lawn)

The children stand in pairs, face to face with hands joined to represent hollow trees. In each hollow tree stands a third player who is the squirrel. The trees with their squirrels should be spaced unevenly about the room.

One extra player is a squirrel without a tree.

When he or she either claps her hands or calls 'Change' all the squirrels hunt for a new tree. The homeless squirrel also tries to find a home during the general change-over. Whoever does not succeed in finding a home then becomes the one to clap or call 'Change'.

Busy Bee (6 plus to 8 plus. Indoors or outdoors)

Each child chooses a partner, and the pairs space themselves out over the playing area. The leader (or you) calls out various commands such as 'Stand side to side' or 'Back to back' or 'Link elbows'. However, when the leader calls out 'Busy bee' each player tries to find a new partner; the leader also tries, and if successful the unlucky one left out becomes the leader and gives the commands.

Jack in the Box (6 plus to 8 plus. Large room or lawn)

At one end of the room or lawn place a mat or hoop on or in which stands 'Jack'. The rest of the players stand in a space at the other end. This can be marked off with a piece of string or rope (see Fig 17). To start, all the players (except Jack) stand in the 'home'. They then walk round and round Jack in his box, singing or saying, 'Jack in the Box, come out and play, catch us now or we'll run away.' Without warning, Jack jumps as high as he can out of his box and tries to tag as many as he can before they reach home. Those tagged drop out. The

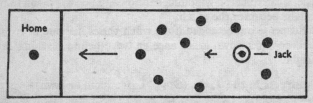

FIG 17

winner is the last person to be tagged; he or she then becomes Jack.

The Hunter and the Rabbits (6 plus to 8 plus. Large room or lawn)

This is a similar type of game to Jack in the Box. The space is divided identically and a mat or hoop is placed on the ground as a 'house' for the hunter.

The rabbits come out of their burrows and walk around the field. When the hunter leaves his house, all the rabbits run behind him and crouch, jump, or bunny-hop in line. When the hunter turns round the rabbits try to keep out of his sight. When he stops, turns round very quickly, and claps his hands, the rabbits try to scoot back to their burrows without being tagged.

Hunt the Slipper (4 plus to 7 plus. Indoors or outdoors)

The children sit in a tight circle with one standing or sitting in the centre. He is given a slipper or a shoe which he hands to one of the players in the circle. He (or all the children) recites out loud:

58

> 'Cobbler, cobbler, mend my shoe,
> Have it done by half past two.'

The centre player then closes his eyes and puts his hands over them. As he does so everyone chants:

> 'Cobbler, cobbler, tell me true,
> Which of you has got my shoe?'

As this chant is going on the children pass the slipper round the circle behind their backs, and whoever is holding it when the last word 'shoe' is said, retains it, holding it out of sight.

The centre player then opens his eyes and by looking round the circle at the expressions on the children's faces tries to guess who is holding the shoe. If he does not guess correctly in two tries, the one who is holding the slipper takes his place in the centre.

If he does guess correctly, he is allowed one more turn as the centre player – but not more.

Hunt the Ring

A quiet game for children from six to ten requiring a fairly long piece of string, tied together at the ends to form a circle, and a small curtain-ring.

All the children, except one, sit in a circle holding the string in their hands. The remaining player stands in the centre of the circle. At a signal to start, the centre player closes her eyes tightly and counts silently up to twenty. She can do this at any speed, but the children must be impressed that the eyes *must* be kept closed and there must be an honest count.

While this is being done, the children in the circle are sliding the ring from hand to hand round the string, all the time trying to conceal it under their hands.

The moment the centre player opens her eyes she must try to guess which player is holding the ring. If she guesses correctly, the person with the ring changes places with the centre player; if she guesses wrongly, the game continues with her in the centre.

If she is unsuccessful after three or four tries, let someone else have a turn in the centre in her place.

Poor Puss-cat (For the younger children, 5 plus to 8 plus, but can be used effectively with mixed teenagers)

All sit on chairs or on the floor in a circle. One player then goes into the centre to become the poor puss-cat. The cat, on hands and knees making cat noises and purring loudly, goes to each person in turn, who must keep a perfectly solemn face, stroke the cat on the head or back and say, 'Poor Pussy, poor Puss-Cat.' Anyone who smiles or laughs while stroking and talking to the cat must take its place in the centre of the circle.

Straight Face

A 'silly' non-active elimination game for children of five to eight years of age. All the players sit fairly close together in a circle. One player is chosen to start the game. He or she then turns to the person immediately on his right and either makes a funny face or tickles his nose or scratches behind his ear – in fact, anything within reason to make him smile, laugh, or speak. The second player then does the identical thing to the player on his right – and so on all round the circle. Anyone who smiles, laughs, or speaks is eliminated. The game continues until all are eliminated except one. He is 'Straight Face' and is given a small prize.

Johnny's Trousers

A non-active elimination game for children of about five to eight years of age. All the players sit in a circle with a leader in the centre.

The leader says, 'Johnny's lost his trousers,' then looks intently at the players in the circle. '. . . And I think I know who's taken them . . . (pause) . . . It's you.' As he says the last words he points dramatically at one of the seated players.

The player addressed must neither speak nor smile, yet must reply immediately by vigorously shaking the head and pointing at another player. Any player who smiles or speaks or does not answer by pantomime immediately drops out of the game.

Each child, of course, tries by his or her pantomime actions, or by the speed of pointing, to eliminate another player.

When a player is eliminated, the leader restarts the game with his original remark: 'Johnny's lost his trousers . . .'

Big Ball

Another non-active elimination game for young children in the seven to ten years age range. The players again sit in a circle or semicircle with the leader standing in the centre.

The leader then calls out either 'Big Ball' or 'Little Ball'.

If he calls 'Big Ball' he holds out his arms with his hands close together indicating a *small ball*; if he calls 'Little Ball' he indicates a *big ball* with his hands.

The players in the circle, however, must do what he says – which is the opposite to what he does.

Anyone who makes a mistake or who does not do the correct action quickly enough is eliminated. This continues until there is only one player remaining – the winner.

The Magician

A very simple, somewhat noisy, game for the very young. Gather the children together and tell them that you are going to pretend to be a magician and that when you wave your magic wand (a stick or ruler) you are going to turn them into all kinds of different things and that they are to imitate whatever you call out. You then proceed to call such things as aeroplanes, trains, buses, dogs, sheep, crows, horses, ducks, frogs, ballet dancers, clowns, and so on.

Wobbling Bunnies

Another simple, competitive game for the very young. All the children hop about the room in the knees-full-bend position with their open hands held upwards by the sides of their heads pretending to be rabbits (the hands represent ears).

Whenever you call out 'Hunter' they must stop moving immediately and keep absolutely still until you call out

'Hunter's gone' when they start hopping about again. The period required for them to remain motionless should vary between five and ten seconds. During this period anyone wobbling or falling over is eliminated from the game which continues until only one player is left. He or she is the winner and should receive a small prize.

Animal Farm

A noisy elimination game for children of five to eight years of age. All the children sit down on the floor. A story-teller then makes up a story about a visit to a farm or a trip to the country bringing in at frequent intervals the names of animals. The moment an animal's name is mentioned all the children make the noise appropriate to the animal. The last to do so each time is eliminated until only one player is left. He or she is the winner and should be given some small prize.

The story-teller should try to bring in surprises by, say, repeating the name of an animal twice in a short time, or by suddenly naming three or four immediately in succession, e.g.:

'As I walked into the farmyard, I saw a black *cat* and a white dog and a grey cat – and a ginger cat, and on a lorry there was a sheep, a cow, a donkey, a sheep – and a sheep – and a horse, a cow, a sheep, a cat, a dog – and a hen, and a cock – and another . . . (pause) . . . hen . . .', etc., etc.

Animal Beano

A noisy and amusing game for players of seven years of age and upwards. The players are divided into equal teams, each with a leader. The teams are then given the names of animals which make easily recognizable calls, such as cows, sheep, ducks, hens, and so on. Prior to doing this, place all over the room in easily seen and not so easily seen places a large number of beans (or buttons).

Each team then tries to collect as many beans as possible but *only the leader* is allowed to pick them up; the members of his team draw attention to any of the beans they find by making the noises of the animal assigned to them. Thus the whole room will be full of moos, baas, cacklings, and quacks.

Royal Court

This 'seething about' game can be adapted for use either with small or large numbers. A pack of cards is needed. Let us suppose there are sixteen players.

In the centre of the room place face downwards on the floor the Ace, King, Queen, and Jack of Spades, Hearts, Diamonds, and Clubs. These should be well shuffled about.

The sixteen players stand round the room while this is being done.

On the word 'Go' all the players rush for the cards, each picking up one. The one who picks up the King of any suit is leader of that suit. He immediately calls the name of his suit and makes for the nearest chair on which he sits. The other three players with cards of the same suit rush to him; the first there sits on his knee with his feet on the ground, the third player sits on the second's knee and the fourth sits on the third player's knee so that the four finish as shown in Fig 18.

FIG 18

The first four players to be seated correctly are the winners.

With one pack of cards, the game can accommodate up to fifty-two players in four courts of thirteen.

Donkey's Tail (6 to any age)

You need a small blackboard, or a piece of hardboard about two feet by eighteen inches plus a piece of string with a drawing pin through one end for this old favourite.

On the blackboard or hardboard draw an 'animal' (without a tail) as large as possible in chalk and mark with a small dot the place where the tail would grow from, like this:

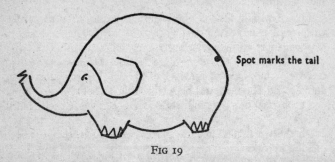

Spot marks the tail

FIG 19

Prop your work of art up on a chair or other suitable place. Each competitor in turn is given the piece of string with the drawing pin in one end and is then placed about six feet away (or two steps) from the animal, where he is either blindfolded or told to close his eyes.

He then steps forward and tries to pin the tail to the exact spot marked on the drawing. (You will find it amazing how many animals develop tails on their ears or under their stomachs!) The one who puts the tail nearest to the correct spot wins the contest. It is advisable to initial the mark made by each competitor so that later there can be no arguments as to who made which mark.

The Vicar's Cat

A quiet game for the ten- to twelve-year-olds. This vocabulary game can be played by any number, but is particularly suitable for groups of four or five.

The first player starts by saying something like the following: 'The vicar's cat is an *angry* cat and her name is *Alice*.'

The second player has then to use an adjective and a name beginning with 'B', e.g. 'The vicar's cat is a *big* cat and his name is *Bert*.'

64

The third player then continues with, say, 'The vicar's cat is a *cheerful* cat and her name is *Caroline*.'

This procedure is followed by each player using the next letter of the alphabet ('X' can be omitted).

Any player who cannot produce a sentence within, say, five seconds, is eliminated.

The game can be made more difficult by insisting that each player produces a sentence for each letter of the alphabet; i.e. in the 'A' round and subsequent rounds each player provides an adjective and a name beginning with 'A' for the vicar's cat, e.g.:

(1) The vicar's cat is an *angry* cat and her name is *Alice*

(2) The vicar's cat is an *awful* cat and his name is *Albert*

(3) The vicar's cat is an *attractive* cat and her name is *Angela*

Make a Rhyme (6 plus to 8 plus. Indoors or outdoors)

Another quiet sitting-down game for younger children.

One player stands up and says, 'I want a rhyme in jolly quick time and the word I choose is Ben.'

Each child in turn then has to give a word which rhymes with Ben, e.g. pen, hen, den, men, ten, and so on.

Any player who cannot answer in, say, ten seconds, loses a 'life'. At the end of the game, when each player has asked for a rhyme, the one who has lost the least number of lives is the winner.

It is a good plan to insist that each questioner must know at least five words which rhyme with the one he or she chooses. This will prevent hold-ups and will also stop unrhymable words such as SILVER and ORANGE being chosen.

The following games are also suitable for children in the age range covered in this chapter: *Musical Spoons* (page 77), *Cat and Mouse* (page 91), *Dressing-Up Race* (page 142), *Musical Torch* (page 77), *Hand-tap Chase* (page 90).

SECTION SEVEN
INTRODUCING GAMES

Introducing games can serve two or three purposes. They can enable guests to get to know each other quickly; they can help to 'warm up' the party in its early stages and, perhaps most important of all, some of them can keep the earlier arrival occupied and free from potential embarrassment while waiting for the other guests to arrive.

Here, then, are a number of introducing games:

GUESSING AND PROBLEM GAMES

These types of games generally involve some previous preparation which should be done well in advance to save last-minute rushing about on the day of the party.

Guess the Place

Paste or pin up on a large sheet of paper some ten to twenty picture postcards or photographs from holiday brochures showing reasonably familiar places either in the British Isles or abroad; any names, of course, should be obliterated with ink or hidden by sticky paper. The pictures should be numbered.

The guest, on arrival, is provided with a pencil and paper, asked to study the photographs and then write down the names of the places.

When all the guests have arrived and have had a chance to write down the names, give out the answers. While the guests are looking at the pictures they should be encouraged to chat about and discuss them among themselves.

Guess the Flowers

This is identical in nature to *Guess the Place* except that the pictures are of flowers cut from seedsmen's old catalogues. The pictures should all be in colour.

Guess the Crests

In this variation, trade marks or crests (such as that of the BBC or those appearing at the tops of newspapers) are pasted on the sheet and numbered as before. About twenty should be provided.

Black-outs

A large sheet of white paper is required. From pictures in magazines trace the outlines of well-known objects such as pans, beds, chairs, vacuum cleaners, wheel-barrows, television and radio sets, petrol lighters, and so on. Transfer these outlines to the sheet of paper and then black in inside the outlines forming silhouettes. The guests are required to guess as many of the objects as possible.

The Face is Familiar

Cut out portraits of well-known television personalities from papers such as the *Radio Times* and *TV Times*. Competitors are required to write down their names.

Who Said It?

This can be used either as an introducing game or a quiz with teenagers and adults. Write down on a large sheet of paper ten to fifteen well-known quotations or current catch-phrases. Players are then required to write down the name of the author or the originator of the saying. Here are some examples:

'Never was so much owed by so many to so few' (Winston Churchill). 'Wait and see' (Asquith). 'Good evening all' (Jack Warner). 'Before your very eyes' (Arthur Askey). 'Friends, Romans, and Countrymen' (Mark Antony). 'We have nothing to lose but our chains' (Rousseau). 'Dr Livingstone, I presume' (Stanley). 'O, to be in England now that April's there' (Browning). 'Oh, what a good boy am I' (Jack Horner).

'The quality of mercy is not strained' (Portia, *Merchant of Venice*).

Sense of Touch

Put a number of small, familiar objects in a shoe bag or a thick stocking so that they can be felt but not seen. Players are allowed to handle the stocking and asked to write down the names of as many of the objects as possible. Some suitable items are as follows: a clothes-peg, a thimble, a nail-brush, a collar-stud, a small sponge, a small potato, a lipstick case, a cork, a small bottle, a large paper-clip, a coin, a wrapped tablet of soap, a piece of coke, a protractor, an egg cup, a pair of *blunt-ended* scissors, a walnut or peanut (unshelled), a toothbrush, a bottle-opener, a crown cork, a blunt-ended nail-file, a handkerchief, a cuff-link, a hair-curler, a comb, etc., etc.

New Angles

Make about ten small drawings of common objects seen from an unusual viewpoint; some examples are given in Fig 20.

As the guests arrive, give each of them a pencil and paper and ask them to study the drawings and to write down what they think the objects to be. Tell them to discuss them with the other guests and get their views as well.

Name the Advert

This is a useful 'introducing game' at the beginning of a party. Beforehand, paste on to a large sheet of paper about twenty advertisements of nationally known articles which can be cut from newspapers or magazines, but *cut out the name of the article*. Number the advertisements from 1 to 20.

Provide every guest with paper and pencil and ask them to study the advertisements and then write down on their papers what they think the advertised articles to be. All the guests are allowed to discuss the advertisements with the others. (They will do, in any case.)

A small prize should be given to the one who produces a complete list when called upon. At least fifteen minutes can be allowed for this game – more if you make a few of the items quite difficult. If no one produces an all-correct result, award the prize to the one with the highest number correct.

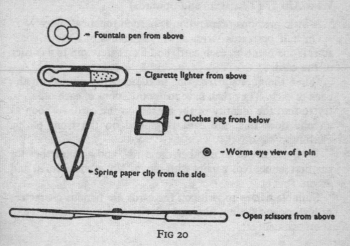

– Fountain pen from above

– Cigarette lighter from above

– Clothes peg from below

– Worms eye view of a pin

– Spring paper clip from the side

– Open scissors from above

FIG 20

Find the Other

Cut a number of old picture postcards or old Christmas cards each into two pieces. As you do so, put one of the pieces of each into a large envelope marked 'Boys' and the matching half into another envelope marked 'Girls'. When the boys arrive give them a half-card from the 'Boys' envelope and the girls, a half-card from theirs. Guests have then to seek out whose card matches the one they have got and talk to them until you start the first game, which should be one for pairs – which are already selected for you.

Zoo

An interesting activity similar to the above for young children. Have two envelopes as before, but in each envelope put cards bearing the names of animals which make noises, e.g. cows, sheep, hens, ducks, etc. Partners then try to find each other by going round the room moo-ing, quacking, clucking, and so on.

Who Am I? (Teenagers and upwards)

A little previous preparation is needed for this 'mixer'.

On half postcards write down the names of famous characters (one name on each card) and fix a safety pin to a corner of the card.

When the guests arrive, one of the cards is pinned on the back of each. They then have to ask questions of each other, to try to find the identity of the person on the card. As soon as anyone does this, the card is pinned on the front of his clothing.

It is also useful to number the cards, and arrange that for the first game, No. 1 pairs with No. 2, No. 3 with No. 4, and so on.

Suitable names to write on the cards are famous characters of history and fiction, film and television stars, sportsmen and sportswomen, etc.

Soul Mates (Teenagers upwards)

This is similar to *Who am I?*, except that cards are prepared containing the names of the men and women involved in the great romances of history and fiction.

Thus a girl, on arrival, might receive a card on which is written 'CLEOPATRA'. She then is due to pair up with 'ANTONY' as and when he searches her out, which he must do, not by shouting 'Where's Cleopatra?', but by going round the girls inquiring from each one.

As soon as all, or most, of the people present are paired off a 'partner' game should be started. Some suggested 'Soul Mates' are: John Ridd and Lorna Doone, Romeo and Juliet, Hiawatha and Minnehaha, Prince Charming and Cinderella, Beauty and the Beast, Adam and Eve, Lord Nelson and Lady Hamilton.

Know your Neighbour (Teenagers upwards)

This is an 'introducing game' which can be made into a competition. Make some small labels (half a postcard will do) and write on each a number; e.g. if there are twelve guests, numbers from 1 to 12 will be required. It will help your preliminary organization if you give odd numbers to the boys and even numbers to the girls.

As the guests arrive, each one is given a number which they pin on themselves and a sheet of paper on which six tasks are written; the tasks for the boys will involve them talking with all the girls in turn, and vice versa.

When all are present each player sets about completing his or her list of tasks as quickly as possible, the first boy or girl to do so being the winner. Here are some suggestions:

Questions for the boys to ask —

    (1) Ask No. 2 the names of the last four films she has seen.

    (2) Ask No. 4 where she has spent her last four holidays.

    (3) Ask No. 6 the names of the last four books she has read.

    (4) Ask No. 8 the names of her four favourite film stars.

    (5) Ask No. 10 what are the four things she likes best of all.

    (6) Ask No. 12 her four greatest dislikes.

Questions for the girls to ask —

    (1) Ask No. 1 who are his four favourite sportsmen.

    (2) Ask No. 3 the names of four places he wouldn't like to go on holiday.

    (3) Ask No. 5 the names of four brands of cigarettes he likes.

    (4) Ask No. 7 the names of his four favourite sportswomen.

    (5) Ask No. 9 the names of his four favourite crime writers.

(6) Ask No. 11 the names of four famous detectives in fiction.

As an alternative to the above type of question, tasks such as given below can be set:

(1) Introduce No. 3 to Nos. 6, 8, and 10.
(2) Introduce yourself to No. 5 and help him to choose three girls whom he would like best to take to the cinema.
(3) Find No. 4, introduce her to No. 5, and get them involved in a discussion about dance music.
(4) See if you can find anyone who is really interested in ballet and opera and get them to tell you why.

If the above type of task is given, the game will be non-competitive but will achieve the aim of making your guests talk among themselves.

Junior Paul Jones (6 plus to 10 plus)

Younger children rarely require 'mixing' games to get to know each other, as most of them are spontaneously friendly. However, this is a simple 'mixer' which might be useful on the odd occasion.

Two concentric circles are formed facing each other, boys in one circle, girls in the other. When the music plays they run or skip round in opposite directions; when it stops they are told to do certain actions with the boy or girl opposite, such as 'Join hands and spin round five times', 'Shake hands with each other, five times with each hand and five times with both', 'Each of you hum a song and ask your partner to guess what it is', 'Find out your partner's name, age, address, and school', 'Girls try to do an Irish Jig and boys a Sailor's Hornpipe'.

Nosey Parker Partner (Teenagers and upwards)

Two concentric circles are formed, the men facing outwards, the girls facing inwards. They then move round in opposite directions (as in a 'Paul Jones') to music, if possible.

When the music stops, each pair facing each other have to try to find out as much as possible about each other before the music starts again. They must find out each other's full name, address, occupation, likes and dislikes, and so on.

The process is repeated each time the music stops.

Circle Talking (Teenagers and upwards)

This is similar to Nosey Parker Partner, except that each time the music stops the pairs facing each other must discuss a topic (announced by the leader) for two minutes. Suggested items or topics for discussion might be such things as:

(1) Give your views on pop music.

(2) Discuss your favourite film stars.

(3) Discuss the latest women's fashions.

(4) Tell your partner as briefly as possible the plot of the last book or short story you have read.

(5) Give your views on 'A woman's place is in the home'.

(6) Discuss 'should women wear trousers?'

(7) Tell each other your three favourite 'likes' and your three biggest 'dislikes' and say why.

End of the Line

An introducing game particularly suitable for a medium-sized teenage party.

Provide a ball of string (bought at the local multiple stores) for each male guest.

Keep hold of one end of each ball of string and then ask each boy to wind the string haphazardly round items of furniture such as chair- and table-legs, finishing somewhere out of the room in, say, the hall. Having reached the end of their balls of string they sit down retaining the ends in their hands.

You then give the ends of the strings which you are holding to the girls in the party – one to each.

Each girl then starts to wind up her string until she finally reaches the boy holding the other end. He then becomes her partner for the next game or dance which you have arranged.

Spill the Beans (Teenagers and upwards)

As each guest arrives, he or she is given five beans (dried peas or matches will serve equally well) and told that the object of the game is to talk to someone and try to make them say 'Yes' or 'No' by asking questions, or by any other means they can think of.

If successful, they hand over a bean to the unfortunate one who has said 'Yes' or 'No', and move on to someone else.

The first person to get rid of all of his or her beans is the winner.

Odd or Even

This game can be used as a 'mixer' or 'introducer' with children or adults. It can also be used as a time-passer at parties with small numbers. Ten beans or dried peas are required for each person.

One player takes a number of his beans in one hand, closes his hand and holds out his clenched fist to any other player and demands 'Odd or even?' The one questioned then says either 'Odd' or 'Even'. If his guess is correct the player holding the beans hands over one of his beans to his opponent. The opponent then goes through the same actions with some of his own beans. If the original questioner guesses incorrectly, he hands over another bean, but if his guess is correct, he in turn collects a bean from his questioner.

Alternatively, if a guess is correct, the questioner can be asked to hand over all the beans in his or her hand.

Players circulate demanding 'Odd or Even' for, say, five minutes, at the end of which each player counts the number of beans in his possession; the one with the greatest number is the winner. If two players have the same number they play off a final until one has lost all his beans. In such a final the alternative method of playing, i.e. handing over all the beans held in the hand, should be used, otherwise the contest might be too long-drawn-out.

SECTION EIGHT
MUSICAL GAMES

———

There are many forms of musical games from simple ones for small children such as 'London Bridge is Falling Down' to advanced musical quizzes for teenagers and adults involving the use of tape recorders and record players.

Some musical and singing games are given in other chapters of this book, but on the following pages will be found a short selection of musical games mainly of the elimination type as in the perennial favourite, straightforward 'Musical Chairs'.

First of all, however, a 'warming-up' or introducing game.

Musical Crocodile

A singing game for the five- to eight-year-olds. Everyone sits down except a leader who walks about the room. As he walks they sing 'John Brown's body . . .'. At the end of the verse they stop. The leader then bows to one of the seated players who joins the leader, walking behind him in step with hands resting on his shoulders. Everyone then sings, 'Glory, glory, Hallelujah', etc. At the end of the chorus, the singing stops again, the leader bows to another person who joins on behind the player already chosen. This process continues until a long 'crocodile' is formed from all players. The crocodile then winds its way around the house with everyone singing as lustily as they can.

With large numbers, two or three leaders can start the game, form short crocodiles and then finally link up into one large one.

Musical Bumps (4 to 7 plus. Indoors)

All the players form a circle. While the music plays, they bob up and down doing little skip jumps. The moment the music stops everyone flops down on to the floor and sits cross legged. The last one down is eliminated. Continue till only one is left.

Musical Mats (6 to 10 plus. Indoors or outdoors)

Place four or five newspapers (or mats) unequally spaced around the room (or lawn). All the players form a large circle, and when the music starts they walk, trip, or skip round the room, always stepping on the mats as they pass them. When the music stops, anyone actually on a mat, even with only one foot, drops out of the game. As the numbers get smaller, the mats should be brought in closer together.

Musical Islands (6 to 10 plus. Indoors or outdoors)

This is similar in style to *Musical Mats*. Papers or mats are placed about the room or lawn. As the music plays, the players walk or skip about, but when it stops they must stand with both feet on one of the 'islands'. Not more than two players are allowed on any one island. Anyone not finding an island is eliminated. Remove one or two islands after each stop.

Musical Rush (6 to 10 plus. Outdoors or in large room)

The players in this game should preferably be all the same sex and about the same age. In the centre of the space available place a number of small objects, e.g. corks, cotton reels, marbles, pebbles, etc. The number of objects should always be at least one less than the number of players. All the players skip round the outside edge of the playing space while the music is playing, but the moment it stops they all rush to pick up one of the objects. Anyone failing to do so drops out.

Musical Arches (6 to 10 plus. Indoors or outdoors)

This is a musical game in which everyone takes part right until the end. Two pairs of children stand, one at each side of the room or lawn, joining hands overhead to make an arch. The remainder of the children line up in pairs round the room all facing one way. When the music begins they walk or skip round the room and pass under the two arches. When the music stops, any pair caught under the arches form arches in turn. The game continues until all have been caught except one pair of children; these are the winners.

Musical Torch

A musical passing game for younger children and particularly suitable for Hallowe'en. Players sit in a circle and the lights are turned out. As the music plays a torch is passed from hand to hand around the circle. The torch should be passed at just under chin-level so that each player's face is lit up in a rather eerie manner. Whoever is holding the torch when the music stops is eliminated.

Musical Spoons

A somewhat boisterous game of the *Musical Chairs* type more suitable for boys and girls in the eight to twelve years age range and requiring a fair amount of room.

In the centre, or at one or both ends of the room place a number of spoons. There should be one or two less than the number of players.

When the music begins the players walk or trot round the room. When it stops they rush to grab a spoon; anyone failing to get one is eliminated.

Reduce the number of spoons by one or two each time.

Musical Arms

A *Musical Chairs* type of game suitable for players of eight years of age upwards.

All the boys (or men) stand in a line behind each other in the centre of the room. The front player stands with his right hand on his hip, the other hand by his side; the second player has his left hand on his hip, his right by his side and so on down the line.

The girls, who should number one more than the men, walk round as the music plays; when it stops they grab the arm of the nearest boy. The one who fails to get an arm drops out, as does one of the men. The game continues until finally two girls are circling one man. The winner is the one who succeeds in grabbing the arm.

Repeat with the girls making the arms and the boys walking round.

Musical Stick

A musical passing game for the five- to ten-year-olds. One (or more) walking-stick is required. All the players form a circle, one holding the stick. When the music begins, the one with the stick taps it on the floor three times and passes it on to the next player who does likewise and so on round the circle. Anyone in possession of the stick when the music stops is eliminated.

With larger numbers two sticks can be used, one travelling clockwise round the circle, the other anti-clockwise.

Musical Couples

A *Musical Chairs* game suitable for teenagers and adults. A row of chairs is placed down the centre of the room; each chair faces the opposite direction to its neighbour. Pairs, consisting of a boy and girl, are formed (there should be one less chair than there are pairs).

They walk round while the music is playing; when it stops each pair rushes for a chair. The boy sits on the chair and the girl sits on his knee. The pair without a chair drops out; a chair is removed and the game continues.

Repeat with the boy having to sit on the girl's knee.

Guide Dog

A game similar to *Musical Couples* and suitable for teenagers and adults. The chairs should be spaced haphazardly around the room, some near together, others wide apart. In this game, however, the man is blindfolded and guided round by his 'dog', the girl. 'Dog noises' add to the amusement. The dog guides the man to a chair when the music stops, and as before, sits on his knee. The game can be repeated with the men as the dogs – all baying like bloodhounds.

Musical Number (Any age from 6 upwards. Indoors or outdoors)

All the players walk or skip round the room as the music plays. When the music stops they rush to form circles or groups of a number given out while the music is playing, e.g. when the music is playing the leader or hostess calls out 'Fives'. The moment the music stops the players form groups of five. Anyone unable to find a place drops out. The leader should count the players to ensure that someone must be eliminated. If there are ten players, for example, he can call 'Eights', 'Fours', or 'Sixes', but not 'Fives'.

Musical Parcel (6 plus to any age)

Place a small present in a little box and then wrap it in seven or eight layers of paper, each layer being tied up with a number of pieces of string.

All the players sit round in a circle and the parcel is given to one of them to untie the knots and unwrap the parcel. As this is being done, the music plays. (Whoever is responsible for the music should not be able to see the players.) The music is stopped at frequent intervals, and the instant this happens, the parcel is passed to the next player in the circle. Whoever succeeds in finally opening the box and taking out the present *while the music is playing* is the winner and receives the present.

Finally, a singing game for teams of players:

Nursery Rhymes (6 plus to 10 plus or older. Indoors or outdoors)

This is a singing game for younger children who are divided into two groups sitting on opposite sides of the room.

One side starts by singing any nursery rhyme, say, 'Little

Jack Horner'. While they are singing this, the other side thinks of another rhyme, and the moment the first side has finished, the second one must start.

This goes on until one side fails to find another rhyme to sing, or starts to sing one which has already been used by themselves or the opposite side.

It is useful for each side to have a leader who calls out to his side the title of the next rhyme, though anyone in the team is allowed to suggest rhymes to the leader.

SECTION NINE

GAMES WITH BALLOONS

Balloon Blow (6 plus to any age. Indoors)

Small teams of about four or five players are needed, plus one circular balloon for each team. The leaders throw up their balloons at the starting signal, and then all the teams try to keep their balloons in the air by blowing at them. The hands or other parts of the body must not touch the balloon. The team that keeps its balloon up the longest is the winner.

Pushing the Pig

This is a race for teams of four or five players. One sausage-shaped balloon and one walking-stick or umbrella per team is required.

Teams stand behind a line or a stick or piece of string laid on the ground. About ten to fifteen feet in front of the teams is a second line.

The first player in each team places his balloon or pig on the floor by his feet and holds the stick in his hand. On the signal to start he proceeds to push or prod his balloon forwards (the prodding must be done only at the ends of the balloon – not in its middle) over the far line and back to the starting line, where he then hands the stick to the second player to do likewise.

The second player hands over to the third and so on until each member of the team has completed the course. The first team so to do is the winner.

Balloon Blowing Race

A course similar to that for *Pushing the Pig* is required, along with one round balloon per team and one drinking straw per player.

On this relay the balloon is blown over the course, the blowing being done through the drinking straw. Alternative methods of blowing are by mouth alone or by bicycle pumps, if such are available.

Balloon Tapping Relay

One balloon and one ruler, short cane, or stick are required for each team. Competitors again cover a short course tapping the balloon upwards and forwards and handing on the ruler to the next in the team.

Balloon Heading Relay

A game more suitable for boys of eleven years and over. Normal relay procedure over a short course with the balloon being headed by each competitor. If possible, have the teams fairly widely spaced apart to minimize the risk of the players bumping heads.

Balloon Overhead Relay

A simple passing race involving a minimum of running and requiring one balloon per team.

Teams stand in line, each member of the team standing close behind the one in front.

The leader holds the balloon. On the starting signal the balloon is passed overhead down the team to the last player, who, on receiving it, runs to the front of the team and continues the overhead passing. This goes on until the original leader has received the balloon at the back of the team and then returns to the front and holds the balloon high above his head.

An alternative method of passing, more suitable for boys, is underneath the legs – or alternately over the head and under the legs – i.e. the first player passes it overhead, the second under the legs, and so on.

Charlie Chaplin Relay

This activity is suitable for children of eight or nine years of age upwards, teenagers, and adults. One balloon, one book, one walking stick per team, plus a fair amount of room are required; a lawn would be suitable.

A short course of about twenty feet in length is necessary. Normal relay procedure is used; each player in the team covering the course and handing over to the next player.

The balloon is held between the knees, the book balanced on the head (a small cushion would also be suitable), and the cane or stick twirled à la Charles Chaplin (see Fig 21). If the

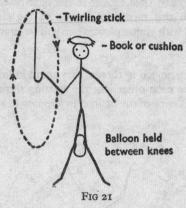

— Twirling stick

— Book or cushion

Balloon held
between knees

FIG 21

balloon is released from between the knees or the book is dropped from the head it must be picked up and replaced by the competitor before continuing the course.

Circle Balloon Race

Teams form circles. These should be of the same size; this can be done, if conditions permit, by drawing circles on the floor, or by making the competitors link arms, or grasp outstretched hands and then release their grips.

The leader of each team holds the balloon in both hands. On the signal to start, the balloon is passed from hand to hand round the circle of players a given number of times, say three. The first team to do this is the winner. An alternative is to pass the balloon behind the backs. If the balloon is dropped it must be retrieved by the one who dropped it and the passing continued.

Balloon Tap-up Race

A circle formation is required for this team race as for *Circle Balloon Race*. Instead of the balloon being passed directly from one player to the other, each person taps it upwards with one hand to at least head height a given number of times (three or four) and then taps it to the next player, who does likewise. With this race two circuits of the circle is quite sufficient, and with young players one will be enough.

Ten Trips

Players are arranged in threes; they stand in line about four feet apart from each other. On the starting signal each three try to make ten trips of the balloon by tapping it with one hand

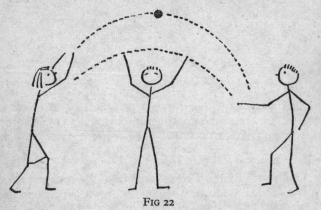

FIG 22

from one to the other as shown in Fig 22 in the shortest possible time. The first three to complete the ten trips are the winners.

With younger children, five or six trips are quite sufficient.

This activity can be done out of doors in summer using a tennis or small rubber ball; the players can then stand farther apart.

Indoor Balloon Ball

This game can be played in almost any normal-sized room by players of any age, by both sexes and by mixed teams of children and adults. There is no running about; in fact, everyone, by rule, must be seated all the time. Two equal teams of six or seven players (or less), one chair or stool per player, and one balloon are required (Fig 23).

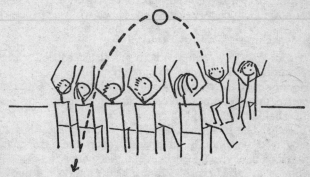

FIG 23

Arrange two rows of chairs (one for each member of the teams) about two short paces apart. The teams sit facing one another. Each team then tries to tap the balloon over the heads of the opposing team *so that it falls to the ground behind them.*

It is advisable not to have a hanging light between the opposing teams!

The rules are simple:

(1) The balloon must always be struck with an open hand; clenched fists or feet must not be used.

(2) A coin is tossed to determine which side shall have first strike.

(3) At all times during the game all the players must be seated. Penalties can be devised for infringement of this

rule, such as giving half a point to the opposing side or removing the offender for a period of one or two minutes.

(4) The game can consist of two halves of not more than four or five minutes each.

Fanning the Balloon

Another simple relay race. One folded newspaper and one balloon per team are required. Each player fans the balloon over the set course with the folded newspaper. The balloon must not, in any circumstances, be *touched* with the paper.

Balloon Bursting Competition

Provide each competitor with an uninflated balloon which he places in his mouth ready to blow up.

He, or she, must then blow it up until it bursts. One can stipulate, to make things more difficult, that one hand or *both* hands should be clasped behind the back.

The first one to burst his balloon – blowing according to rule – is the winner. From the spectators' and the competitors' point of view, the delight of this activity is in watching the others' agonized expressions just before a balloon is due to burst.

SECTION TEN

TAGGING AND CHASING GAMES

———

Tagging and chasing games are generally only suitable for playing in large rooms, out in the open during picnics or on garden lawns.

When playing games in the garden involving the use of balls, it is essential that due regard should be paid to the protection of both windows and flowers in flower beds. If a game involves a ball being thrown, it should be so arranged that the throwing is done away from and not towards windows.

Whenever possible take the same precautions with regard to flower beds; alternatively, protect them by placing a length of small-mesh wire netting across the front of beds.

If, however, the air-flow type of ball is used the precautions suggested above will hardly be needed as this type of ball will cause little or no damage to windows or flowers.

French Tag (5 plus to 10 plus. Indoors or outdoors; large room, lawn, or beach)

The chaser tries to touch one of the other players on an awkward part of the body, such as the knee, ankle, or foot. Wherever the one who is tagged is touched, a hand must be kept constantly on that spot until he, or she, in turn tags another player.

Hopping the Tag (5 plus to 10 plus. Indoors or outdoors; large room, lawn, or beach)

As the title implies, all movement by the players, chaser or chased, is done by means of hopping on one leg. Legs, however, can be changed at will. When a player is not being chased he is allowed to stand on both feet for a rest.

Walking Tag (5 plus to 10 plus. Outdoors)

This is a useful tag variation when conditions are a little crowded. All moves must be by walking; there must be no running about whatsoever.

Pairs Tag (5 plus to 10 plus. Indoors or outdoors)

Two players join hands and try to tag the other players. If they succeed in tagging one player, a chain of three is formed, but the moment they tag another one, the four split up into two pairs. The last person to be tagged is the winner.

Double Jump or Bunny-hop Tag (5 plus to 10 plus. Indoors or outdoors)

All movement by the players must be made by jumping off both feet, which should be kept together.

Bent-knees Tag (8 plus to 12 plus. Indoors or outdoors)

All movements must be made with the knees in the full-bend position. Players are, however, allowed to stand up when not being chased. This is an extremely strenuous activity, and should be played for only a few minutes at a time.

Chain-tag (6 plus to 10 plus. Indoors in a large room or outdoors on a lawn or beach)

At the start of the game, two players join hands as in *Pairs Tag* (above) and try to tag the other players. As tags are made, a gradually increasing 'chain' is made until all are caught except one, who is the winner.

Fox and Geese (5 plus to 10 plus. Large room, lawn, or beach)

Groups of five or six players are required for this active game. One player represents the 'fox', the rest Mother Goose and her young ones. Mother Goose stands with her arms held out sideways, her young ones form a line behind her holding each other round the waist. The fox tries to catch the back gosling, but Mother Goose turns from side to side with her goslings behind her to stop this happening. The grip round the waist must not be broken.

Snake's Tail (5 plus to 10 plus. Large room, lawn, or beach)

One or more groups of five or six children required. The groups form lines holding each other round the waist. The front player in the group, i.e. the 'head' of the snake, tries to twist round and tag the back player, the 'tail'.

Hot Ball (6 plus to 10 plus. Indoors or outdoors)

One fairly large rubber ball required. All the players except one form a circle facing inwards and pass the ball round the circle from hand to hand. The remaining player runs round the outside of the circle trying to tag the ball. If he succeeds, whoever was holding the ball at the time tries to do the tagging, the original player taking his place in the circle.

Circle Tag Ball (8 plus to 10 plus. Indoors or outdoors)

A large rubber ball is required. All the players except one form a circle facing inwards. If the space permits, the children should be four or five feet apart. The remaining player stands in the centre of the circle. The players throw the ball to each other across the circle, while the centre player tries to tag it as it is thrown. If a successful tag is made the thrower changes places with the centre player.

Circle Number Tag (6 plus to 12 plus. Large room, lawn, or beach)

All the players stand in a circle with hands joined and number off by threes, fours, or fives, according to the number playing (Fig 24). The leader then calls out a number, say, 'three'. Immediately all the threes in the circle chase each other in a clockwise direction round the outside of the circle; each one trying to get back to his original place without being tagged by the one behind. Each number should be called during the game two or three times.

Hand-tap Chase (6 plus to 12 plus. Large room, lawn, or beach)

All the players except one make as large a circle as possible, facing inwards and clasping their hands behind their backs. The remaining player runs round the outside of the circle

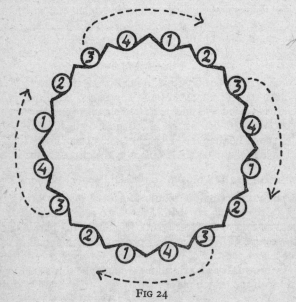

FIG 24

and taps the hands of one player. Immediately the one who was tapped chases after the tapper and tries to tag him before he reaches the gap in the circle left by the chaser. If no tag is made, the chaser continues to run round the circle and taps another player's hand in turn. If, however, a tag is made the chaser goes back to his place in the circle and the original runner tries again with some other player.

A variation is for the one who is tapped to chase round the circle in the opposite direction to try to get back to his own gap in the circle before the tapper reaches there.

Dropping the Handkerchief (6 plus to 12 plus. Large room, lawn, or beach)

This is an almost identical game to *Hand-tap Chase*, except that instead of a hand tap being given, a handkerchief is dropped behind one of the circle of players. The odds here are heavily weighted in favour of the one who drops the handkerchief. With such being the case, the game is useful for a party with children of different ages; the younger ones could drop the handkerchief, while the older ones would use the hand-tap method.

Cat and Mouse (6 plus. Indoors or outdoors)

A running about game in which all take an active part but only two children are running at any one time.

All the players except two join hands in a circle. Of those remaining, one becomes the 'cat' and has to chase the other, who is the 'mouse'.

The problem is made a little difficult for the cat, who must follow the mouse, i.e. he must go in and out of the circle through the same gaps as the mouse, and, in addition, whereas the children lift up their arms to allow the mouse to get through easily, they lower them or move them up and down to hinder the cat's progress.

If the cat shows no aptitude for mousing he should be replaced – or if both get a little tired, let two others take their places. In any case, all the children should have a turn at being cat or mouse – or both.

Fox and Hound (6 plus to 11 plus. Large room or lawn)

This is a chasing game especially suitable for large numbers, for though everyone must be alert and ready to participate at any moment, only two players are actually running about.

The players stand about the playing space in groups of three. The centre players are designated foxes. Two extra players are chosen, one of whom is the 'hound', the other a 'fox'. The hound chases the fox who can escape by touching another fox who then seeks to escape in a similar manner. It adds interest if the changes are made as frequently as possible, i.e. short runs to safety.

If the hound tags the fox before he reaches safety, their roles are reversed, the hound becomes a fox and vice versa.

Dog and Rabbit (6 plus to 10 plus. Indoors or outdoors)

This game is suitable both for indoors or outdoors if sufficient space is available. A double circle is formed, and two of the children are chosen, one as the 'dog' and the other as the 'rabbit'.

The rabbit can reach safety by standing either in front of or behind any of the pairs in the circle. If he stands in front of a pair, the rear player immediately becomes the rabbit and is chased by the dog. If the rabbit stands behind a pair, the front player becomes the rabbit to be chased.

If the dog should succeed in tagging the rabbit before sanctuary is reached, the rabbit immediately becomes the dog and vice versa.

The children should be encouraged to run only very short distances so as to make the changes as often as possible.

Two Dogs, One Bone (6 plus to any age. Indoors or outdoors)

A ball, quoit, rubber bone, or just a duster is all that is required.

The players are divided into two equal teams, who sit on chairs in line facing each other at least six to eight feet apart. They then number off down the line, starting at the right-hand side of each team. Midway between the two teams, on the floor, is placed the 'bone' (Fig 25).

The leader stands at one end of, and midway between, the two lines. He then calls out any number, say 'Two'. Number Two from each team then dashes out, tries to grab the bone and get back to his own seat again without being tagged by his opponent. If he succeeds in doing this, his side scores one point. If he fails, the opposing side scores one point.

A tag cannot be made unless the bone is being held by one of the dogs. If two dogs arrive at the bone simultaneously, there is no need for an immediate grab to be made; both can use cunning, moving their hands about very close to the bone without actually touching it until one can catch the other momentarily off guard.

If the game is played out of doors, the space between the lines should be made as wide as possible.

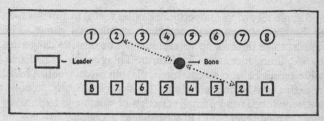

FIG 25

After each grab the bone is replaced centrally. Play goes on for a given time or until one team has scored a previously determined number of points, usually an odd number such as 11, 15, or 21.

It is advisable that the leader should have a pencil to note down the scores and absolutely imperative that he should call out all the numbers in the team two or three times each.

He can, and should, try to keep the players on tenterhooks by varying his method of calling. For instance, if he called out 1, 2, 3, and 4 successively, it is almost certain that 5 would be expecting the next call, and certainly 6, 7, and 8 would be very alert. An element of surprise could then be introduced by calling out 1, 2, 3, or 4 again, even though some of the players had not yet had a turn. It is quite useful, too, to call the same number twice on occasions and to call it almost before the two players concerned have had time to sit down after their efforts at grabbing the 'bone'.

SECTION ELEVEN

THROWING AND AIMING GAMES

Simple throwing competitions can be useful as time-passers or breaks between more energetic or hilarious games. The objects to be thrown, however, must not be missiles dangerous to life, limb, furniture, or pictures. Things such as balloons, table-tennis balls, cigarette cards, playing cards, woollen balls, and the new perforated plastic balls are eminently suitable. Below will be found a small selection of suitable games; many more can be invented to fit a particular occasion.

Cards in the Bucket (6 plus to any age. Indoors or outdoors)

A bucket, large basin, or similar vessel is placed on the ground about ten feet in front of a line. Each player is given ten playing cards which he tries to flick into the bucket. If players are given cards of a different suit, four can take part at any one time without counting muddles arising. The one who gets the most out of ten in the bucket is the winner.

Space Ships (6 plus to any age. Indoors or outdoors)

Each competitor is provided with a balloon. Circular ones will do, but sausage ones are better. Standing behind a line, each player blows up his or her balloon as high as possible and then holds the mouth of the balloon with the fingers to prevent the air from escaping. When the signal to go is given, the fingers are suddenly released and the escaping air propels the balloon forwards. The one whose balloon travels the farthest distance is the winner. If desired, each competitor can have three attempts, the best of the three to count.

Card Flicking (6 plus to any age. Indoors or outdoors)

One pack of cards per four players is required. Though the game can be played by six or eight players simultaneously, four or less at a time is best.

The four players, each with thirteen cards, stand behind a line about ten or twelve feet from a wall. Holding one card at a time horizontally between the first and second fingers, they flick their cards in turn on to the ground close to the wall.

Any player whose card falls even partly on to another card already lying on the ground takes the whole of the cards which are already lying there.

The game continues, either for a given time, when the one who is holding the greatest number of cards in his hand is the winner, or until all except one have lost all their cards. If a player has no cards in his hand when it is his turn to flick he is automatically eliminated.

In the absence of playing cards, cigarette cards or small pieces of cardboard cut to the size of cigarette cards will suffice, or even drinking straws can be used.

The elimination process can also be speeded up, if so desired, by reducing the initial number of cards given to each player.

Another variation is to place a specific card such as the Ace of Diamonds on the floor at the beginning of the game, and the cards on the floor are picked up only by the one who flicks a card on to this target card.

Cork Flicking (6 plus to any age. Indoors or outdoors)

This is another simple contest which can be played by everybody at the same time, in fours, or between pairs. One small cork per player is required. Players stand behind a line and place the cork on the flat palm of the left hand. By using the thumb and first finger, they then flick the cork as far forwards as possible, the one achieving the greatest distance being the winner.

Corks in the Bucket (6 plus to any age. Indoors or outdoors)

Using the same flicking method as in *Cork Flicking*, each player tries to flick his cork into a bucket about ten feet distant. The one with the highest score after a stated number of flicks (say ten) is the winner.

Ringing the Bottle (6 plus to any age. Indoors or outdoors)

One lemonade bottle and one or more rubber rings or quoits are required. Each player in turn stands behind a line and tries to drop the ring over the lemonade bottle placed upright on the ground about ten or twelve feet away. Each player has ten throws (or less), and the one who has 'ringed' the bottle the greatest number of times is the winner. The bottle must not be knocked over for a 'ring' to count.

Pennies on the Plate (6 plus to any age. Indoors or outdoors)

An aluminium or enamel plate is placed on the floor and competitors try to pitch pennies on to it from a distance of about six to nine feet. Each competitor has a previously decided number of throws; the one who gets the most pennies on the plate being the winner. Here again the difficulty is not in hitting the actual target but in throwing the pennies in such a way that they do not shoot off. Crown corks from lemonade bottles, or playing cards, can be used instead of pennies if so desired.

Target Bounce (6 plus to any age. Indoors on a hard surface)

An egg carton and a ping-pong ball are required. The egg carton is placed on the floor and players try to bounce a ping-pong ball into the compartments. These can be numbered, if so desired, so that balls bouncing into certain compartments score more than others. If such is done, a target of, say, twenty-five or fifty should be set, the first player to reach that score being the winner. Each player, of course, throws in turn.

Ball in the Basin (6 plus to any age. Indoors or outdoors)

A large basin and a ping-pong ball are required. Players take turns at trying to throw or drop a ping-pong ball into a basin from a distance of about four or five feet. The difficulty is not so much in getting the ball to drop into the basin as in getting it to stop there. Each player has a total of ten throws taken one at a time in turn, the player with the highest score being the winner. If two or more players are equal at the end of ten throws they each have another five throws to decide the winner.

Bounce Bucket Ball (6 plus to any age. Indoors or outdoors on a hard, smooth surface)

Any number can take part. This is a similar game to *Ball in the Basin* except that a bucket is used and the distance of the thrower from the bucket should be about six to nine feet. Each player in turn tries to *bounce* a ping-pong ball into the bucket. After ten tries the player with the highest score is the winner.

Hole in the Bucket (6 plus to any age. Indoors or outdoors on a lawn)

If a golf putter and a golf ball are available they should be used, but a walking-stick and a tennis ball, perforated ball or ping-pong ball can be used quite effectively. A child's bucket, a small basin, or large tumbler is placed on its side on the ground. Players take turns putting the ball with the club or stick into the receptacle from a distance of ten or twelve feet. The one with the highest number of successful putts after ten attempts is the winner.

Penny Roll (6 plus to any age. Indoors)

This game is identical in principle with *Hole in the Bucket*, except that each player tries to roll a penny into the receptacle from a line about ten feet or so distant. A bowling action with the penny rolling off the first finger should be used.

Pennies in the Circle (6 plus to any age. Indoors on a smooth or polished floor)

Each player requires four pennies. The game is best played in pairs. Eliminate normally to get two into the final, who then play off to decide the winner of the game. About six inches from a wall draw a circle in chalk about six inches in diameter. The players kneel down about ten feet from the circle and in turn slide their four pennies along the floor trying to get them in the circle. The one who gets the most in goes on to the next round. It is permissible, of course, to try to knock your opponent's pennies *out* of the circle. If the aim is so bad that no pennies finish up in the circle the ones nearest to it score.

Penny Bowls (6 plus to any age. Indoors on a smooth or polished floor)

This is another pairs game, similar in principle to *Pennies in the Circle*, except that no circle is required. A halfpenny or sixpence is placed on the floor about a foot away from a wall, and the players, in turn, slide their pennies along the floor trying to get them as close to the target coin as possible. If only two are in the game a score, say, of eleven or fifteen can be decided on, the first one to get that score being the winner.

Penny on the Line (6 plus to any age. Indoors on a smooth floor)

Any number of players can take part at the same time, but six or eight are the most convenient numbers. Each player has six or eight halfpennies or pennies. A line is drawn on the floor (a crack between two boards will serve equally well). The players kneel on the floor about eight or ten feet from the line or crack. They then slide one of their coins along the floor, trying to make it stop on the line or as near to it as possible. The one whose coin is on or nearest to the line wins all the other coins. The game continues for a stated length of time, at the end of which the player with the most coins in his possession is the winner. Alternatively, the game can go on until one player has won all the coins.

Dropping Beans (Any age from 6 plus. Indoors or outdoors)

A simple quiet partner competition to pass the time between more active games. Eight or more can play at any one time. Place four one-pound jam jars on the floor. Provide four lots of ten peas or beans (or even ten large paper clips will do).

One player plays against another. Each in turn stands almost astride the jam jar, holds a pea or bean at nose height and tries to drop it in the jam jar. The one who gets the most out of ten in the jar is the winner. Let winners play winners and losers play losers, or run the game as a simple knock-out competition.

Magic Square (6 plus to any age. Indoors or outdoors)

This is similar in principle to *Holey Board* except that less preparation is needed.

On a piece of paper or cardboard rule out nine squares, each about six inches square, and write numbers in each as shown in Fig 26. (The numbers in each row add up to fifteen.)

The board is then laid *flat* on the floor and competitors pitch pennies or crown corks on to the board from about nine

4	9	2
3	5	7
8	1	6

Fig 26

99

feet away. Missiles which fall on lines (i.e. they are not completely in a square) do not count.

Each competitor has a total of nine throws, one at a time in turn; the one with the highest score being the winner.

Indoor Bowls (Any age from 5 plus. Indoors)

This is a useful wet-day game requiring nothing more than nine marbles (for two players at a time) or four marbles per player plus one for the 'jack' – and a fairly large book.

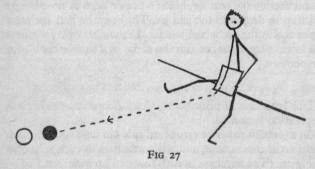

FIG 27

The game is best played on a fairly smooth carpet. The 'jack' is either rolled or placed in position at one side of the playing space on the carpet (the jack should be a marble of distinctive colour). Each player in turn, sitting with his legs astride and holding the book as shown in Fig 27, rolls one of his marbles down the book and tries to get it as near to the jack as possible. (It is advisable for each player to have marbles of a distinctive colour so that each knows which are his own and which are his opponent's.)

After each has rolled his four marbles the score is counted. The marbles nearest the jack count one point. The maximum score for each 'end' that a player can make would be four, when all his marbles are nearer the jack than any of those of his opponent.

The game can be decided on either the highest score from a

given number of 'ends' (i.e. each player playing four marbles counts as one 'end') or the one who first reaches a given number of points, say twenty-one.

Roll for Goal (8 plus to any age. Indoors)

This is a game played on a table with pennies. Make a goal at one end of the table by placing two small books about three inches apart. Now try to roll a penny across the table and into the goal. The penny should be supported (by one finger only) upright on the edge of the table farthest from the goal, and only this one finger should be used to roll the penny.

Each competitor has a total of ten rolls, the one with the highest number of goals being the winner.

A similar game can be played on the carpet, rolling the penny down a book as in *Indoor Bowls* (see page 100). Another variation is to have more than one goal with differing scores for each, the goal in the centre counting the highest number of points. The goals can be made from books as suggested above or cut out of a cardboard box as shown in Fig 28 below.

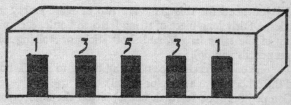

FIG 28

In the case of a box goal, the slits can be small, not more than half an inch to an inch wide.

Another alternative is to use marbles for rolling instead of coins.

SECTION TWELVE
RACES AND COMPETITIONS

These are races for any number of players, all of whom are doing the same thing at the same time. Usually the competitors start side by side in line. The advantage of individual competitions is that they can be used when the numbers at the party are small and team competitions are not possible; the disadvantage is that if you wish to avoid having only one or two players performing at any one moment, while the rest watch, you become involved in preparing more materials for certain of the activities.

Milk Bottle Race (Any age above 10. Indoors or outdoors)

All you need for this game are two or more empty milk bottles, a fairly long piece of string for each bottle, each piece being of the same length, and short sticks or walking sticks (even pencils will do).

Tie one end of each piece of string firmly to a milk bottle and the other end to a stick (or pencil).

Competitors (one for each bottle) sit on the floor or on a chair holding the stick across their knees. On the starting signal they twist the sticks to wind up the string; the first one to get the bottle up to touch the stick is the winner. Heats and finals can be run if so desired.

Paper Stepping Stones (10 plus to any age)

Each competitor is provided with two half pages of newspaper and is required to travel over a given distance or course always being on one of the two pieces of newspaper. Standing on one piece, he puts the other down in front of him, steps on to it, picks up the piece he has just left and places that in front of him, steps on to it – and so completes the course.

Sir Walter Raleigh Race (10 plus to any age)

This is a variation of *Paper Stepping Stones* for pairs – a boy and girl. The girl does the walking on the newspapers; the boy does the moving of them only. To add amusement, you can insist that he lays each one down with a sweeping bow and words appropriate to the occasion such as 'Prithee, walk on my cloak, O Queen' or merely 'Step on it, Liz'.

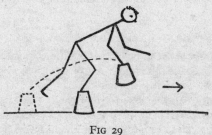

FIG 29

Plant Pot Race

A game more suitable for lawns than lounges. The principle is identical with that of *Paper Stepping Stones* except that reasonably large plant pots are used to step on. The course should not be more than fifteen to twenty feet in length, as progress tends to be slow due to the amount of balancing required from competitors (see Fig 29).

Indoors, large old books could be used instead of plant pots.

Potting the Beans

Each player is provided with two cups or bowls, half a dozen beans (or peas) and a ruler or table knife.

One cup containing the six beans is placed on the starting line by the feet of each player, the other cup is placed a short distance away (the distance must be the same for all competitors).

The object of the race is to transfer the six beans one at a time to the empty cup, using only the implement provided to do so.

Nose Ball

Each competitor is required to push a ping-pong ball over a short course using his nose only. More amusement is caused if the course is an out-and-home one, for the player then has to turn his ball round a corner.

An alternative is *Blow Ball* when the ping-pong ball is blown round the course; a straw should be provided for each competitor for this purpose.

Sheepdog Trials (8 to 80. Indoors or outdoors)

Though this game can be played in quite a small room, it is much more effective in a larger room or on a lawn where several 'dogs' can be in action at any one time.

The object of the game is for one player (the shepherd) to guide another player who is blindfolded (the sheepdog) round a series of obstacles and into a pen by giving verbal instructions only.

In a small room, a single short course can be devised in which the sheepdog negotiates obstacles such as cushions, books, stools, etc., and finally enters a pen consisting of two chairs, one chair width apart, set against a wall.

When only one shepherd and his dog are in action at any one time a watch should be used to take the time required to negotiate the course. The pair which does it in the shortest time are the winners.

In a large room or on the lawn, three or four courses can be in use at the same time; this not only makes the trials more exciting to watch, but adds amusement, because the dogs are apt to obey the commands of the wrong shepherds when all are calling instructions at the same time.

The dogs are blindfolded before the actual course is set up. They are then led to the starting line by their shepherds and turned round three times. From that moment onwards the shepherd remains on the starting line and the dog follows his instructions, e.g. 'Three paces forward, one pace to the right, two paces forward; one pace to the left' and so on.

Once a command has been given, the dog must carry it out (even if the shepherd realizes he has made a mistake) before another command can be given.

The only exception to this rule is if the command as given is leading the dog into actual danger.

In mixed parties it is a good thing to have girls acting as shepherds to their boy friends (or vice versa) or grandchildren guiding grandparents.

Fanning the Kipper (6 plus to any age)

This can be used as an individual contest or as a team relay race. If played as an individual contest, one folded newspaper and one 'kipper' (a piece of tissue paper about nine inches by four inches cut into the shape of a fish) per player is required; for a relay race, one kipper and one newspaper fan per team is needed.

Each competitor is required to waft or propel his kipper over a predetermined course by fanning just behind it with his newspaper.

Pegging the Clothes (Teenagers and upwards. Indoors or outdoors)

A boy and girl partner contest. A piece of string or clothes line and six handkerchiefs and one dozen clothes-pegs per pair competing are required.

The line is fixed at a convenient height and the competing pairs stand facing it about ten or twelve feet distant, the boy holding the twelve pegs, the girl the six handkerchiefs.

Partners race to the line; the girl takes one peg at a time from the boy and pegs up the handkerchiefs with two pegs to each. When they are all pegged, the boy unpegs them, one peg at a time. He passes the pegs (one at a time) to his partner, but retains the handkerchiefs. When they are all unpegged, the pair race back to the starting point, the first pair to get there being the winners.

Tip the Bottle Relay (6 plus to any age)

The players are arranged in equal teams. Normal relay procedure. In front of each team and ten or twelve feet (or more) distant place an empty milk bottle the right way up. The first player in each team runs to the bottle and turns it upside down, balancing it on its neck. He then dashes back to his team and touches the second player, who runs forward and places the bottle the right way up, the third player reverses it and so on. The first team to finish is the winner.

Blow the Ball Race (6 plus to any age. Indoors)

Players are divided into equal-sized teams. One ping-pong ball per team plus one drinking straw per player are required; normal relay procedure.

Each player blows (by means of his straw) the ping-pong ball over a there-and-back course, the first team to finish being the winners.

One-handed Doll Dressing (12 plus up to any age. Indoors)

This very amusing competition for pairs is very suitable for mixed parties, particularly in the teenage range.

Two dolls complete with clothes are required; the number of garments on each doll should be the same.

Contestants, who work in pairs, should be a boy and a girl.

The problem with which they are presented is a simple one. They are required to dress the doll as quickly as possible between them – *but*, and this is the snag, *they must each only use one hand*, the other one must be kept behind their backs all the time that they are working. It doesn't matter which hand they choose to work with, but once having made the decision, they must not change hands.

Front and Back Race (6 plus to any age. Indoors or outdoors)

Two saucers and a dozen buttons, beans, shells, or similar small objects per team are required.

This is an amusing and often exciting team race in which everyone is busy, but no one is rushing about.

Teams of equal numbers stand sideways in line. On the floor by the leader of each team are two saucers or similar receptacles, one containing the twelve (more if desired and available) small objects, the other empty.

On the starting signal, the leader picks up one object at a time and passes it to the second in the team, who passes it to the third, and so on down the line. When the object reaches the last player he begins to pass it back down the line *behind* his back, thus at the same time some objects are being passed in one direction in front of the body, and others are being passed in the opposite direction behind the body. When the leader receives the objects behind his back he puts them into the second and previously empty saucer. He must also count them as they come back to him, so that the instant he knows the last object has come back and been placed in the saucer he can shout 'Up' to indicate that his team has completed the race.

The number of objects to be passed can be varied at will, but whenever possible it should be at least twice the number of players in the team, so that automatically every player will be involved, at some period of the competition, in passing objects in both directions at the same time.

Plate and Marbles Relay (8 plus to any age. Indoors)

Equal teams stand in line behind their leader, who is holding in both hands a small cardboard plate containing five to ten marbles, the number being the same for each team. The plate is then passed overhead down the line, each player grasping and passing the plate with two hands. When the back player receives it he runs to the front of the line with it (each member of the team moves back one place) and again passes it overhead to the back player, who runs to the front and so on until the original leader becomes the last player. When he receives it he runs to the front, holds the plate above his head and calls 'Up'. The first team to finish with all the marbles on the plate are the winners.

If any marbles drop off the plate during the race they must be retrieved and put on the plate, which must not be passed until it has its right number of marbles.

Arch and Straddle Plate and Marbles (8 to any age. Indoors)

The procedure in this team relay is identical with *Plate and Marbles Relay*, except that the plate is passed alternately over the heads and under the legs all down the line. The rear player must remember when he goes to the front of the line that he must pass it differently from the way he receives it. If he receives it overhead he must pass it under the legs, and vice versa.

Over and Under Plate and Marbles (8 plus to any age. Indoors)

Procedure as in the two relays above, except that the plate is passed alternately over the head and under the legs by the players each time it goes down the line. The leader passes it overhead, where it is taken by the second player, who passes it under his legs to the third player, who passes it overhead, and so on.

With younger children modifications should be made; the receptacles should be somewhat deeper than a shallow plate, or solid objects such as books, rubber quoits, or tennis balls, can be substituted for the plate and marbles.

Drop the Lot Relay (6 plus to any age. Indoors or outdoors)

For this race you will need six or seven empty matchboxes or cigarette packets for each team; clothes-pegs will do, but you will require about a dozen per team if you use them in preference to boxes.

Equal teams stand in line. The leader has the matchboxes on the ground in front of him. On the starting signal he gathers them up in his hands and drops them from not lower than knee height at the feet of the second player, who in turn picks them up and drops them at the feet of the third player. This procedure continues until the last player picks them up; when he does so, he races back to the leader, drops them in front of him, and scoots back to his place.

The number of objects to be picked up will depend largely on the age of the competitors; there should be enough of them to make a really awkward double handful.

Peas on a Knife Race (6 plus to any age. Indoors)

Two cups, ten dried peas, and one flat lollipop stick per competitor are required. The cups are placed on the floor about six feet apart, and in one of the cups are placed the ten peas. Using the lollipop stick only, each competitor transfers the ten peas to the empty cup. The free hand should be kept behind the back. With younger children the number of peas can be reduced to five or six, otherwise the competition may drag on too long.

Chopsticks Race (8 plus to any age. Indoors)

This race is a variation of *Peas on a Knife Race*. Each player has two saucers, with ten grains of uncooked rice in one of them, and two knitting needles or cocktail sticks. Using these as chopsticks, he has to transfer the grains of rice, one at a time, to the empty saucer. Both hands can be used to manipulate the needles on this occasion, if required.

Marble Race (6 plus to 11 plus. Indoors or outdoors)

This is a variation of the well-known *Potato Race*. Each child stands on a line (or at the edge of the lawn). At his feet he has a cup or mug. In front of him at one-yard intervals are four marbles. All the competitors race forwards, pick up a marble, run back, and drop it in the vessel; they repeat this action with each marble in turn. When they have collected the four marbles, they hold the cup containing them them above their heads. The first one to do so wins the race.

With older children the number of objects to be picked up can be increased to six or seven, or the distance from the starting line to the first object can be lengthened. Do not make this more than four or five yards, however, or the children will become quite exhausted. With five marbles at one-yard intervals and a distance of five yards from the start line to the first marble, the child has to run a distance of seventy yards!

Ring Gathering (10 plus to any age. Indoors or outdoors)

A dozen small curtain-rings and two garden canes or walking-sticks are required for this competition.

Lay out the curtain-rings in two equal-length rows of six; each curtain-ring should be about a foot from the next one.

The contestants stand facing the rings holding the canes. They are then required to pick up the six rings on the stick, and they are not allowed either to touch them with their hands *or to bend their knees*. The first ring is easy to pick up, but the next five are much more difficult.

Make this into a knock-out competition, the winner of each pair going on to the next round.

Bang, Bang Relay (6 plus to any age)

One small paper bag per player is required. Two equal-numbered teams are chosen and sit on chairs in line, facing each other about six to eight feet apart. On the seat of each chair is a small paper bag, about the size which will hold half a pound of sweets (see Fig 30).

On the starting signal the first member of each team jumps up, dashes down the front of his team, round behind the chairs, and back to his place. He sits down, picks up his paper bag, blows it up, and then bursts it by hitting it hard with the hand. This bursting of the bag is the signal for the second player to start. He repeats the same performance as the leader and sets off the third player by bursting his bag. Each member of the team does exactly the same. The bursting of the last runner's bag is the signal that the team has completed the course, the first team to finish being the winner.

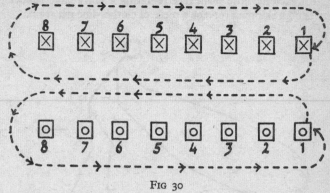

FIG 30

Boat Race (5 plus to 12 plus. Large room, lawn, or beach)

At least two groups of from six to eight are needed. A 'boat' is made by five or seven players in knees-full-bend position behind each other, each with his hands on the shoulders of the person in front. The remaining player, the 'cox', stands facing the 'boat' holding the hands of the first player.

The 'boat' moves forwards by all the players hopping together off both feet, the 'cox' helping by calling out the rhythm so that they all move in unison. 'Boats' race against each other over short distances. During the race, any 'boat' which 'breaks', i.e. anyone losing grip on the shoulders, is considered to have sunk and is disqualified.

Duck Race (5 plus to 12 plus. Large room, lawn, or beach)

This is almost identical with *Boat Race*. Groups form up in a similar manner, but instead of hopping forwards they walk forwards in the knees-full-bend position. The leader helps the rhythm by calling out 'left-right-left' to keep them all in step.

Dragging the Ball (6 plus to any age. Indoors or outdoors)

An exciting little team race requiring a fairly large rubber ball and a skipping rope or a piece of clothes-line per team.

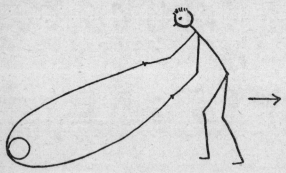

FIG 31

The object of the race is for each member of the team to drag a ball over a short there-and-back course by means of the rope as shown in Fig 31. This race is particularly suitable for a lawn, where the slight unevenness of the grass makes the ball more difficult to pull along.

Chin-chin or Adam's Apple (8 plus to any age)

This team passing game is particularly suitable for teenagers, but it can be played with equal amusement by both children and adults.

Teams form lines; where possible have girls and boys alternately so that a boy passes to a girl, and vice versa.

Now present the leader of each team with a large apple or orange, and inform them that at the word 'go' the apple has to be passed to the end of the team and back without the hands being used at all – in fact, it must be passed from chin to chin.

The leader is allowed to place the apple in position with his hands, the position being on the shoulder, with the chin pressing firmly on the apple (see Fig 32).

From then onwards it is chin to chin!

There is only one other rule. If the apple drops to the ground during the contest (as it inevitably will) the passer must pick it up and not the receiver.

FIG 32

Spoon Ball

This is a variation of *Chin-chin*. Teams are arranged as before, but one spoon per player and one table-tennis ball or marble per team is needed.

The leader, holding the spoon handle in his mouth, places the ball in the bowl of the spoon, turns round and passes the ball to the next in line, and so on (see Fig 33).

Ping pong ball in a spoon

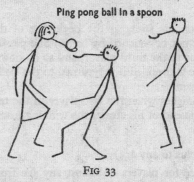

FIG 33

If the ball is dropped (it will be), it must not be picked up by hand but by the spoon *still held in the mouth*.

Thimble Race

A simple team passing race suitable for players of any age above about eight years, similar to *Spoon Ball*, in which one thimble per team and one plastic drinking 'straw' per member of each team are required.

Equally numbered teams form up in lines; the leader holding the thimble. On the starting signal, he puts the straw in his mouth and the thimble on top of the straw.

He then turns round to face the second player in his team, who, with the straw in her mouth, takes the thimble from the leader's straw (Fig 34). (From the moment the leader places

FIG 34

the thimble on his straw at the beginning of the race the thimble must not be touched by hand.) She passes it on in a similar manner to the third player, and so on down the team. If the thimble is dropped it is returned to the leader and that team starts again.

The race finishes when the last player in the team has the thimble on the end of his straw; the winning team is the one to finish first.

A-tissue (7 plus to any age)

A team race for players of almost any age from seven to seventy. A piece of tissue paper about six inches square per team is required together with one drinking straw for every player.

Each team arranges itself either in a line or in a circle. The team leader places the tissue paper over the end of his straw, one end of which is in his mouth, and draws in his breath, causing the tissue paper to stick to the end of the straw (see Fig 35). He then turns to the next player and passes the paper on to him, the secret of passing being that he must exhale gently as the receiver inhales. In an identical manner the paper is passed all along the team, the first team to finish being the winner.

FIG 35

At no time during passing must the paper be touched by hand. If, however, it is dropped, the one who allowed it to fall is permitted to pick it up by hand and place it back in position on *his own* straw.

Nosey Parker Race (6 plus to any age. Indoors or outdoors)

Some empty matchboxes are required. This can be either a team race or one between pairs. A short there-and-back course is decided upon, and couples line up on the start line. The two members of each pair face each other and support a matchbox cover between them by their noses. Keeping the matchbox in position and not touching it with the hands (except to pick it up and replace it, should it be dropped) they race to the end line or mark and back to the start. Because of having to keep the matchbox in position, they will be compelled to run sideways.

If the competition is run as a team race the members can split up into pairs, handing over the matchbox to the next pair on return, or the first and second can go together, then the second and third, third and fourth, and so on.

Blind Potato Race

A game for volunteers of any age requiring a bag and four small objects such as potatoes, nuts, or buttons per competitor.

The competitors kneel on the floor behind a line or close to the wall. They are each given a fairly large paper bag which they place on the floor by their sides and behind the line.

In a straight line in front of them, about two or three feet apart are placed the four objects.

The players are then blindfolded.

On the signal to start, each one crawls forward and tries to find the first object; having done so he crawls back to the starting line with the object and places it in his paper bag (if he can find it). He then crawls forward to find the second object and so on until he has collected the four and placed them in his bag.

The first person to succeed in doing this is the winner.

It may well happen, of course, that competitors get a little mixed up during the game and pick up someone else's objects or place their own in the wrong bag. This merely adds to the fun. If there are more than four volunteers, the game can be run on a heats and final basis. The overall winner should receive a small prize.

Do This, Do That (8 plus to any age)

This game is highly popular with children, but can prove amusing also to teenagers and adults. The players space themselves out quite freely in front of a leader.

Whenever he says 'Do this' and performs some action, such as stretching his arms upwards or clapping his hands, all the players must instantly copy him. If, on the other hand, he performs an action and at the same time says 'Do that' the players must ignore the command and continue doing what they were told to do when the order 'Do this' was given.

Anyone who makes a mistake is eliminated. Similarly, if a player does not move quickly enough when 'Do this' is said he or she is eliminated also. The leader should give the orders in fairly rapid succession, and the movements should be simple ones. The game continues until all but one are eliminated; the last person 'in' being the winner.

Quite Contrary (6 plus to 12 plus. Indoors or outdoors)

This is an 'active' game, but one which does not involve the children tearing about all over the place; it is also, like *Do This, Do That*, a test of alertness.

It can be played with the children working as individuals or in teams. The leader stands where he or she is plainly visible to all the players and performs a series of simple activities. The children are required immediately to do exactly the opposite. If the leader swings up the left arm the children do the same with the right, if he or she hops on the right foot, they hop on the left, and so on. Anyone making a mistake or taking too long to start the proper movement is eliminated, the last remaining person, or the last team with anyone remaining in it, being the winner.

If the children are pretty bright and alert the movements can become more complicated, e.g. one arm up, the other sideways, patting the head with one hand and rubbing the stomach with a circular motion with the other, etc.

A time limit can also be imposed, particularly if a team competition is being run, the team with the most players remaining at the end of a given time being the winner. This will help to prevent the demonstrator from becoming completely exhausted.

All Change (6 plus to 11 plus. Indoors or outdoors)

All the players except one sit in a circle, either on chairs or on the floor; the one remaining stands blindfolded in the centre of the circle. All the seated players then take the name of a well-known town or city, calling out the one they choose, such as London, Manchester, Bristol, Glasgow, Leeds, etc. (The leader, or whoever is running the game, should make a mental or written note of these towns.)

The leader then chooses two towns sitting opposite each

other and calls out, 'The train is now going from London to Manchester' (or any other two places). Manchester and London get up and quietly change places; as they do so, the blindfolded one tries to catch one of them as they pass. If, after a few change-overs, no catch has been made, the leader calls, 'All change,' when everyone must cross to the opposite side of the circle. In the confusion that results the centre player is pretty certain to catch someone who then takes his place in the centre, while he becomes one of the 'towns'.

Winking (11 plus to 15 plus. Indoors)

This is an age-old favourite with young boys and girls. A circle of chairs is made facing inwards. A girl sits on each chair except one, which is left empty. Behind each chair, including the empty one, stands a boy with his hands resting on top of the chair but not touching the girl sitting in it.

The boy standing behind the empty chair starts the game by winking at one of the girls, who must immediately try to leave her chair and dash to the empty one. The boy standing behind her, however, must try to stop her from going by putting his hands on her shoulders. If he does this quickly enough she must remain where she is and wait for another chance when she is winked at again. If she does succeed in getting away, the boy who failed to keep her must then wink at some other girl in an effort to fill the chair in front of him. Whichever boy is doing the winking must use guile and cunning to obtain surprise. For instance, his wink can be almost imperceptible (except to the girl who is looking for it) or he can gaze steadily towards one part of the circle for a few seconds, then quickly turned his head and wink at a girl on the other side.

After all or most of the girls have been winked at, change over; let the boys sit down and the girls stand behind the chairs to have their turn at winking.

Blow Football (6 plus to any age)

This is a table game played between two sides or teams of equal number. A drinking straw is required for each person.

In addition, a table-tennis ball and four matchboxes or small books (to make goals) are needed.

The players group themselves round the table (which should have a cloth on). They can be in any order, but it is preferable that one team should be towards one end of the table and the other team at the opposite end (see Fig 36). The matchboxes or books are then arranged as goals, about six inches wide.

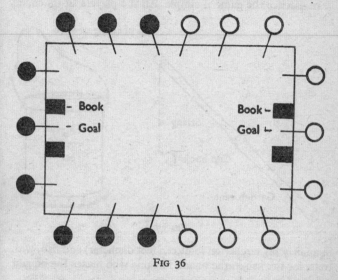

FIG 36

The table-tennis ball is placed in the centre of the table, and on the starting signal each side tries to score goals by blowing the ball into the opposing goal.

The rules are simple:

(1) There must be no pushing, shoving, or elbowing round the table.

(2) All blowing must be done through the straws.

(3) After each goal, or if the ball falls off the table, the game is restarted by placing the ball in the centre of the 'pitch'.

Fish in the Pond (6 plus to any age. Indoors or outdoors)

Though this game needs a little previous preparation, it is well worth while, as it can cause considerable amusement without any upset – and can be used as an interlude between more strenuous activities. It can also be played by players of almost any age, boys or girls, men or women.

In essence the game is simple. All the players sit on chairs

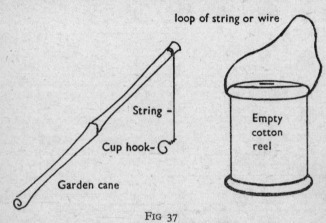

loop of string or wire

String –

Cup hook–

Garden cane

Empty cotton reel

Fig 37

in a fairly big circle (ten to fifteen feet diameter) and fish, with rods, for the fish in the pond. The one who makes the biggest catch is the winner.

The rods are made from either pieces of dowelling or from garden canes about four feet long. The line should be a piece of string, also about four feet long, to the end of which is attached the 'hook', which can be a blunt-ended piece of wire, or better still (and less trouble) a round brass cup hook (see Fig 37).

The 'fish' are empty cotton reels, to the top of which is attached a loop of string or wire (Fig 37).

The 'fish' (about twenty, if possible) are placed on the ground in the centre of the circle of seated players, and on the starting signal each player does his utmost to hook as many of the 'fish' as he can.

With younger children, the winner can be decided simply on the number of fish caught, but with older children and adults, additional interest can be raised by making each 'fish' of a different 'weight', the angler with the highest poundage taking the prize. The 'weights', e.g. 'pike 5 lb', 'tiddler, $\frac{1}{2}$ ounce', are written on small pieces of paper, rolling these up and slipping them into the central hole of the reel. If the reels are of various sizes it is often a good idea to put the largest 'weight' into one of the smaller reels. Fishing goes on for a given time or until all the 'fish' are caught.

Find the Leader (8 plus to 12 plus. Indoors or outdoors)

One player goes out of the room. While he is out the others choose a leader, and then they all sit in a circle. The leader starts any simple movement, such as patting his stomach, opening and shutting his mouth, waving his hand, and so on. The other circle players copy his movements, changing when he does.

The player who has been outside now comes and stands in the centre of the circle. His task is to find which of the circle players is the leader. The leader will, of course, not normally change a movement while the centre player is looking in his direction. When the centre player finds the leader, he takes his place in the circle, the leader goes out of the room and a new leader is chosen.

If the centre player does not discover the leader after two or three minutes he should be told who it is; another player would then be sent out of the room and a new leader chosen.

Find the Whistle (8 plus to 10 plus. Indoors or outdoors)

This old favourite, suitable for both boys and girls, has many variations. Here is a simple form.

Two or three victims who have not played the game before go out of the room, the rest form a fairly close circle all sitting facing inwards on chairs.

The first victim is then brought in and told to kneel in the centre of the circle. He or she is then blindfolded; while this is being done, a small wooden whistle (one from a cracker will do), which is attached to a piece of string about twelve inches long on the end of which is a safety pin, is attached surreptitiously to the back of the victim's coat or dress.

Some rigmarole is then told about the Fairy Queen's (or Demon King's) whistle having been stolen and that it is suspected that one of the fairies (demons) in the circle has taken it. The victim has been called in to help find it. It has got a rather unusual note, and if he (the victim) concentrates hard he may be able to hear it. At this, one of the circle players gently lifts the whistle, blows it, and lets it drop equally gently.

The blindfold is then removed. Immediately this is done, another player behind the victim blows the whistle. The victim will automatically turn round and accuse someone of having it, which will be hotly denied – and, as proof, the whistle sounds again from the opposite side of the circle.

It may be quite a time before he realizes that the whistle is attached to his own back.

When he does find out, allow him the privilege of 'telling the tale' to the next victim to be brought in!

Spinning the Plate (8 plus to any age)

The plate should be either a metal one or a wooden bread board. All the players sit round in a fairly wide circle, either on chairs or on the floor. They then 'number off' round the circle.

The leader or host goes into the centre of the circle and spins the plate on the ground. He then calls out any number, and the player in the circle with that number dashes forward to catch the plate before it stops spinning. If he is successful he starts the plate spinning again and calls out another number before he returns to his place in the circle.

Anyone who fails to catch the plate either 'loses a life' or drops out. What often happens is that while someone is laughing at somebody else's attempts at catching the plate, his or her number is called. This fact may not be realized at all, or only at the very last instant when there is a terrific dash into the centre to catch the very last moments of the spin.

Tip It (Up Jenkins) (8 plus to any age. Indoors)

It doesn't really matter whether you call this game *Tip It* or *Up Jenkins*, it's fun either way.

Two teams, preferably of the same number of players, sit in line facing each other on opposite sides of the table.

One of the teams (chosen by tossing) passes a threepenny piece or a sixpence from hand to hand under the table. The leader of the opposite team, after a few seconds calls out 'Up' (or 'Up Jenkins'). Immediately the team passing the coin bring their hands with fists clenched from under the table simultaneously and hold them about a foot above the table. On the second command, 'Down' or 'Down Jenkins', the clenched hands are slapped down on the table with palms flat. (Under one of them, of course, is the coin.)

The captain or leader of the opposite team advised by his team now has two courses open to him to find the hand covering the coin. He can either be quite definite about it, point to one of the hands and say 'Tip it' (if he is wrong the coin-holding side score a point and have another go) or he can say 'take that hand away'. If there is no coin under it, he then proceeds to order other hands to be removed from the table, one at a time. If, however, he orders a hand to be taken away and the coin *is* underneath it, the coin side wins again.

He can, if he so wishes, after having successfully moved off several hands, make another outright guess to say under which hand the coin is held. If he is successful, his side gain a point – and the coin, to try to baffle the original coin holders.

If desired, instead of the leader giving all the orders, each member of the guessing team can give them in turn.

A further variation which can be added, and which often causes considerable amusement, is for the guessing side, once in a game, to order 'Creepy Crawlies'. When this is given the hands which are flat on the table must be shuffled forwards about six inches by slightly raising and lowering the palm of the hand. The fingertips and the thumb are, of course, kept flat to prevent any chance of the coin being seen by the guessing side, who really hope that they may be able to hear the coin 'chink' on the table as the hands are moved. It rarely does!

The winning team is the one first to score a previously agreed number of points, usually an odd number such as seven, nine, or eleven.

SECTION THIRTEEN

HIDING AND FINDING GAMES

Hunt the Thimble (4 plus to 8 plus. Indoors)

Traditionally, a thimble is used for this old favourite, but any other object, such as a coin, button, or a cork, can be used. One player leaves the room while the thimble is hidden, the others remain seated. The seeker comes in and begins to hunt for the thimble. Help is given by the onlookers calling out 'ice cold', 'cold', 'warmer', 'fairly warm', 'very warm', 'hot', and 'boiling' as the searcher gets nearer and nearer to the thimble.

The first searcher, when the thimble is found, then has the privilege of hiding it for the next person to find.

As an alternative to calling out 'warm', 'cold', etc., the children can hum or buzz like bees, varying the loudness or softness as the seeker approaches or recedes from the hidden object.

How Green You Are

A singing variation of *Hunt the Thimble*.

When the seeker comes in to look for the thimble, the children sing over and over again, 'How green you are, how green you are,' the volume of noise increasing or decreasing as the seeker gets nearer to, or moves away from, the thimble.

Find and Sit or 'Blindman' (4 plus to 10 plus. Indoors)

This is another variation of *Hunt the Thimble* in which all the players are seeking at the same time. All taking part leave the room for a few moments while the object is placed in a not too inconspicuous spot. They then enter the room and try to find the object. The moment they see it they do not say a word, or show by any expressions that they have seen it, but sit down quietly on a chair or on the floor. The last person to discover the hidden object is the 'Blindman', but he then has the privilege of hiding it for the next round.

Musical Blindman

A singing variation of *Blindman*. The thimble is placed in a reasonably visible spot. The children return and look for it. The moment any child sees the thimble he sits down and starts to sing 'Three Blind Mice'. This process continues until all are sitting down singing, except one; he or she is the 'Blindman'.

Ten Coins

A game for children from about eight years upwards. While children are in one room or in the garden, place ten sixpences (or ten beans will do) in various places in another room. They must be so placed that they are reasonably visible if one looks hard, e.g. on top of a picture frame; half projecting from the leaves of a book; in the centre of a flower, and so on.

The children are then given paper and pencils, told that ten coins are hidden and that they are to try to find them. When they discover a coin, they do not tell anyone else about it, but write down its location on the sheet of paper.

The first player to bring a correct list of all the places is the winner.

Wool Gathering

A seeking game for summer parties in the garden. Before the children arrive or while they are indoors at tea, drape thirty or forty (make it a definite number) pieces of green wool about four or five inches long on bushes and plants around the garden.

The game continues until all the pieces have been found, the winner being the one with most pieces of wool.

Hidden Numbers (6 plus to 12 plus. Indoors and/or out-doors)

Pencils and paper are required. In this seeking game the object is to find a number and write down to what the number is attached. While the guests are playing a game which confines them to one room, or while they are having tea, arrange for a series of cards bearing consecutive numbers from 1 to 20 to be placed on or attached to various objects in the house and in the garden, if weather conditions and the time of year permit. Thus No. 1 could be placed on the piano or under the piano lid, No. 2 on the back of a settee, No. 3 on a rose tree in the garden, No. 4 on the door of the airing cupboard, and so on.

The children are given sheets of paper and pencils and told to write the numbers 1 to 20 down the left-hand side. When they have done this they are all sent off together to find the numbers and to write down on the paper where or on what the numbers are placed.

The first child who produces a correct list, or the one who produces the most in a time of ten minutes, is judged to be the winner.

One thing must be remembered; the numbers must be so placed that they can be seen or reached by even the smallest child in the game, otherwise the tall child will always have the advantage.

Finding the Proverbs

A game for children of about eight-plus upwards, needing some previous preparation. Suitable for small parties. Prepare a number of postcards by writing on each one part of a proverb; thus on one card you might write 'A rolling', on a second card 'stone gathers', and on a third card 'no moss'.

If you have ten guests you will need thirty cards over which you have spread ten proverbs.

Previously hide (not too inconspicuously) two cards of each proverb and at the party give each player the remaining card.

His first task will be to decide what proverb he is looking

for, and his second task will be to find the other two cards to complete it. The first player to produce a complete proverb is the winner.

No one is allowed to ask any questions; it is also good strategy not to indicate to the others that you have found a card that does not belong to the set you require. Merely glance at it surreptitiously and replace it.

If you wish to let the game last a fair amount of time, continue until the last player has completed his proverb when he, once again, becomes 'Blindman'.

Spot the Squeeze

Another 'finding' game for the seven- to ten-year-olds. All the players except one stand in a circle, fairly well spaced out and holding hands to the front of their bodies so that their hands are plainly visible to the remaining player who stands in the centre of the circle.

One of the circle players (instructed secretly by you) squeezes the hand of the player next to him or her. This squeeze is then passed on round the circle, but its direction can be changed at will, i.e. it can move clockwise or anti-clockwise.

The task of the centre player is to spot an actual squeeze being made. If he does so, the one detected becomes the centre player for the next turn.

Flap-Ears

A game somewhat similar in nature to the previous one in which one player stands in the centre of a circle of children facing inwards. It is suitable for children of six or seven years of age and upwards.

All the circle players place their hands with palms facing forwards and fingers stretched upwards by the sides of their ears.

When the centre player has his back turned towards them, the circle players flap their fingers about like ears in a strong wind, but when he is facing them they keep their fingers absolutely still.

It is the task of the centre player to catch someone actually waggling their fingers. He can, of course, turn round slowly or quickly in any direction he chooses.

Anyone caught 'flapping' changes places with the centre player.

Ankle Guessing (12 plus to any age. Indoors)

This guessing game can often cause some amusement, particularly to teenagers and adults. A large screen, or something similar improvised from an old blanket or sheet, is required. The boys go out of the room while the girls sit behind the sheet with just their feet and ankles protruding from underneath. (The shoes should be removed.) The boys then come in and are given pencils and paper on which they write down the identities of the girls judged from the ankles on view. The girls should be numbered, say, from left to right. Each boy would then put down the numbers and, by the side of each, a girl's name.

The one with the most correct is the winner.

The same thing can then be done the opposite way round, the girls guessing the identities of the boys. Only have volunteers for this game; someone might have a hole in his sock and not wish to display it!

Hand Guessing (12 plus to any age. Indoors)

This game is almost identical with *Ankle Guessing*, except that the girls hold one hand up above the top of the screen; the palm of the hand should be shown and not the back, as the colour of nail varnish might give away an identity. Rings and wrist-watches should also be removed for the same reason.

Repeat the game with the boys behind the screen.

Bloodhounds (10 plus to any age. Indoors)

Get a number of small paper bags and punch a few tiny holes in them. Place inside each bag something which has a distinct or characteristic smell; tie up the necks of the bags and suspend them in line from a piece of string.

Each competitor, provided with a piece of paper and a

pencil, then goes along the line of bags sniffing at each one and writing down what he thinks it contains. The one with the most correct wins a small prize. Suitable things to put in the bags are: mothballs, scented soap, a piece of orange peel, some grated nutmeg, a piece of cut onion, lavender, some peppermint sweets, cinnamon, a small piece of gorgonzola, a small piece of sponge soaked in Eau de Cologne or a well-known perfume, etc.

Noises Off (8 plus to any age. Indoors)

The host goes behind a screen and produces certain noises which have to be guessed and written down by the competitors. The one with the most correct wins. Some suggested noises are: removing a crown cork from a bottle, shuffling a pack of cards, tearing a piece of paper, cracking a nut, tapping the thumbnails together, brushing a shoe or a coat, dropping a sugar lump in a cup of liquid, rubbing a bunch of keys, scratching a bottle or piece of glass with a pin, snapping a piece of wood, smoothing and folding a piece of brown paper, tapping a tumbler with a fingernail, snapping a cigarette lighter, etc.

Pom-Pom Relievo

A variation of normal *Hide-and-Seek* which will be played almost indefinitely by children from about seven to ten years of age. It is particularly useful for small numbers.

One child, the seeker, stands in a corner facing the wall with eyes closed and counts up to 50 (or 100) while the rest of the children scatter throughout the house and hide.

Having counted up to the required total, the seeker goes looking for the hiders. The first one to be found becomes the seeker, BUT if any child manages to get back to the corner in which the seeker stood to count, without being spotted and named by the seeker, he or she calls out 'Pom-Pom Relievo' and the game starts all over again with the same player acting as the seeker once again.

Witch-Hunt

A form of *Hide-and-Seek* specially suitable for children of eleven years of age and upwards for a Hallowe'en party. Children who are known to be nervous should not be coerced to join in.

One person, chosen to be the witch, goes out into the garden or, if the weather is not suitable, hides somewhere in the house – *with all the lights turned out.*

After a suitable lapse of time, the witch hunters go looking for the witch. If they call out, 'Where are you, Witch?', the witch answers by giving an eerie or ghostly cackle, and then slips quietly away to some other spot in the dark.

Whoever succeeds in catching or cornering the witch becomes the witch for the next round.

Murder (Teenagers upwards)

This is an old game but is always popular with teenagers. Select as many playing cards as there are players. Included in the playing cards must be an ace and a jack. The player who draws the jack is the murderer, the person who draws the ace is the detective. All the lights are turned out. The players move round the house not knowing who the victim will be. The detective stays in one lighted room. The murderer selects a victim, puts his hands round the victim's neck and whispers, 'I am the murderer, you are dead.' The victim waits for a count of ten, and then screams, during which time the murderer has time to move away from the scene of the crime. After the victim has screamed, the detective turns on the lights; the players are not allowed to move. The detective makes notes of which player was in which part of the house or flat. Then all the players return to the main room where the questioning takes place.

During the questioning, all the players must tell the truth – only the murderer can lie.

From the answers given, the detective then tries to deduce who did the murder. When he is convinced that he knows who it is, and not before, he says, 'I accuse you of murdering Mary Jones.' If his accusation is correct the murderer – for the first time – is required to tell the truth, and the detective wins. If, however, he definitely accuses the wrong person the murderer wins and the mystery remains unsolved.

Treasure Hunts (Suitable for any age above 10 plus. Indoors or outdoors)

Treasure Hunts need some careful thought and preparation, particularly in the devising of clues, which must neither be too hard nor too easy for the age of the players taking part.

The principle of the game is simple. The players, generally in pairs, are each given a written clue to start with. The solution of the first clue leads them to the second clue, the second to the third, and so on until they finally reach the 'treasure', which can be a small prize for each of the pair. The game can be played indoors or outdoors or can go from indoor to outdoor locations, and vice versa.

As every house and every garden is different, it is obviously impossible to lay down a set of concrete instructions, but the following *Treasure Hunt* types of clue will indicate the sort of thing required for children of twelve to fourteen years of age.

Each pair is given a small slip of paper on which is written: 'Where the mouse ran up in a small bedroom.'

The smarter ones will immediately think of the nursery rhyme 'Dickory, Dickory, Dock, the mouse ran up the *clock*'. They must therefore look for a clock in a small bedroom in the house. Behind the clock is another slip of paper, written on it is: (Mixed up) '*Motor Ad*'. This may cause a little trouble, but someone will soon see that the letters when rearranged make 'DOORMAT', and it is under the doormat that the next clue is found. This clue says, 'Submarines sink under the sea. Leave out the submarines and almost go into reverse'. This when solved becomes 'Sea (see) under the sink' – so into the kitchen they go for clue 4, which reads 'It's under 14 lb near a rose bush.' It will not take them long to realize that 14 lb is a *stone*, so off they go turning up stones near rose bushes – and sure enough under one of them is the fifth clue.

'You'd be in a jam if you found the next clue on a pantry shelf'. This is a relatively easy one. They've got to find a jar on a shelf in the pantry.

Clues can be very simple in direction, but difficult to find. For instance, a clue could merely say 'It's under a chair'. This will then involve the searchers looking under every chair in the house – and when they do find it, it is pinned underneath the seat!

The only other necessary rules are:

(1) All clues must be left where they are found.

(2) The solutions to the clues must not be given to the other treasure hunters.

(3) All cupboards, drawers, etc., must be closed if they were found so.

SECTION FOURTEEN
'SILLY' GAMES

'Silly' games can cause lots of hilarity at a party but, unless care is taken, they can also cause a lot of embarrassment.

It is wise to avoid games in which items of clothing are removed or, if they are included, make them for volunteers only. Even a game which merely requires shoes to be taken off could embarrass someone who has a hole in his sock!

I have also avoided games of the 'practical joke' type in which players' faces are blacked. This form of humour can not only be embarrassing but can also spoil clothing.

Straight Face (Any age from 6 upwards)

With teenagers and adults the game can be given the alternative name of *Dead Pan*.

Five or six boys are seated in a row; facing them are an equal number of girls. The girls have the task of trying to make the boys smile, the boys have to keep a 'straight face' or 'dead pan'.

At the start of the game each girl concentrates on the boy opposite to her, and by posturing, grimaces, making stupid noises, etc., she tries to make him smile. The moment any boy smiles or laughs, he drops out, and the six girls then devote their attention to the remaining five, and so on until finally there is only one boy left – he, of course, being the winner. It then becomes the task of the boys to make the girls laugh by using similar methods.

Finally, the winner from the boys and the winner from the girls try to make each other laugh. Obviously, as both have considerable control over their features, some ingenuity will have to be shown by each to get the other to smile –

generally to the great amusement of the other guests who are watching.

Okay for Sound (6 plus to any age. Indoors or outdoors)

A sitting-down game, useful between two energetic games. The players all sit in a circle or in a line while the storyteller (almost certainly yourself) makes up a story mentioning various sounds. As each one is mentioned, each child in turn has to imitate the sound to the best of his ability. Anyone failing to do so either loses a 'life' or drops out; at the end of the story the one who has lost the least number of 'lives', or who is last in, is the winner. A typical story might start like this (the sounds to be imitated are in italics):

'One dark and stormy night as the wind *whistled* round the house, I heard an owl *hooting* in the trees, then somewhere a dog *barked* and a cat *mewed*. I listened for a moment. What was that? It was someone *scratching at the door*! Then there was a low *growl* and I thought I could hear someone *crying*. I got up from my chair and started to go to the door. To pretend I wasn't afraid, I started to *hum* a song, but just as I got into the hall, I heard the *scratching* and *crying* noise again, and then someone started to *cough* as well. . . .'

Other noises which could be introduced are: a train *whistled*, a motor car *started its engine*, a bell *rang*, a clock *struck three*, a *clap* of thunder, a lion *roared*, a duck *quacked*, a cock *crowed*, a horse *whinnied*, a pig *grunted*, and so on.

The story is not of vital importance with adults; in fact, the sillier it is the better, but with children it is better to try to make it reasonably interesting or dramatic.

Feed Your Friend (8 plus to any age. Indoors or outdoors)

Two bowls, some contents for the bowls, two wooden spoons, and two aprons or overalls are required for this 'silly' game, which is a useful time-passer for the odd moments before a meal or between two hectic rushing-about games. It is also a game for volunteers only – and volunteers who do not mind looking temporarily ridiculous.

Two players, wearing overalls to protect their suits or dresses, are seated on chairs facing each other about three or four feet apart. In their left hands they hold a small basin in which can be put some dry cereal, or broken biscuits, or if outdoors, some cereal and milk, cold rice pudding, or in extreme circumstances, some treacle. (Discretion *must* be used on the contents of the basin.) In the right hand, each player holds a wooden spoon. They are then blindfolded.

The game is quite simple. Each tries to feed the other! Don't keep them at it too long, or something somewhere will be ruined – and do make certain, particularly if liquid is involved, that their clothes are well protected.

Feeding Time

This is a 'silly' competitive game for boy/girl pairs who should be volunteers. A chair, a baby's bottle or medicine bottle with teat, and a napkin or small hand towel per pair are required.

The girls or women taking part sit on chairs at one end of the room holding the feeding bottle half full of milk (all bottles should contain the same measured amount) and the napkin.

The boys or men stand opposite their partners in a line at the opposite end of the room.

At the signal to start, the men rush across to their partners and sit on their knees. The girls then tie the napkins round their partners' necks and hold the bottles while the men drink the milk as quickly as they can. (The men are not allowed to touch the bottles with their hands.) As soon as the bottle is emptied, the girl unties the napkin and both then race back to the line from which the men started. The first pair to do so are the winners.

An alternative method of finishing is for the 'baby' to pick up his partner and carry her back to the starting line.

136

Bun Biting (Any age from 8 upwards. Indoors or outdoors)

This game is definitely for volunteers. Suspend one small bun (they must all be about the same size) for each competitor on a string.

Each competitor is then required to eat his bun without touching it with his hands. The one who does it first is the winner.

Bob Apple (8 plus upwards. Indoors or outdoors)

This is an almost identical game to *Bun Biting*, except that *peeled and cored* apples are suspended from the rope instead of buns.

Feeding the Baby (A silly game for adults who volunteer)

Four babies' feeding bottles, complete with teats and half full of lemonade, milk, or other drinkable liquid, are suspended (teat downwards) on pieces of string at just below head height. The competitor who succeeds in emptying his or her bottle first (it must not be touched by the hands) is the winner.

Duck Apple (7 plus to 14)

This traditional game is more suitable for boys than for girls. Take a large bowl and fill it just above halfway with water. Place the bowl on the floor (if the game is being played indoors, a waterproof groundsheet or some thick towels will prevent the carpets from getting wet). In the bowl place one or more apples, according to the number of contestants, who should definitely be volunteers. The object of the game is quite simple, to get the apples from the water without the use of the hands.

Dusty Miller

Definitely a game for male volunteers only, this is a dry variation of the perennial *Duck Apple*.

Place a large dust sheet on the floor and in the centre of it place a medium-sized enamel or plastic bowl in which has been put sufficient flour to half fill the bowl.

Stir into the flour half a dozen or so threepenny bits which have previously been thoroughly scrubbed and well dried.

Provide your volunteers with an effective overall, then ask them, one at a time, to try and remove as many threepenny bits as possible in, say, two minutes, *with their teeth*!

The enthusiastic volunteer will push his face hopefully deep into the flour; the cunning one will blow gently until a threepenny bit is exposed and then remove it delicately with little or no trouble nor mess to himself or the carpet.

Fizz-buzz (6 plus to 10 plus. Indoors or outdoors)

This is a silly little game, but useful for filling in five minutes or so between two active games or for calming down just before a meal.

All the players sit in a circle. One starts counting by saying 'One', the next says, 'Two', but the third one, instead of saying 'Three', says '*Fizz*'. The fourth player says 'Four' but the fifth one says '*Buzz*'.

So the counting goes on; when a number is a multiple of three the word '*Fizz*' must be used, and when a multiple of five, the word '*Buzz*'. When a number is a multiple of both five and three, then '*Fizz-Buzz*' must be called. Thus the numbers from eleven to twenty would be called: 'Eleven, *fizz*, thirteen, fourteen, *fizz-buzz*, sixteen, seventeen, *fizz*, nineteen, *buzz*'.

Sardines (Any age from about 8 years upwards)

This is a variation of the universally known *Hide-and-seek*, and is particularly popular with teenagers.

The first person sent off to hide is told 'in secret' where he has to go. It might be under the stairs, under a bed, in a large cupboard or wardrobe – anywhere in fact where a number of people can crowd together if they pack themselves in very tightly. The second player (who does not know where the first one has been told to hide) then goes seeking, but is told that when he has found the first person, he does not shout out, but hides along with him. At short intervals the remaining players go seeking and are given the same instructions.

By the time half a dozen or more are packed tight like 'sardines' they will have the utmost difficulty in preventing themselves from giggling, laughing, or even screaming and thereby disclosing the hiding place.

It's pointless – but almost invariably it's fun.

Reading in the Train (10 plus to any age. Indoors)

For this competition a number of newspapers are required; it is preferable that they should all be the same paper. Having got the papers (one is required for each contestant), rearrange

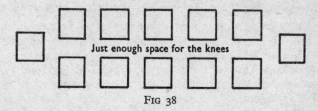

Just enough space for the knees

Fig 38

the page order in them. They must all be rearranged identically; inserting some upside down adds to the fun.

A line of chairs is then made with the chairs as close together as possible, and the competitors sit on them. They are then given the disarranged newspapers and told to put all the pages in the correct order as quickly as possible. The first one to hand up his newspaper with this done is the winner. An alternative chair arrangement which makes conditions even more cramped and difficult is shown in Fig 38.

Morning Rush

Another 'silly' game for volunteer pairs (boy and girl or man and woman). A newspaper and a man's hat is required for each pair. The men stand at one side of the room with their jackets over their arms, their waistcoats (if worn) and ties unfastened.

The girls stand at the opposite side of the room, at their feet a folded newspaper and a hat.

When the word 'Go' is given, the girl rushes over to her partner, ties his tie, fastens up his waistcoat, and helps him on with his jacket. She then dashes back for the hat, returns and puts it on his head, rushes back for the newspaper and hands it to him. Together they race for the door where she kisses him goodbye, then pushes him out of the room.

The first pair to accomplish this wins the competition.

Even more amusement can be created if the man accompanies the actions of his partner by agitated, appropriate shouts such as 'Where's my hat? I've forgotten my hat! Where's my paper?' etc.

Steeplechase (About 10 upwards. Indoors or outdoors)

A short 'obstacle' course is laid out on the floor or on the lawn. The obstacles can be cushions, books, a chair laid on its side, a bucket, and so on; they should be placed about one stride apart. Two or three 'horses' are then selected and sent out of the room. The horses should be players who do *not* know the game.

One of the horses is then brought into the room, shown the course, and then told that he has to walk along the course blindfolded and in no circumstances must he touch any of the obstacles.

After being given a few minutes to study the course, he is blindfolded. This should be done with a lot of chatter – and done quite slowly – but the moment the blindfold is in position, *the obstacles are very quietly removed*.

The amusement comes from watching his antics as he tries to step over the non-existent obstacles. Vocal encouragement can be given if necessary by the watchers calling out such things as 'Careful, George!' or 'Ooh – you nearly touched that one!' or 'Mind your left foot', and so on. When he has travelled the required distance, the horse has his blindfold removed – his expression on seeing that he has been stepping over precisely nothing is also part of the fun. The obstacles are then replaced and the same procedure gone through with the remaining horses.

Grand Chain

A silly musical 'warming-up' game suitable for teenagers and adults. One balloon per person is required; half the number of balloons should be one colour, the other half a different colour. Alternatively, provide a number of different colours in pairs. These are given out at random alternately to the boys and girls, so that if a boy is given a blue balloon another blue one is given to a girl and so on. A girl with a blue balloon then seeks out a man with a blue one for a partner; a man with a red balloon finds a girl with one of the same colour.

All the partners then form a grand chain holding hands.

The balloons are then gripped by the knees of each player. When the music starts (a piano or record player) the whole assembly parade round the room, walking as best they can with the balloons between their knees. The pace of the music should be varied, first slow, then a little quicker and so on; the players must increase or decrease their speed accordingly.

If anyone drops or bursts their balloon, the pair is eliminated. Continue until a winning pair is obtained.

Balloon Dance

This is a variation of *Grand Chain* particularly suitable for teenagers. Each member of the party is given a balloon (the colour is immaterial). Girls form a circle in the middle facing outwards, men in a circle on the outside facing inwards.

From this point follow the normal procedure for a Paul Jones, except of course that during the parading and *dancing*(?) the balloons must be retained between the knees. If a balloon falls to the ground, it must be replaced between the knees.

End the event by making it an elimination dance; any dancer dropping a balloon involves the elimination of both his partner and himself.

As an alternative to this, eliminate only the one who allows the balloon to fall; the partner remaining then tries to find another dancer who has lost his or her partner.

Dressing-Up Race

A relay race suitable for players of any age from seven or so upwards, but particularly suitable for teenagers and adults. Small teams (not more than five or six in each) are formed. Opposite, and a short distance away from, each team place a basket, bag, or plastic bucket containing items of clothing such as an old hat (man's or woman's), a scarf, an old jacket, an old nightie, an old pair of flannels, and so on. There must be, however, similar items of clothing in each container.

On the signal to start, the leader of each team dashes up to the basket and puts on (say) the hat, gloves, trousers, and nightie as quickly as he can. He then picks up the now empty basket, runs round the back of his team, and replaces the basket in its original position. Having done this, he removes all the items of clothing he has put on, pops them back into the basket then runs back to his team to touch the second player, who repeats the same procedure.

The first team to finish is, of course, the winner.

Baby's Bed Time

A 'silly' race particularly suitable for teenagers and adults. Equal teams form up in lines, each facing a chair or table on which there is a candlestick and a box of matches, a doll or teddy bear and a shawl or cloth.

At the signal to start, the leader of each team dashes out, lights the candle (which should be fixed very firmly in the candlestick), wraps the 'baby' in the shawl or cloth, then carrying both the candlestick and the baby runs round the rear member of his team, puts the candlestick back on the table, blows out the candle, takes the shawl off the baby and puts them down side by side in their original positions on the table. Having done this, he runs back to his team and touches the next player who repeats the whole procedure. The leader meanwhile goes to the rear of his team.

The first team to finish the race is, of course, the winner. If at any time during the race a candle goes out, then the person carrying it must go back to the table and relight it before continuing.

Chain Stores (Adults. Indoors)

This is a team game for the second half of the party, by which time everybody should be well acquainted with each other.

Two equal teams are formed; each team, if possible, should have the same number of both men and women.

The host then says that he is going shopping at one of the big chain stores in the High Street. There are (as everybody knows) two of these stores almost next door to each other, 'Cottonworths' and 'Stains & Fencer's', and what he can't buy in one, he hopes to buy in the other. He then designates one of the teams as 'Cottonworths' and the other as 'Stains & Fencer's' and goes on to explain that he is going to call out a list of articles he requires, one at a time. Each time he calls out an item, both teams (or stores) must try to be the first to supply him with the article called for, the one which does so scoring one point; the winning store will be the one which gets the highest score.

The amusement in the game, of course, lies in the frantic rushing around to find the article demanded and to get it first to the host. Articles (which must all come from members of the team) such as the following should be demanded:

A pair of men's shoes	A key ring without any keys on it
A pair of women's shoes	
A collar	Ten aspirin tablets
A tie	A diary
A pair of men's suspenders	A cigarette case (empty)
A pair of braces	A belt
A lipstick	Two collar studs
A powder compact	A pullover or cardigan
An eyebrow pencil	A silk scarf

Twenty cigarettes of a named brand

A handkerchief with spots on it

A box of matches containing 40 matches

Three twopenny stamps

Two bus tickets

A luminous watch

A bottle of scent

A coloured pencil

The Chocolate Game (6 plus to any age. Indoors)

Three or four bars of chocolate, each one on a plate, and a number of knives and forks and a dice are required for this 'silly' game.

All the players sit cross-legged in a circle on the floor. In the centre of the circle is a bar of chocolate on a plate, by the side of which are a number of knives and forks.

Each player in turn shakes and throws the dice, but the moment anyone throws a six, that player dashes to the centre, picks up a knife and fork and, still sitting cross-legged, begins to try to eat the chocolate with the knife and fork.

In the meantime, the other players are still throwing the dice. As soon as another, player throws a six, the one who is busy with the chocolate dashes back to the circle and the new player, with another knife and fork, continues eating what remains of the chocolate, trying to finish it before someone else throws another six. Several rounds should be played, the winner of each round being the player who actually finishes each bar of chocolate.

Alternatively, the game can be made into a team competition, in which case the children would sit facing each other in two parallel lines, in the centre of which would be two plates, each containing a bar of chocolate, one for each team. Two dice would also be required, each team throwing independently of the other. In this case, the first team to finish its own bar of chocolate would be the winner.

The Horror Game (Teenagers upwards)

This game can cause a considerable amount of amusement among teenagers and adults, but discretion must be used on whether to introduce it at a party, as the very squeamish or those with a known tendency to fainting may well find it most distasteful. Some considerable preparation is also required, as will be seen.

All the players sit round a table in complete darkness. The storyteller, being as dramatic and sepulchral as possible, tells a story of how a murder was committed and how the murderer, to hide the body, dismembered it. As each part of the body is mentioned an object is passed round under the table for each one to feel. Not until the object reaches the story-teller again does he continue his account. He might say, for instance, 'First of all the murderer chopped off the victim's head'. He then passes a cabbage or a melon round. 'Then he gouged out the eyes . . .' (two soft grapes go round the table) 'and then the brains were removed' (a damp sponge is passed from hand to hand), and so on.

Some suitable things for various parts of the body might be as below:

Hands. Rubber gloves stuffed with earth.
Toes or fingers. Small, thin carrots.
Ears. Dried figs or apricots.
Hair. Hank of wool or silk.
Tongue. Piece of rubber or plastic material, etc.

The Health of Colonel Bogey (14 plus to any age)

This game can be enjoyed by everyone at a party – and all can join in, young and old. A Master of Ceremonies, who has practised the whole series of movements, is the leader.

Everyone is sitting down and has a glass with a drink (according to choice) in it. The Master of Ceremonies, who should be clearly visible to everyone, goes quite quickly through the first movements of the whole nonsense, closely watched by all the others, who are expected to do exactly as he did the moment he finishes.

The movements are these:

(1) He stands up, picks up his glass with his thumb and *one* finger, raises it shoulder high, and says, 'I drink to the health of Colonel Bogey for the first time.'

(2) He takes a short drink, sits down, and puts his glass on the table with *one* clear tap.

(3) He wipes his moustache (real or otherwise), the right side with his right hand, the left side with his left.

(4) He taps the table on the right-hand side of his glass with his right hand, and on the left-hand side with his left hand.

(5) He taps under the table, first with the right hand and then with the left.

(6) He stamps the floor, first with the right foot, then with the left, and finally –

(7) He rises a few inches from his chair and sits down again.

When all the audience have attempted to do the same, the MC rises holding his glass with the thumb and *two* fingers and says, 'I drink to the health of Colonel Bogey for the second time.'

He then goes through the whole series of motions again, but this time he does everything *twice*, i.e. he takes two short drinks, taps twice with his glass on the table, wipes each side of his moustache twice, taps the table on each side twice, and so on, finally rising from his chair and sitting down twice.

The audience try to emulate the procedure.

The ceremony continues with everything being done *three* times (the glass being held by the thumb and three fingers) and finally *four* times, when the opening sentence is, 'I drink to the health of Colonel Bogey for the last time.'

Whatever is left in the glass must be finished off on this final toast.

SECTION FIFTEEN

GAMES FOR SMALL NUMBERS

When the numbers at a party do not exceed more than six or eight guests, many team games are well-nigh impossible to run as the sides, obviously, could not exceed four players.

Relay races which take a relatively long time to complete can be run, however, as can various types of competitions, some of which are described in this chapter.

In general, the types of games particularly suitable for small parties are those in which the members compete as individuals or in pairs such as Pencil and Paper Games, Quizzes, Treasure Hunts, Time-Passers and Problems, Hiding and Finding Games, Musical Games, simple Table Games and Card Games.

They can also take part in games such as Indoor Golf, Darts, simple throwing and aiming competitions and Singing Games.

Here then are some suggestions:

Floppy Coat Race

A simple and amusing relay race for boys and girls of about four to seven years of age. One adult overcoat or raincoat is required for each team taking part. Normal relay procedure.

Children form teams of equal numbers. Each leader holds one of the overcoats. On the starting signal, the leader puts on the over-large coat, buttons it up (all coats should preferably have the same number of buttons, but if this is not possible, then stipulate the number of buttons to be fastened) and then runs, or shuffles, over the prescribed course, takes off the coat and hands it over to the next player who repeats the process – and so on all down the team.

Big Slipper Race

Another simple relay race similar in nature to *Floppy Coat Race*, except that the players run the race wearing adult slippers, Wellingtons, or shoes. If a slipper is lost during the race it must be put on again before continuing.

Rebecca Race

Normal relay race procedure. One cushion per team is required. Competitors run over the course balancing a cushion on their heads. With older children a book can be substituted for the cushion and the race retitled 'Model Race'.

Quack-Quack!

A game for small numbers of young children. One of the children (or perhaps even better still, an adult) starts the game by being the Mother Duck who is blindfolded. Mother Duck stands in the centre of the room and every few seconds she calls out 'Quack-Quack' as if calling her ducklings. When the other children hear the call, they run or creep in close to Mother Duck and try to touch her and dart away again without being caught. Any player who is caught becomes Mother Duck and the game continues.

The game can cause lots of fun, particularly if Mother Duck varies her manner of calling, sometimes softly, sometimes plaintively, stridently, angrily, and so on.

Scratch-cat

Another game for small numbers of young children of the same type as *Quack-Quack!* except that the centre player, 'Scratch-Cat', need not be blindfolded.

Scratch-Cat walks about on all-fours round the room. The rest of the players dart in and try to touch him on the head or back or legs. If when doing so, however, Scratch-Cat tags any of them with either of his hands, then the person tagged becomes Scratch-Cat in turn.

Catch your Tail

A game for six or eight players from six to eleven years of age, similar to *Fox and Geese*. All the players form a line behind the leader, clasping the waist of the player immediately in front. The leader then has to swing round to try to tag the last player in the line. At no time must the grasps be broken. If the leader succeeds in tagging the Tail, the end player becomes the Head and the game continues.

Chopstick Race

A game for players of any age above seven to eight. Five beans, two plastic drinking straws and a saucer or small jam jar are required for each competing player.

The players stand side by side in line. By the feet of each player is placed the saucer or jam jar, and about ten to twelve feet from the jars five beans (or peas) are placed on the floor. Each player holds two straws representing chopsticks.

On the starting signal, each player runs forward to his or her pile of beans and using the chopsticks only, picks up one of the beans and carries it back to the jar into which it is dropped. She then returns for the second, third, fourth, and fifth.

The first player to put the five beans in his or her jar is the winner and should be given a small prize.

At no time during the race must the beans be touched by hand; if at any time they are dropped, the chopsticks only must be used to retrieve them.

The game can, of course, be used with large numbers of players by having heats and finals.

With younger players the number of beans can be reduced to three and the distance which they have to be carried can be shortened as desired.

Musical Hats

A quiet (no rushing about) Musical Chair-type of game requiring a paper hat for all the players except one.

149

Competitors sit in a circle wearing the hats; one player, of course, does not have a hat. When the music starts, the players pass the hats round the circle. When the music stops, all those with a hat put them on their heads. The one without a hat drops out.

One hat is then taken away and the game continues until finally only two players remain passing a hat between them. As the numbers decrease the players should move in closer together so that the hats can be passed without the players having to get up.

Get Away

A tagging game (suitable for players from about seven to twelve years of age) for small numbers, which does not involve a lot of movement or chasing, hence is also suitable for a relatively small space either indoors or outdoors.

Six or more players join hands to form a circle facing inwards, then loose their hands and hold them open behind their backs. An extra player (yourself) then starts to walk round the outside of the circle carrying any small object such as a ball, or a clothes-peg, or even a rolled-up newspaper. This is quietly placed into the hands of one of the circle players who, on receiving it, tries to dash out of the circle formation before he or she can be tagged by one or both of the players on each side of him. The players trying to make the tag are not allowed to move their feet, but, of course, may twist and bend as much as they wish.

If a tag is made, the one tagged becomes the person to walk round the circle; if he is not tagged, he merely returns to his place in the circle and the game then continues as before.

Hedgehog

Provide each competitor with a washed, but unpeeled, potato and a saucer of pins. Each player – *wearing gloves* – is then required to pick up the pins one at a time and stick them into the potato. The one who achieves the greatest number in three minutes (or any other stated time) wins the competition.

Guess How Many

A simple guessing competition requiring a little previous preparation. Pencils and paper are also required. Prepare beforehand items such as the following: a part-empty matchbox containing a known number of matches, a saucer with, say, about 120 grains of rice on it, an ashtray containing fifty or sixty pins, a jam-jar containing a known number of peas or beans, a parcel of known weight and a sealed box containing about a dozen marbles.

Competitors are then required to estimate the numbers of items in, or the weight of, each item and to write their answers on the paper provided. The matchbox and sealed box must not be opened, an estimation having to be made by shaking them.

The competitor with the most correct, or nearest correct, guesses is the winner.

Tasty Dish (12 plus and upwards. Indoors)

This is yet another guessing game. Volunteers are asked for and they go out of the room. They are then led in blindfolded one at a time and are told that they are going to be given six things to taste and they have to guess what the substances are. They must be assured that there is no catch in the game, that all the things they are given are perfectly harmless and can be tasted without fear.

Previously, there should be prepared a tray containing six saucers holding a small quantity of substances such as are named below. A minute amount of each is then given to the competitor; if you can obtain a number of small, flat, wooden ice-cream spoons, so much the better, for a fresh one can be used for each volunteer.

Suitable substances are: salt, sugar, ginger, breadcrumbs, ground nutmeg, grated cheese, milk powder, cocoa, mint, small pieces of lemon rind, sherbet powder, lemonade powder, desiccated coconut, ground almonds, and blancmange powder.

The Pin-drop Game

All the players sit with their backs to the leader, who drops a series of common objects on to a table. The players have to guess what each object is and write its name down on the slip of paper provided. Objects such as the following are quite suitable, and not likely to damage the table surface: a pin, needle, drawing pin, thimble, small book, sponge, tennis ball, toothbrush, button, coin, paper clip, packet of cigarettes, a full and an empty box of matches, and so on.

The player who gets the most right is the winner.

MEMORY GAMES AND QUIZZES

There are many variations of the memory game, but basically they all require the players to memorize an increasing number of items of phrases. Here are two examples; many more can be devised at will:

Ten-Up

Players sit in a circle. The player chosen to start says 'One Onion.' Everybody in turn repeats this. When the turn of the leader comes again he says 'One Onion and Two Tomatoes.' Everybody in turn repeats this. The list of items is gradually increased and any player making a mistake or forgetting an item is eliminated. Here are some suggested phrases, which may, of course, be changed at will: One Onion, Two Tomatoes, Three Thirsty Thrushes, Four Fat Fried Fish, Five Famous Filmstars, Six Sizzling Sausages, Seven Satisfied Sailors, Eight Energetic Elephants, Nine Nasty Nitwits, Ten Tasty Tadpoles.

Tongue Twisters

The same procedure is followed as in *Ten-Up*, but the leader tries to add a new tongue twister to the list each time his turn comes round; e.g Red leather, yellow leather, Six thick thistle sticks, Pick a peck of pickled peppers, A puzzled apothecary's apprentice, etc.

Each player must repeat these phrases as quickly as possible *three times* each.

Even more amusement can be added to this game – and to other similar games – if it is also stipulated that during the competition each player must have a sweet in his or her mouth.

Nursery Rhyme Quiz (4 plus to 8 plus. Indoors)

This is another quiet 'in-between' game. All the players sit comfortably in a line or a circle. One of the grown-ups then asks a series of simple questions based on Nursery Rhymes. The children are asked in turn; anyone giving the right answer scores a point. Suppose you say, 'Who was it who found the cupboard bare?' (or empty). If the first child does not know the answer you ask the second child. If he gives the right answer, you address the next question to the third child and do not start with the first again.

The questions can be worded or phrased in such a way that the game can become quite suitable for children of varying ages. Some examples are given below, the first question in each case being suitable for four- or five-year-olds, the second for, say, children of seven or eight.

(1) a. Whose dog didn't get a bone?
b. Name a lady whose dog was hungry } Mother Hubbard

(2) a. Who made the girls cry when he kissed them?
b. Who didn't like playing with boys? } Georgie Porgie

(3) a. Who was it who lived in a shoe?
b. Who didn't know what to do about her large family? } An old woman

(4) a. Who had her nose pecked off by a blackbird?
b. Who was injured while hanging out the washing? } The maid

(5) a. Who wandered upstairs and downstairs?
b. Who threw an elderly gentleman down some stairs? } Goosey Gander

153

(6) *a.* When the sheep were in the
    meadow, who was in the corn? ⎫
b. What animal caused damage in a ⎬ The cow
    cornfield? ⎭

Any child who answers correctly scores one mark; at the end of three or four complete rounds, the child who has got the most marks gets a small prize.

With six- or seven-year-olds, this can be made into a paper and pencil game. Ten or more questions are asked, then the children write down the short answers required. At the end, children change papers and mark them as the answers are called out.

Musical Sound Quiz (10 plus to any age. Indoors)

Pencils and paper are required. This quiz can be used only when a gramophone is available. Prior to the party, select about ten records. These can be a mixture of serious, light classical, or popular music according to the taste of the major-ity of the members of the party. Play them through and select a portion of the music which you think might be a little puzzling; part of the verse of a popular song, for example. Make a chalk mark or stick a tiny piece of paper on the record to mark the section you have chosen.

Play these small selections to the contestants, who merely have to write down the name of the tune from which the music has been taken. Do not, of course, make them all difficult; put in one or two which can be recognized fairly easily, but intersperse these among the harder ones. If you are the for-tunate possessor of a tape recorder you can prepare a tape in advance, which will save you the trouble of having to change records during the quiz.

Tape recorders can, of course, be used to make up a variety of sound quizzes on such things as bird songs, sports noises (an extract from a motor race, a football match, and so on), common sounds such as a dripping tap, water running out of a bath, a cork being pulled out of a bottle, a match being struck, sausages frying, or even a shovelful of coke being put on a boiler fire.

Annual Quiz (Teenagers and upwards)

Pencils and paper are required. This type of quiz is particularly suitable for Christmas or New Year's Eve parties. Devise ten or a dozen questions based on events which have happened during the year, but with each question give three suggested answers, one of which is the correct one. The players are then merely asked to write down the answer they think is right. Below are given some specimen questions of this type:

(1) The Boat Race was rowed on February 18th, April 5th, May 3rd?

(2) When did the Blankshire Conspiracy Trial take place, February, May, or July?

(3) When did the violent gale occur—the first week in January, the third week in March, or the second week in April?

(4) Did England beat the West Indies in the third Test Match by ten wickets, two wickets, or an innings and twenty-one runs?

(5) Who won the Marathon at the Olympic Games: John Brown, Herbert Black, or Augustus Green?

Even though you suggest the correct answer in each case, you will be surprised at the short memories of most of the members of your party.

Similar quizzes can be devised to suit all ages and tastes; sport, popular music, serious music, books, etc., can all form the subjects for a series of simple questions.

Topical Quiz (Teenagers and upwards)

Pencils and paper are required. Prior to the party make up a list of about ten or a dozen simple questions based on items which have been headline news during the previous three or four weeks. The answers to these questions should not require more than two or three words each.

Call out the questions, allowing half a minute or so for an answer before going on to the next. The player who has the most correct wins a small prize.

The type of question chosen can be varied to suit the ages and known tastes of the members of the party. With young people questions on sport, popular singers, dance music, etc., can be chosen; with older people, political views, trials, scandals, and so on, can be introduced. Some types of questions are given below:

(1) Which team won the County Cricket Championship this year?

(2) Who won the FA Cup and what was the score?

(3) Give the names of the winners of the Men's Singles and Ladies' Singles Championships at Wimbledon.

(4) What tune was top of the Hit Parade last week?

(5) What is the name of the famous singer who was at the Palladium last week?

(6) Give the name of the film which had its première a fortnight ago and who were the stars of the film?

(7) Name the person who was found guilty at the big trial at the Old Bailey this week.

(8) Who became French Premier a fortnight ago?

(9) What is the name of the prominent foreign statesman who is visiting this country at this moment?

(10) What was the headline news three days ago?

Historical Character Quiz (14 plus to any age. Indoors)

Pencils and paper are required. A series of ten or twenty questions, the answer to each of which is a well-known historical character, is given. The one with the most correct wins a small prize. Here are some examples:

(1) Who was the lady whose lover expected every man to do his duty? (Lady Hamilton)

(2) He had to have his cloak washed but his action gained him favour. (Raleigh)

(3) He had a wart on his nose and he didn't like baubles. (Cromwell)

(4) She was a most distinguished fruit seller. (Nell Gwynne)

(5) By shooting arrows high in the air, his men hit more than a bull's eye. (William the Conqueror)

(6) As a widow she lived for a long time on the Isle of Wight. (Queen Victoria)

(7) His footwear is still worn a lot in winter. (Wellington)

(8) He didn't let foreigners interrupt a ball game. (Drake)

(9) A place for devotions on high ground suggests his name. (Churchill)

(10) A bird that didn't build a nest but buildings. (Wren)

Fiction Character Quiz (12 plus to any age. Indoors)

Pencil and paper are needed for each competitor. This quiz is almost identical with the one above, except that all the characters are from well-known fiction. Here are ten examples:

(1) She was Irish by name and red by colour. (Scarlett O'Hara: *Gone with the Wind*)

(2) He was a giant in one city and a dwarf in another. (Gulliver)

(3) His character was not golden but his name was quite valuable. (Long John Silver: *Treasure Island*)

(4) She was an outlaw's daughter who married a Devon man. (*Lorna Doone*)

(5) He sounds as if he plays a musical instrument. (Hornblower)

(6) Did he ever sell crazy headgear? (The Mad Hatter: *Alice in Wonderland*)

(7) His horse was black and so was his character. (Dick Turpin)

(8) An apple disagreed with her but a royal person made her well again. (Snow-White)

(9) A lot of Frenchmen looked in a lot of places for him. (*The Scarlet Pimpernel*)

(10) His Christian name wasn't Smith, Jones, or Brown, but it was the other even on an island. (*Robinson Crusoe*)

SECTION SIXTEEN
GAMES FOR THE GARDEN

During the summer months many suitable party games can be played in the garden, providing there is a reasonable amount of lawn area. This need not be very large; a space some thirty feet by fifteen to twenty feet will provide ample room for quite a variety of games. If more, or less, space than this is available some of the sizes given in the list of games which follows may have to be – and can be – modified to suit individual requirements without detracting from the enjoyment of the games suggested.

Garden games can be divided into two main categories: set games such as clock golf and deck tennis, and free games which may or may not require some equipment, but which can be played quite freely on any convenient space of lawn. These free games include such things as races, aiming or throwing competitions, circular musical games, and so on.

EQUIPMENT FOR GARDEN GAMES

Though one can purchase at quite moderate prices equipment for games such as clock golf and deck tennis, much can be done with improvised equipment. For instance, a length of clothes-line or a narrow piece of pea or bean netting stretched between two long canes stuck in the ground makes a perfectly serviceable net. Putters for clock golf can often be picked up quite cheaply at auction sales, in second-hand shops, and at lost property offices.

Repainted golf balls can also be bought quite cheaply from many sports stores.

The following items of easily-obtained equipment are then

suggested as being adequate for a wide variety of games and activities:

Two to four fairly thick six-foot canes.

A twenty- to thirty-foot length of plastic-covered clothes-line.

Four to six small rubber balls or old tennis balls or air-flow balls.

Four to six used or repainted golf balls.

Four rubber or rope quoits.

Two or three old putters.

In addition to the above, three or four fairly large plastic or rubber balls will be found useful.

All this equipment should be stored *together* in a convenient shed or in the garage. It is important to insist that the equipment is always put away in the correct place after use to save it getting lost or deteriorating.

When using balls in the garden it is essential that due regard should be paid to the protection of both windows and garden flowers in the flower beds.

Games involving throwing a ball should be so arranged that the throwing is done away from and not towards windows. Whenever possible, take the same precautions with regard to flower beds or alternatively protect them by placing a length of small-mesh wire-netting across the front of the beds when games are being played.

If, however, the air-flow type of ball is used whenever possible, the precautions suggested above will be largely minimized or even rendered unnecessary as this type of ball will cause little or no damage at all, either to windows or flowers.

Though the games in this chapter are designated as being mainly for playing on a lawn, some of them can be played equally as well in a large room or hall. This is indicated in the text where necessary.

Racing Against a Ball

An extremely simple chasing game for the very young. It is quite suitable for the three- to six-year-olds. The leader (you), standing at one end of the lawn with all the players behind or alongside, rolls a largish ball across the lawn. The instant the ball leaves her hand the children race across the lawn and try to reach the far side before the ball gets there. Considerable judgement must be used to see that the ball travels at such a speed that the fastest children stand a fair chance of winning the race.

Wicked Witches

A simple, noisy, chasing game for the five- to eight-year-olds which is particularly suitable for girls. Two or three of the players are chosen to represent witches and they crouch or huddle together in their 'den' in one corner of the lawn. The rest of the players skip freely about the lawn. The leaders of the game, after a few seconds, howling and shrieking, race out of their corner and start to tag the skipping players. The moment a tag is made, the witch concerned calls out 'Stone', and the person tagged must remain as still as possible in the position and pose in which she was tagged until everyone has been turned into stone. The last two to be tagged become the witches for the next round.

Queenie

An old favourite with girls in the seven to ten years of age range, requiring one rubber or tennis ball.

A girl is chosen to be 'Queenie.'

She stands, holding the ball at one end of the lawn, with her back turned to the rest of the players. She then throws the ball backwards over her shoulder; the other girls race to get it. They then stand still, holding their hands behind their backs and shout 'Queenie.'

Queenie then turns round and tries to guess, by looking at their faces and positions, which girl has the ball. If she guesses correctly the girl holding the ball becomes 'Queenie'. If her guess is incorrect she continues as 'Queenie.'

Catch and Throw (Girls 7–10 years)

The players stand fairly close together in the centre of the lawn; one of them has a ball. She throws the ball high in the air, calling out the name of one of the players as she does so. The moment the ball is thrown up all, except the one called by name, scatter as widely as possible. The named girl tries to catch the ball. The moment she does so (or picks up the ball) she calls 'Stand' and all the players must immediately stand still. The girl with the ball then tries to 'tag' one of the standing players by rolling the ball along the ground towards her. If she is successful, the girl tagged becomes the one whose name is called when the ball is thrown up again by the thrower. If she fails, the ball is thrown up by the original thrower and she is named again as the one to catch the ball.

Keep the Basket Full

A very simple chasing game for younger children from about five to eight. A number of small tennis balls and a box, tin, or basket is required. If the balls are not available a number (twenty or more) of clothes-pegs will serve quite well.

The pegs are placed in the box or basket in the centre of the playing space. The leader (yourself) then takes out one peg at a time and throws them varying distances about the lawn. The children chase after the pegs and return them as quickly as they can to the box, their aim being never to let the box become empty.

The game should be played for two or three minutes only. If, by that time (or before), you have succeeded in emptying the box, then you have won the game; if you have not done so, then the children have won.

Ring the Stick

A game for five or six players at any one time, particularly suitable for the eight to twelve age group. One quoit per player is required and a small cane about two feet high.

The cane is stuck upright in the ground in the centre of the lawn or playing area. Round it, and at varying distances from it, a number of throwing bases are marked. This can be done by putting down small sticks or clothes-pegs. A typical course with eight throwing bases is shown in Fig 39.

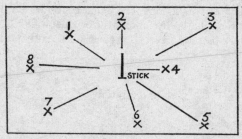

FIG 39

Each player stands at each base in turn and attempts to throw his quoit so that it falls over the stick. If he throws it over the stick at the first attempt, he then moves on to the next base and throws from there. If he fails at the first throw, then he must continue throwing until he rings the stick. The number of throws at each base is counted and the player with the lowest total of throws for the whole eight (or more) bases is the winner of the game and is awarded a suitable prize.

Spry

A simple team throwing and passing game which can have many variations and which is suitable for players from about ten to fifteen years of age. A small ball or quoit is required for each team which should consist of about six players. Fig 40 shows an arrangement for two teams.

Each team stands evenly spaced over a definite distance which can be marked by a length of rope or two small canes stuck in the ground. The leader also stands at a fixed spot marked by, say, a hoop or a small cane. The distance of the leader from his team should be, if possible, about twelve to fifteen feet.

On the starting signal being given, the leader throws the ball to No. 1 who returns it to him. It is then thrown to Nos. 2, 3, and 4 who return it. When No. 5 receives the ball, however, he does not return it but runs with it to occupy the leader's place. At the same time, the leader runs to the opposite end of the line and all the other members move one place to the left. No. 5 now acts as leader. The game continues until all the players have acted as leader and the original leader has finally received the ball and returned to his original centre position.

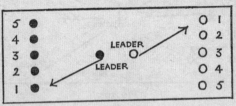

FIG 40

Garden Golf

A game for players of about ten to twelve years of age and upwards played either in pairs or fours. A walking-stick or cheap putter and one small rubber or tennis ball *or air-flow ball*, or old golf ball per player is required.

A course of any convenient number of 'holes' is laid out on the available lawn area. The holes, however, are not cut in the lawn, but are made of such things as a small pail or a large jar lying on its side, an enamel bowl or biscuit-tin standing upright, a small hoop or rubber quoit lying flat on the ground or a shoe-box with a fairly large rectangular hole in one side.

'Bunkers' or 'obstacles' can be made with such things as bricks, garden rakes, an old sack, and so on.

The game is played as in actual golf and the scoring done on a hole basis or on the number of strokes required to complete the round.

Garden Skittles

A garden (or indoor) game suitable for players of all ages from about seven upwards. Three small rubber or tennis balls are required and ten 'skittles'. These are merely empty 'cleaner' tins or the plastic containers which have contained washing-up liquids and which have been saved up for party occasions.

The length of the bowling pitch or 'alley' can be varied at will and will be dependent upon the length of lawn available and/or the age and skill of the players concerned.

The skittles should be set up in the form of a pyramid with four in the front row (nearer the bowler), three in the second row, two in the third, and one at the rear. If only six skittles are available, they should be arranged three, two, one. There should be a space of about six inches between skittles and between rows.

The rules are extremely simple:

(1) The winner is the first person to score a previously determined number of points, say fifty.

(2) Each player in turn has three bowls at the skittles; the number he knocks down are added to his score.

If with the first ball he knocks down all the skittles, they are set up again for his second shot. If he does the same with this second shot, they are again reset for the third and final shot of his round.

When all the participating players have had their turns, the first player starts the second round. This procedure is repeated until a player reaches the required target number.

Garden Bowls

A game for groups of four suitable for children of ten-plus, teenagers and adults, requiring one tennis or small rubber ball per player and one golf ball or air-flow ball per group. Several groups can play at the same time on a lawn of reasonable size.

Each group of four consists of two sets of partners who play against each other.

One player pitches the golf ball or air-flow ball on to the lawn about three or four yards from where he is standing. This is the 'jack'. Each player in turn then pitches or lobs his tennis ball and tries to get it as near as possible to the jack. The player whose ball finishes nearest to the jack scores one point for his pair. If both balls of any pair are nearer to the jack than both those of their two opponents, they then score two points. The first pair to score fifteen points is the winner.

With large numbers of players the competition can be run on a knock-out basis with a small prize for each member of the winning pair.

If desired, foursomes instead of pairs can compete with each other.

Quoit Tennis

A game for two or four a side requiring one rubber or rope quoit. There is no need for any complicated rules. One player standing twelve to fifteen feet away from the net pitches the quoit over the net. If it is caught by a member of the opposing side it must be returned over the net immediately.

The object of the game is to ground the quoit in the opposing team's half of the court. If this is done one point is scored. A point is also scored if the opposing side fail to return the quoit over the net.

Other rules:

(*a*) The quoit must be caught and thrown with one hand.

(*b*) The quoit must be returned *immediately* it is caught, from the spot where it is caught. In other words, no steps must be taken while holding the quoit.

(*c*) A side continues to serve so long as it wins a point. If the serving side loses a point, it becomes the turn of the opposing side to serve.

(*d*) The first team to gain a previously decided number of points, say seven, nine, eleven or fifteen, wins the game.

At a party where there are, say, sixteen guests, short games of seven points can be played on a knock-out basis so that everybody has a chance of playing without having to wait too long. These short games also have the advantage that short periods of fairly energetic play are followed by a rest.

Team Hand Tennis

A game for teams of six or eight from about the age of ten up to about fifteen. A fairly level piece of lawn and one tennis ball is required along with an improvised 'net' about three feet to three feet six inches from the ground.

The object of the game is to bat the ball over the net and within the bounds of the previously decided court so that the opposing team is unable to return it.

The following simple rules should be applied:

(1) The ball remains in play so long as it is bouncing. It becomes 'dead' only when it rolls, is knocked out of court or knocked into or under the net.

(2) 'Services' are taken by players in turn from the back of the playing area; they bat the ball by hand over the net into the opponents' court.

(3) The ball need not be returned immediately over the net, but may be batted to another player more advantageously placed to return it.

(4) Scoring can be as in real Lawn Tennis or the game can be won by a side first scoring a previously decided number of points, say eleven or fifteen.

SECTION SEVENTEEN

ACTIVE GAMES FOR LARGE NUMBERS

Parties for large numbers are usually held out of doors or in large rooms such as church halls. Nevertheless, when conditions are crowded, and particularly if the guests are young children, chasing games can lead to tumbles and collisions causing nasty bumps and bruises.

The ideal type of active game is one in which all the players are taking a direct interest but only a few or even one or two are actually rushing about at top speed at any given moment.

On the following pages is given a selection of such games including some involving the 'Change System'.

The Change System is one whereby very active team games can be played in a relatively small space for the numbers involved because, though all the players are taking a direct part in the game and contribute to their team's success or failure, only a section of the team is really rushing about at any one time.

Dog and Rabbit

A game for children in the seven to ten years age range. All the players, except two, join hands in a circle facing inwards. One of the two remaining players is the 'rabbit' and stands inside the circle; the other, the 'dog', stands outside the circle. To the music of a piano or a record player, the circle players skip or gallop sideways for a few seconds. When the music stops, they stop and let their hands drop to their sides. Immediately this happens, the dog darts into the circle after the rabbit who darts outside. The dog tries to catch and tag the rabbit, but he must follow the exact course taken by the rabbit, who zigzags in and out of the circle players. If after a few seconds, the dog hasn't caught the rabbit, allow the dog to change places with a circle player and restart the game. If, however, the dog does catch the rabbit, the dog becomes the rabbit, the first rabbit joins the circle and a new player from the circle becomes the dog.

Passing the Matches

A game for any number of players of any age above six, divided into equal teams. Two boxes of matches, one safety matches, the other with red or different-coloured heads, per team are required. There should be the same number of matches in all the boxes.

The teams stand in lines; the first player in each team has the box of safety matches, the last player the box with matches of a different colour.

On the starting signal, each of the two players with the matches starts taking them out one at a time and passes them down the line, i.e. each player passes the matches to the person next to him. Thus the red matches will be travelling in one direction and the safety matches in the other direction and crossing each other somewhere along the line. The players holding the matchboxes will be gradually emptying their boxes of one colour and filling them with those of the other.

The first team to complete the change-over wins the race. With younger children the leader only need have a box containing matches; the end player would be provided with an empty box. The matches would then be passed from the full one to the empty one. If desired, once the end box is full, the matches can then be passed back, one at a time to the leader until his box is again filled.

In the absence of matches, tins containing peas and beans can be used.

Roll them Over

Another simple passing game for players of almost any age except the very young, requiring one very shallow metal or enamel plate and six marbles or ball-bearings per team of six to eight players.

Teams of equal numbers sit with their legs stretched out forwards on the floor in lines. The leader of each team holds the shallow plate with the marbles on it in his or her lap. On the starting signal, the plate is passed backwards over the head down the line to the rear player and then forward to the leader. No player must turn round either to pass or receive the plate. The first team to complete the passing with all the marbles intact is the winner.

If, during the passing, any marbles fall off the plates they must be replaced before the plate continues its movement along the line.

In the absence of shallow plates and marbles, a similar race can be done using six dried peas on a playing card or piece of cardboard of similar size.

Roll-a-Bowl

A passing race similar in nature to *Roll them Over*, requiring a small enamel or thick china basin and one marble per competing team of six or eight players.

The members of each team stand in line behind each other about a couple of feet apart. The leader holds the bowl containing the marble. When the signal to start is given, the leader starts the marble spinning round the inside of his basin and then turns round (but without moving his feet) and passes it to the player behind, who in turn keeps the marble rotating and passes it to the player behind, who in turn keeps the marble rotating and passes it on – and so down the line to the end player and back again down the line to the leader. If the marble spins out of the basin at any time during the race, it must be replaced and started spinning again before the basin can be passed.

Thread the Needle Race

Another passing race of a similar nature to the two previous ones. This is particularly suitable for teenagers and adults. One fairly large-eyed needle and a piece of cotton about two feet long per team are required. Teams form up in lines as before with the leader holding the needle in one hand and the cotton in the other. The race starts with the leader of each team threading the needle and then unthreading it. He or she then passes it to the second player who does likewise and so on down the line to the end player and back again down the line to the leader who, having threaded it for the second time, holds it above his head to indicate that his team has completed the race.

An alternative form of the race is to provide the leader with a very large darning needle and a piece of fine cotton and every other player in each team with a similar piece of cotton.

The leader then threads his needle and passes it on *threaded* to the second player who threads his piece of cotton in the needle and so on down the line. The race finishes when the last player in the team has threaded his cotton and holds up the needle containing the six or eight pieces of cotton, one for each member of the team.

Twos and Threes

A chasing game for any number of players of any age above seven. This game is suitable for warm or hot days either outdoors or indoors (providing there is ample space) in that though everybody is taking an active interest in the game, only two are moving at any one moment.

All the players except two arrange themselves in a double circle in pairs as shown in Fig 41.

Of the two players not in the circle one 'A' becomes the chaser and the other 'B' the one to be chased.

To escape being tagged by 'A', the player 'B' runs to stand *in front of* one of the pairs of players in the circle (as shown in Fig 41). Immediately he does this, the rear player of the pair becomes the one to be chased and thus 'A' must now chase 'C' who can escape in a similar manner to 'B'.

If, however, 'A' tags 'B' before 'B' has reached sanctuary, then 'B' must turn round and chase 'A'.

Players should be encouraged to run only short distances and then seek sanctuary so as to give as many players as possible a chance either to chase or be chased.

If a chaser begins to show signs of fatigue or is unable to make a tag after, say, a couple of changes, allow him or her to change places with one of the players in the circle.

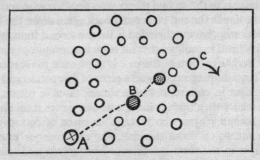

FIG 41

A variation can be added to the game by allowing the player being chased to stand either in front *or behind* the two players. If he stands in front it is the back player's turn to be chased, but if he stands behind the rear of the two, then the front player must run.

Fox and Rabbit

This game, for any number of players, is a variation of *Twos and Threes* and is particularly suitable for the seven to twelve age group.

This time, the players arrange themselves in pairs haphazardly about the playing space, as shown in Fig 42. There should be a distance of at least three feet between the two people forming a pair who should also stand facing each other. This space is the 'rabbit hole' in which the one being chased seeks sanctuary.

The game starts off as before with 'A' chasing 'B' who seeks sanctuary by standing between two players as shown.

If, however, he stands sideways to the two players *neither* of them must move. The moment, however, that 'B' turns to face one of the pair, then that player becomes the one to be chased by 'A'.

As before, the players should be encouraged to run as little as possible and to make frequent changes so that everyone gets a chance to chase or be chased.

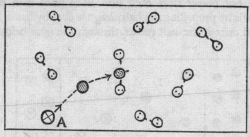

FIG 42

It is also a good thing to insist that once a player has sought sanctuary in a rabbit hole, he must not spend too long in the neutral position but must turn to face one way or the other within, say, five seconds. If this is not done, then he must be considered as having been tagged and must become the chaser.

Change Handball

An active game for any number of players (ten to fourteen years of age) either indoors in a small hall or outside on a lawn. This is much more suitable for boys than girls. One small football or large rubber ball and four skittles or similar markers are required. Let us assume that the game is being played indoors where it is possible to mark lines on the floor with chalk. In a garden, lengths of rope could be used for the same purpose. Let us also assume that some thirty players are involved.

Two teams of fifteen are chosen and these are further subdivided each into three groups of five. The hall or playing area is marked out, as shown in Fig 43, by drawing a chalk line across the width of the hall about three feet six inches from each end. In the centre of each line a goal is made about nine feet wide by placing skittles or any available form of marker.

The first group of five from each team arrange themselves about the court as shown. (One acts as a goalkeeper.) The other

173

two groups of five stand behind the chalk lines ready to join in the play when called.

The game is started by the ball being dropped on the floor between one player from each side. Each team then tries to score goals by propelling the ball *along the floor* by hand. A goal is scored only if the ball passes through the goal below knee height.

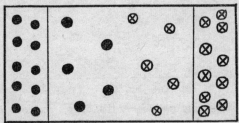

Fig 43

No pushing, tackling or rough play of any kind is allowed.

After about two minutes' play, the referee or leader calls 'Change' whereupon the players 6–10 rush on to the court and take up the play, while *immediately* the original players dash behind the base lines to await their next call. When the word 'Change' is called again, players 11–15 take the court and players 6–10 leave it.

The winning team is, of course, the one which has scored the most goals at the end of a previously decided length of time, usually about ten minutes.

Finnish Handball

A game particularly suitable for large numbers of boys in the eleven to fourteen years age range which can be played in a fairly restricted area. It is a game in which only a few players are moving about freely at any one moment, but all the remaining players are also *actively* engaged in the game and not merely standing waiting to take part. A large rubber ball, small football or a tennis ball is required. The court or playing area is marked out and the players disposed as shown in Fig 44.

174

Two teams of equal numbers are chosen and at the beginning of the game all the members of each team stand in line with their arms linked on their own goal line immediately behind the 'neutral area'. The ball is placed in the centre of the playing area.

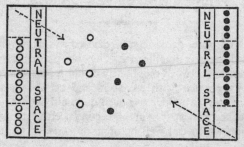

FIG 44

On the signal to start being given, a previously determined number of players (four, five, or six) from one end of each line of players dash out and try to propel the ball by hand over their opponents' goal line at below knee height.

The defenders (who must remain linked all the time they are defending the goal line) try to stop the ball passing over the line by blocking it with their feet and legs; they must not actually *kick* the ball. The whole line of defenders will need to move sideways along the line to close the undefended gap left by the players in the centre space. After a few minutes, the leader or umpire shouts 'Change', whereupon the centre players immediately leave the ball and dash to the opposite end of their defending line from which they came and the next group of four, five, or six race out and take up the play. After a minute or two the signal to change is again given and so on, for a period of, say, ten minutes or more. Other rules: When the ball is in the neutral space, it can only be touched by a member of the defending side in whose space it is.

There must be no rough play; no bumping, charging, or striking the ball with the fist.

SECTION EIGHTEEN
PENCIL AND PAPER GAMES

———————

Pencil and paper games can be devised to suit people of all ages and degrees of intelligence. They are particularly useful as 'quieteners' between more noisy or boisterous games; they are usually popular with teenagers and can be introduced with discretion with older and even quite old people.

Some of the games given in this section need a little previous preparation which can well be done by some of the teenage members of your family.

Consequence Drawing (6 plus to 10 plus. Indoors)

Pencils and paper required. This is a silly little drawing game for younger children. Each child starts off by drawing a face and neck, which can be a serious one or a funny one as desired. It is essential, however, that the drawing must be done as secretly as possible, and certainly so that the next child cannot see it. When this is done, the top of the paper is folded over so that only the bottom of the neck is visible (see Fig 45). The paper is then passed to the next child, who draws a body

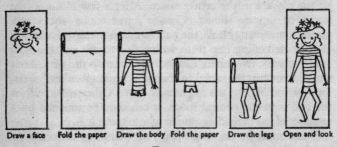

Draw a face   Fold the paper   Draw the body   Fold the paper   Draw the legs   Open and look

FIG 45

and arms. The paper is again folded and passed to a third child, who adds on the legs and feet.

The papers are then opened out, and to children the results are more often than not most hilarious.

Blindfold Drawing (6 plus to any age. Indoors)

A sheet of paper and a pencil for each competitor. The players sit round a table, or have something firm on which to rest their papers. Each player is then blindfolded. The leader then asks them to draw something relatively simple, such as a house or a tree. When they have all finished this and almost certainly think the competition is over, the leader asks for some additions to be made, e.g. 'Put a bird on the tree and a hill in the background' or 'Put some curtains on the windows of the house and a motor car standing in front of the garage.' If they were originally asked to draw a face, they might well be asked to put a collar and tie on the figure, or a pipe in its mouth, and so on.

The winner of the competition can be either the person who has produced the best drawing or the one whose efforts are considered to be the most amusing.

Making Words (11 plus to any age)

The competitors are given a reasonably long word, which they write down at the top of their sheet of paper. They are then given a specified time – about ten minutes – in which to make up as many words as they can from the letters of the given word. The letters may be used in any order and for as many words as desired, but no word made must contain less than three letters. It is not usual to allow the scoring of plural words which are formed by the simple addition of the letter 's'.

In selecting the original word it is advisable to choose one with at least two or three vowels and the same number of consonants. Suppose the word chosen was 'BALUSTRADE'. A competitor might make words such as BALE, LUSTRE, TRADE, DARE,

BLUSTER, DART, RAT, BARE, BUST, ART, RUST, TALE, STARE, BAT, BAR, BUT, etc.

Some useful words for this type of competition are:

ABROGATE	AUSTRALIAN	CANDIDATE
UNDERSTAND	ABORIGINE	FUNDAMENTAL
CATHERINE	TREMENDOUS	IMPERSONATE
RUSTICATE	COMBINATION	ILLUSTRATE

Find the Animals (8 plus to 14 plus. Indoors)

Each player is given a sheet of paper and a pencil. A number of short sentences are read out, which each player writes down. (Alternatively, a number of typed copies of the sentences can be prepared beforehand and handed out.) Hidden in the sentences are the names of animals which the players are asked to find. The one who discovers the most in a given time is the winner. Some sample sentences, along with the answers, are given below:

> I would rather be rich than poor. (RAT)
> I do hope that you will be a very good girl. (BEAVER)
> You must try to add the numbers together. (TOAD)
> There were ten pigeons in the loft. (PIG)
> I think I made Eric understand. (DEER)
> Winston Churchill is a famous Englishman. (MOUSE)
> Alec owed John three shillings. (COW)
> She was very early but he came late. (CAMEL)
> How many times have I told you not to slam both doors. (LAMB)
> I was told that I must go at nine o'clock (GOAT)

Find the Jewels (8 plus to 14 plus. Indoors)

This is identical with *Find the Animals* except that precious and semi-precious stones are hidden in the sentences. Five specimen sentences are given:

> I have told you that you must not rub your eyes. (RUBY)
> The horse had to gallop all the way. (OPAL)

In Siam and Cambodia, Monday is the day of rest. (DIAMOND)

When you go through a gate, close it after you. (AGATE)

John said, 'I must disappear like a flash.' (PEARL)

Consequences (10 plus to 14 plus)

This is an old favourite, but one which never fails to amuse younger children.

The leader of the game says, 'Write down the name of a girl.' Each child does so, folds over the top of the paper and passes it to the next person on the right. The leader then says, 'This girl met a boy. Write down his name.' This is done, the papers are then folded again and passed on. 'Write where they met' is the next order. Again the papers are folded over and passed on. A further series of orders is given such as, 'Write what the girl was wearing'; 'Write what the boy was wearing'; 'Write what she did'; 'Write what he did'; 'Write what she said'; 'Write what he said'; 'Write what were the consequences.'

Each child is encouraged to write humorous answers to the questions or orders. At the end the papers are unfolded and the answers, or stories, are read out. Most of them are just complete nonsense, of course – but they are often highly amusing to the guests. The sort of result that is obtained is as below:

Mary Jones met Johnny Brown on top of a bus. She was wearing a swimming costume; he was wearing a striped suit and football boots. She cried out in terror, he laughed like mad. She said, 'Will you take me to the cinema?' He said, 'I think Bolton will win the cup,' and the consequences were that they both caught shocking colds.

Alphabetical Plants (10 plus to 14 plus)

A letter of the alphabet is chosen at random. (A good way to do this is to open a book at any page and take the first letter of the first word on the page.) Everyone then has to write down in five minutes as many names of plants as he can think of, beginning with the chosen letter. Suppose the letter were 'B'; the lists would then contain plants such as bluebell, buttercup, briar, blackberry, belladonna, blackthorn, etc.

At the end of the time allowed, the lists are marked.

This can be done in two ways. A mark can be scored for every plant written down, or, alternatively, points can be scored only for those plants which no others have got on their lists.

Geographical Games (10 plus to 14 plus)

The paper is divided into four or more vertical columns. Down the left-hand column write under each other the following words: (1) country, (2) river, (3) mountains, (4) port, (5) lake, (6) sea, (7) town, (8) island, (9) race, (10) valley.

A letter of the alphabet is then chosen at random and the competitors have to try to find an appropriate word beginning with the chosen letter, which they write down in the second column. Suppose the letter chosen were 'A'. A list might then read: (1) Albania, (2) Avon, (3) Alps, (4) Antwerp, (5) Loch Awe, (6) Atlantic, (7) Andover, (8) Australia, (9) African, (10) Aylesbury.

At the end of, say, five minutes the lists are marked and the scores placed at the bottom of the columns. Another letter is then chosen and the words put in the second column, and so on, until all the columns are completed. The player with the largest total at the end of the game is the winner.

Find the Town (10 plus to any age)

This is a simple jumbled-letter game. Each player is given a list of, say, ten or fifteen places with their letters all jumbled up. They are then given, say, ten minutes to try to find the actual names of the places and to write them down alongside the jumbled letters. Here are two examples: RRHWOA when rearranged becomes HARROW, and EEARMCHNST becomes MANCHESTER.

Below are given more examples from which a selection can be made:

FICFDRA	= CARDIFF	IBRINGHMAM	= BIRMINGHAM
LOOENT	= BOLTON	BUHGENRID	= EDINBURGH
VREDO	= DOVER	RILECSLA	= CARLISLE
GNLEAI	= EALING	TSEBAFL	= BELFAST
FFHESEIDL	= SHEFFIELD	ONLNLDDUA	= LLANDUDNO
AHGSNITS	= HASTINGS	LLPOOERVI	= LIVERPOOL

The player who gets the most right in the given time is the winner.

Sentences (10 plus to any age. Indoors)

All the competitors are asked to write the longest sentence they can without using words of more than four letters. With older children or adults one can reduce the number of letters to three. Here are two examples:

Four-letter words: 'Mary and Tom went for a walk down the road and saw a shop that sold peas, dogs, cats, etc.'

Three-letter words: 'Tom saw Jim on a big old log at ten to two and hit him on the ear.'

To make the game more difficult still (if you want it more difficult) ask the players to write a sentence, every word of which must consist of three letters, e.g. 'The sly dry old dog was mad, but Mum saw him run out and pat the fat red cow.'

And there will be many sillier sentences than that!

Join Them Up (10 plus to teenagers. Indoors)

Prepare a slip of paper for each guest with two lists of three-letter words such as are shown below. (Carbon copies will save a lot of writing.) Provide them also with a piece of paper and a pencil each.

The problem is to match up words from the first column with those in the second column to form six-letter words. The first player to complete the list of twenty, or the one with the most done in, say, five minutes, is the winner and should be suitably rewarded.

Column 1	Column 2
PAR	LET
CAR	RAY
ERR	MAN
FAT	ROW
BET	SON
IMP	ANT
HAM	HER
FUR	ART
ROT	KIN
BAR	BIT
TEA	WIT
DOT	PET
SET	AGE
DON	TEN
COW	HER
NAP	BOY
BUT	KEY
TIT	POT
OUT	TEE
RAT	TON

(PARSON, CARPET, HAMLET, BARMAN, BETRAY, FURROW, DOT-
AGE, ERRANT, FATHER, IMPART, NAPKIN, ROTTEN, TEAPOT,
TITBIT, SETTEE, OUTWIT, DONKEY, RATHER, COWBOY, BUTTON.)

Your Face is Familiar (10 plus to teenagers)

How many times have you had to say 'Your face is familiar
but I can't remember your name'? Here is a quiet game based
on that phrase. A little previous preparation is needed.

Cut out from an old magazine about a dozen pictures
of men and women and paste them on postcards. Now make
twelve small slips of paper and on each one write a name such
as ROBERT, ROGER, JANET, JOAN, and so on.

Place the pictures on the table, and place one of the names
under each one. Allow the players three or four minutes to
study the pictures and names; take them all away for one

minute and then *replace the pictures only* in a different order. Each player has then to try to identify the pictures by name and write them down in their present order. The one with the most right wins.

To be absolutely sure *you* know the right answers put numbers on the back of the postcards and corresponding numbers on the back of the name slips.

Heads and Tails (10 and upwards)

The players are given five minutes in which to write down as many words as possible of four or more letters which begin and end with the same letter, e.g. *rubber, test, denied, libel, fluff, cynic, blurb, tenet, going, hurrah, kick.*

One point is given for each word; the player with the most points is the winner.

If desired – and with older players – two points can be given for those who can include words with *two* letters the same at the beginning and end, and three points if they include words with three letters which are the same, e.g. *decide, reassure, verve, deride, underground, tsetse, entertainment, ionization.*

Jumbled Proverbs

Suitable for players from ten years upwards. Previously prepare sheets of paper containing a number of proverbs each one of which has been jumbled up, e.g. WORTH THE THE A IS IN IN BIRD TWO HAND BUSH (A BIRD IN THE HAND IS WORTH TWO IN THE BUSH). Leave enough space under each proverb for the correct answer to be written.

Then either give the competitors, say, ten minutes to try to unscramble the jumbled words and write out the correct versions (the one with the most correct wins) or make the winner the one who gets them all correct first.

To ensure fairness, all the papers must be identical.

A list of proverbs from which a selection can be made will be found on pages 185 and 186.

Proverbial Answers

A game for players of ten years of age upwards.

Devise a number of questions (some examples are given below) to which all the answers are to be found in proverbs, e.g. What two things wait for no man? *Answer*, Time and tide.

What animal may look at royalty? *Answer*, A cat (may look at a king).

The player with the most correct answers is the winner.

Q. What is it that saves nine? *A.* A stitch in time.

Q. What should one do when the sun is shining. *A.* Make hay.

Q. Who sees most of the game? *A.* Lookers on.

Q. Which is the shortest way home? *A.* The longest way round.

Q. What happens when the feline quadruped is missing? *A.* The mice will play.

Q. Who is the mother of new ideas? *A.* Necessity.

Q. What is no recommendation? *A.* Self-praise.

Q. What makes the loudest noise? *A.* Empty vessels.

Q. What wears away a stone? *A.* Constant dripping.

Q. What does it require two to make? *A.* A quarrel.

Q. What never reaches 100° C? *A.* A watched pot.

Q. What makes light work? *A.* Many hands.

Q. Who or what laughs at locksmiths? *A.* Love.

Finishers

A game for players from about nine to ten years of age and upwards. Pencils and paper are required. Ten or more of the following phrases or sayings are read out and competitors are merely required to write down the missing word or words:

As hungry as a — (hunter)

Shining like a — (new pin)

Clean as a — (whistle)

Brown as a — (berry)

Mad as a — (hatter)

Thin as a — (rake)

As brazen as — (brass)

As stubborn as a — (mule)

To cackle like a — (hen)

Like a — in a china shop (bull)

Like a red rag to a — (bull)

As dead as a — (doorpost)
As innocent as a — (new-born babe)
As blind as a — (bat)
Grunting like a — (pig)
Like a fish out of — (water)
Pouring down — (cats and dogs)
As black as — (night, ink)
As pure as — (driven snow)
As mischievous as a — (monkey)
As dull as — (ditchwater)
As heavy as — (lead)
As miserable as — (sin)
To sleep like a — (log)
As poor as a — (church mouse)
As slippery as an — (eel)
As playful as a — (kitten)
As sharp as a — (needle)
As happy as a — (sand boy)
As weak as a — (kitten)
As old as the — (hills)
As brave as a — (lion)
As proud as — (punch)
To lean over — (backwards)
To be down on one's — (luck)
As bald as a — (coot)
Singing like a — (lark)
Too big for his — (boots)
As cool as a — (cucumber)
To bellow like a — (bull)
As sober as a — (judge)
As light as a — (feather)

Complete the Proverbs (10 and upwards)

Ten or more of the uncompleted proverbs selected from the list of fifty below are read out and the competitors are required to write down the missing words. The player with the most correct answers is the winner.

Little children should be seen — (and not heard)
You can't make a silk purse from — (a sow's ear)
Look before — (you leap)
He who hesitates — (is lost)
Absence makes the heart — (grow fonder)
Out of sight — (out of mind)
The early bird catches — (the worm)
Time and tide — (wait for no man)
When the cat's away — (the mice will play)
A rolling stone gathers — (no moss)
A friend in need is — (a friend indeed)
You can't have your cake — (and eat it)
Half a loaf is better than — (no bread)

Lookers on see — (most of the game)
Penny wise — (pound foolish)
Still waters — (run deep)
Even a worm — (will turn)
It's a long lane that has — (no turning)
Least said — (soonest mended)
Too many cooks — (spoil the broth)
Many hands — (make light work)
Self-praise is — (no recommendation)
More haste — (less speed)
A cat may look at — (a king)
One good turn deserves — (another)
A bird in the hand is worth — (two in the bush)
It takes two to make — (a quarrel)
Constant dripping — (wears away a stone)
Jack of all trades — (master of none)
Enough is as good as — (a feast)
An Englishman's house is — (his castle)
Those who live in glass houses should not — (throw stones)
Do not put all your eggs — (in one basket)
Set a thief to — (catch a thief)
Honesty is the — (best policy)
Still waters — (run deep)
A miss is as good as — (a mile)
Spare the rod — (spoil the child)
It's an ill wind that — (blows nobody any good)
In for a penny — (in for a pound)
Familiarity breeds — (contempt)
Empty vessels make the — (most sound)
A watched pot — (never boils)
Make hay while — (the sun shines)
The longest way round is — (the shortest way home)
Don't look a gift horse — (in the mouth)
You can't burn the candle — (at both ends)
Silence is — (golden)
Let sleeping dogs — (lie)
A wink is as good as a nod to — (a blind donkey)

Anagrams

A quiet competition requiring one previously prepared post-card and a pencil for each player.

Down the left-hand side of the postcard write, say, ten jumbled-up words, i.e. the letters are all out of order.

The players are then given five or more minutes (according to age and word difficulty) to try to find out and write down the correct words made from the jumbled letters.

For younger children, three- and four-letter words are quite long enough; older or adult players can be given longer or more difficult words.

Two examples (with the answers) are given below:

Card for Younger Children	*Card for Older Players*
HRSOE (HORSE)	RCCAAILF (FARCICAL)
LMUE (MULE)	PEDNIHUMIL (DELPHINIUM)
EEGNR (GREEN)	GBOEIAN (BEGONIA)
ALBCK (BLACK)	CAHTKSIMBL (BLACKSMITH)
HEOS (SHOE)	SLÉFFUO (SOUFFLÉ)
KOBO (BOOK)	VETOMOOCLI (LOCOMOTIVE)
EADRB (BREAD)	AHSEOVNIC (ANCHOVIES)
CONAB (BACON)	AAEAZL (AZALEA)
ACTR (CART)	SILNMEOIU (LIMOUSINE)
LMEDA (MEDAL)	MURUBECC (CUCUMBER)

Guess in the Dark

An amusing but quiet game for players of any age from about ten years upwards. All the players sit round a table and are provided with a pencil and paper. The lights are switched off and an object is passed round the table from hand to hand. The lights are then switched on and the players write down what they think the object was. After, say, ten or twelve objects have been passed round, the person who has written down the most correct answers is the winner.

Unusual objects should be selected, whenever possible; here are some suggestions: A small fluffy animal, a brussels sprout, a small sponge, a dog's rubber bone, a small torch battery, a shell, a wrapped meat cube, a coin or medal, a large paper-clip, the lid of a scent bottle, an empty walnut-shell, a toy mouse, sugar tongs, a piece of pumice stone, a car plug, a crochet needle, a cork, a pair of socks tucked together, a thimble, a shampoo sachet, etc., etc.

The Memory Game

A quiet pencil and paper game for older children and adults. The game is basically a simple one designed to test the memories of the players. A short topical news item or report containing a number of facts is read out slowly and distinctly to those taking part.

Then a number of questions on the paragraph (say, ten) are given which require answers of not more than two or three words.

The player with the most correct answers is the winner.

USE YOUR INTELLIGENCE

Pencil and paper games for players of ten years of age and upwards.

The games can be of many kinds, but basically they all require answers of not more than one or two words, which should of course be written down. Here are some examples:

Analogies

Consider the following sentence: Man is to woman as boy is to —. The obvious answer is, of course, 'girl', which would be written down as the answer.

Here are some examples which are read out to the players. Many more can be devised. (The answers are in brackets.)

The player with the most correct answers wins the competition.

(1) Black is to white as night is to — (day)
(2) France is to Paris as America is to — (Washington)
(3) Dexter is to cricket as Matthews is to — (football)

(4) England is to an Englishman as Holland is to a — (Dutchman)

(5) Aeroplane is to — as ship is to sea (sky)

(6) Six o'clock is to eight o'clock as nine o'clock is to — (eleven o'clock)

(7) Calf is to cow as — is to sheep (lamb)

(8) Feet are to shoes as hands are to — (gloves)

(9) Nephew is to uncle as — is to aunt (niece)

(10) Orange is to peel as banana is to — (skin)

(11) Food is to famine as water is to — (drought)

(12) Author is to book as — is to statue (sculptor)

(13) Scuttle is to coal as — is to tea (caddy)

(14) Cow is to beef as pig is to — (pork)

(15) Revolver is to holster as sword is to — (scabbard)

(16) Inside is to outside as interior is to — (exterior)

(17) Eskimo is to igloo as Red Indian is to — (wigwam)

(18) Lodge is to beaver as — is to badger (sett)

(19) Flock is to sheep as — is to lions (pride)

(20) Gaggle is to geese as — is to porpoises (school)

Odd Man Out

In this type of quiz or competition a list of items is usually given, one of them being a stranger or 'odd man out' in the group. Here are two very simple examples:

(a) Apple, pear, orange, potato, plum.

'Potato' is the odd man out, because it is a vegetable: all the others are fruits.

(b) Snowdon, Ben Nevis, Mont Blanc, Vesuvius, The Matterhorn.

'Vesuvius' is the odd one, because it is the only one which is a volcano.

Below are given twenty examples; many more can be devised. Competitors merely write down the word they consider should not be there. The odd man out is printed in italics.

(1) Ridicule, mock, *praise*, scorn, taunt

(2) Red, *green*, yellow, blue (green is not a primary colour)

189

(3) Rome, Paris, *Ottawa*, Oslo, Brussels
(4) Rectangle, square, *circle*, parallelogram, triangle
(5) Roach, perch, *newt*, minnow, pike
(6) Shark, swordfish, *whale*, cod, herring
(7) Dublin, London, Madrid, *New York*, Cairo
(8) Volga, Rhine, Danube, Tiber, *Amazon*
(9) Silver, iron, lead, *brass*, copper, tin
(10) Priestley, *Picasso*, Shaw, Dumas, Verne
(11) Cormorant, seagull, *eagle*, albatross, puffin
(12) Sett, warren, lodge, den, *prison*
(13) Motor car, bus, *bicycle*, taxi, train
(14) Disraeli, Bonar Law, Chamberlain, Churchill, *Heath*
(15) Trombone, flute, *concertina*, saxophone, whistle
(16) Seal, walrus, polar bear, *penguin*
(17) High Jump, Shot Putt, Pole Vault, Hammer Throw, *Hurdles*
(18) Penalty Area, Goals, Full Back, *Fairway*, Cross Bar
(19) Bogey, Birdie, Eagle, Driver, *Bails*, Blaster
(20) Tay, Tyne, Humber, Liffey, *Ullswater*, Avon

Initial Proverbs

A pencil and paper game for teenagers and upwards. The initial letters of ten or more well-known proverbs are either dictated to the players, or supplied to them already written out on postcards or slips of paper. The competitors are then given five to ten minutes to write down as many of the proverbs as possible, at the end of which time the answers are called out and the one with the most correct is the winner.

A specimen selection of ten is given below along with the answers. Further proverbs will be found on pages 185 and 186.

Proverb Initials	Proverb
(1) L.b.y.l.	Look before you leap
(2) T.m.c.s.t.b.	Too many cooks spoil the broth
(3) M.h.m.l.w.	Many hands make light work
(4) A.s.i.t.s.n.	A stitch in time saves nine
(5) A.r.s.g.n.m.	A rolling stone gathers no moss

(6) L.s.d.l.	Let sleeping dogs lie
(7) I.a.l.l.t.h.n.t.	It's a long lane that has no turning
(8) E.i.a.g.a.a.f.	Enough is as good as a feast
(9) H.w.h.i.l.	He who hesitates is lost
(10) Y.c.h.y.c.a.e.i.	You can't have your cake and eat it

Spelling Quiz

Ten or more somewhat-difficult-to-spell words are dictated slowly. Allow a few seconds between words to give the players reasonable time in which to write down the words.

Players then change papers for marking. A small prize should be given to the one who has most words correctly spelled.

The words chosen must be suitable for the age of the participants. If necessary, particularly with younger children, a sentence containing the word can be given as a help to their understanding, or, alternatively, give a short definition, e.g. 'Pane – made of glass'.

Here are two lists of words from which a selection can be made, one for younger players, the other for adults:

List 'A' – Younger Players

ADDRESS, WEATHER, WHETHER, VANE, VEIN, THERE, THEIR, SENTENCE, EDIBLE, PARALLEL, COOLLY, MATTHEW, RECEIVE, GALLOP, TUNNEL, BELIEVE, RAIN, REIN, GRAMOPHONE, DELICIOUS, INOCULATE, BELIEF, DECEIVE, PATHETIC, JEWEL, MURMUR, ASPIDISTRA, CHASM, PERPETUAL, ACCIDENT, SUPPOSE

List 'B' – Adults

ASSASSINATE, EMBARRASSMENT, ACCOMMODATE, PHENOMENON, MAINTENANCE, SOLILOQUY, HARASS, NAPHTHA, DIPHTHERIA, ANNIHILATE, PARALLELOGRAM, INFALLIBLE, HANDFUL, PSYCHIATRIST, INACCESSIBLE, CANNIBAL, SCHISM, CHAOTIC, FAC-SIMILE, RESUSCITATE, FUCHSIA, HYDRANGEA, FORSYTHIA, NON-CHALANT, CONSCIENTIOUS, FLACCID, ACQUISITIVE, SCINTILLATE, LOQUACITY, HYPOCHONDRIAC, SOPORIFIC, SUPERCILIOUS, LIQUEFY, EPHEMERAL, OBLOQUY, INNOCUOUS, ONOMATOPOEIA, PNEUMONIA,

Make a Word (10 plus upwards)

Dictate to the players fifteen to twenty endings of words – say, the last three letters, e.g. ore, ent, eny, hic, eue, tal, eur, etc., etc.

The players are then given five minutes (or less) to complete the words; the one with the greatest number of correct words being the winner.

Using the endings given above, the words could be: bef*ore*, ev*ent*, d*eny*, grap*hic*, qu*eue*, capi*tal*, pos*eur*.

Fivers (Teenagers upwards)

This game is a variation of *Make a Word*, but in this instance the first and last letters only of a word are given. The object is to complete the word by adding three letters to complete a five-letter word; e.g. suppose the letters G–S were given, a five-letter word could be made by inserting ATE, or ALE, or IRL. A fairly large number of words should be set (forty to fifty) and a time of about ten minutes allowed for the players to try to complete their list. The one with the most words completed at the end of the given time is, of course, the winner.

The following words might prove useful:

*Late*X, *Pani*C, *Livi*D, *Bigo*T, *Yach*T, *Wris*T, *Prim*P, *Gnom*E, *Eart*H, *Past*Y, *Leve*L, *Stud*Y, *Tric*K, *Nabo*B, *Blur*B, *Comi*C, *Fluf*F, *Heat*H, *Mada*M.

Books and Authors Quiz

A quiz suitable for players of ten years of age and upwards. Read out the names of twenty or so well-known books; the players are merely required to write down the names of the authors of the books.

Obviously the books selected must be the ones which are familiar to the members of the party, e.g. for children of ten or twelve years of age popular classics or semi-classics can be chosen. Adults can be given the names of more modern books or those which they are likely to have read during adult or teenage life.

Given below are two lists of books along with the names of their authors. List 1 is suitable for the ten to fourteen years of age group. List 2 is for teenagers and adults.

List 1

(1) Robinson Crusoe
(Daniel Defoe)
(2) Treasure Island
(R. L. Stevenson)
(3) Gulliver's Travels
(Jonathan Swift)
(4) Lorna Doone
(R. D. Blackmore)
(5) Silas Marner
(George Eliot)
(6) Heidi
(Johanna Spyri)
(7) Alice in Wonderland
(Lewis Carroll)
(8) Black Beauty
(Anna Sewell)
(9) Moby Dick
(Herman Melville)
(10) Round the World in 80 Days (Jules Verne)
(11) Little Women
(Louisa M. Alcott)
(12) Jane Eyre
(Charlotte Brontë)
(13) The Black Tulip
(Alexandre Dumas)
(14) Ivanhoe
(Sir Walter Scott)
(15) Oliver Twist
(Charles Dickens)

List 2

(1) Bulldog Drummond
(Sapper)
(2) Huckleberry Finn
(Mark Twain)
(3) The Wooden Horse
(Eric Williams)
(4) Rebecca
(Daphne du Maurier)
(5) The Scarlet Pimpernel
(Baroness Orczy)
(6) The Dam Busters
(Paul Brickhill)
(7) The Small Women
(Alan Burgess)
(8) Dark Duet
(Peter Cheyney)
(9) Ten Little Niggers
(Agatha Christie)
(10) Seal Morning
(Rowena Farre)
(11) For whom the Bell Tolls
(Ernest Hemingway)
(12) Seven Pillars of Wisdom
(T. E. Lawrence)
(13) A Ring of Bells
(John Betjeman)
(14) Under Milk Wood
(Dylan Thomas)
(15) A Pattern of Islands
(Sir Arthur Grimble)

Who Wrote It?

A pencil and paper quiz more suitable for teenagers and adults. A number of quotations are read out and the competitors are asked to write down the names of the authors. A sample collection of quotations is given below, along with the answers:

(1) I wandered lonely as a cloud (Wordsworth)

(2) Full fathom five thy father lies (Shakespeare)

(3) Drink to me only with thine eyes (Ben Johnson)

(4) Go and catch a falling star (John Donne)

(5) The curfew tolls the knell of parting day (Thomas Gray)

(6) Tiger, tiger, burning bright,
In the forests of the night   (William Blake)

(7) My heart leaps up when I behold a rainbow in the sky (Wordsworth)

(8) Water, water, everywhere, nor any drop to drink (Coleridge)

(9) Season of mists and mellow fruitfulness (Keats)

(10) What was he doing, the great god Pan
Down in the reeds by the river? (Elizabeth Barrett Browning)

(11) Come into the garden, Maud
For the black bat, Night, has flown (Tennyson)

(12) O, to be in England
Now that April's there (Browning)

(13) O Mary, go and call the cattle home (Charles Kingsley)

(14) Under the wide and starry sky
Dig the grave and let me lie (R. L. Stevenson)

(15) God of our fathers, known of old –
Lord of our far-flung battle line (Kipling)

SECTION NINETEEN

TALKING GAMES

Simple Spelling Bee (6 plus to any age)

Teams sit opposite each other in two lines. The leader calls out a word from a prearranged list. The first player of one team tries to spell it. If he fails he is eliminated and the *same* word is given to the leader of the second team. If he fails he is eliminated also. If, however, he spells the word correctly another word is given to the second player of the first team. If he in turn gets this one right, the next word is given to the second player of the second team and so on. The game ends when all the players of one team are eliminated.

In selecting words for the *Spelling Bee*, the leader is advised not to choose difficult technical ones, but words in fairly common usage which are often spelt wrongly such as PARALLEL, JUDGEMENT, BATTALION, HARASSED, EMBARRASSED, ELLIPSE, ERRATICALLY, DIPHTHERIA, HALLUCINATION, ATTACHABLE, ATROCIOUS, LITERARY, REHABILITATE, STATIONARY, STATIONERY, CORRESPONDENCE, and OVERREACH.

Younger players should be given simpler words or be asked to spell words which are pronounced the same as other words but spelt differently. In such cases the definition of the word should be given, e.g. PAIN, PANE; VAIN, VANE, VEIN; THERE, THEIR; WHETHER, WEATHER, WETHER; HORSE, HOARSE, etc.

Backward Spelling (8 plus to 14 plus. Indoors or outdoors)

All the players sit in a line or circle. The leader calls out a common word, and the first person in the line tries to spell it backwards in, say, ten seconds. If he fails he loses a 'life'. Each person in turn is given a word, and at the end of five or six rounds the one who has lost the least number of lives is the winner.

The Old Oak Chest (8 plus to 12 plus)

This is an alphabetical game in which players have to think of words beginning with the letters of the alphabet in their correct order.

The players sit in a circle, and the leader starts the game by saying, 'Up in the attic there's an old oak chest, and in that chest there's a big rosy Apple' (or some other article beginning with 'A'). The second player then says, 'Up in the attic there's an old oak chest, and in that chest there's a big white Apron' (or, like the first player, any other item he can think of beginning with 'A'). Everyone must think of something beginning with 'A' until it becomes the leader's turn again, when he must give a word beginning with 'B'.

The game continues until all except one are eliminated, a player being eliminated, of course, if he fails to think of some item beginning with the correct letter and which has not been used by the previous players. If necessary, 'X' and 'Z' can be omitted, as there are very few words beginning with these letters.

What Are We Shouting? (10 plus to 14 plus. Indoors or outdoors)

A noisy game, but one which can be quite amusing. Players divide into two roughly equal teams. One team then selects a proverb or saying, say, 'Too many cooks spoil the broth', and one word is allocated to each player. Thus, if there were six players, the first would be allocated 'Too', the second 'many', the third 'cooks', and so on. If there are more players than there are words in the proverb or saying, the same word is given to two or more players. For example, if there were eight in the team, the seventh player as well as the first would be allocated 'Too' and the eighth player as well as the second would be given 'many'.

All this preliminary arrangement is done quietly and out of

earshot of the opposing team. When it is done, at a signal from the leader, the team all shout out their words at the same time, and the opposing team have to try to guess the proverb or saying. If they fail to get it on the first shout, they are allowed two more calls, and if by then they do not know what it is, the shouting team pick another proverb or saying and repeat the procedure. If, however, the listening team get the right answer, it becomes their turn to do the shouting. Whichever team gets five points first is the winner. Some suitable phrases and proverbs for this game are given below:

Under the spreading chestnut tree.
Jack and Jill went up the hill.
A stitch in time saves nine.
John Brown's body lies a-mouldering in the grave.
Hark the Herald Angels sing.

The Queen's Kitchen (6 plus to 10 plus. Indoors or outdoors)

Everyone sits comfortably. One player starts the game by saying, 'I am the Queen of Spain, and in the kitchen of my castle in Madrid, there is an oven of gold' (or any other item which may be found in any kitchen).

The next player repeats exactly what the first player said and adds another item. The sentence might now be: 'I am the Queen of Spain, and in the kitchen of my castle in Madrid there is an oven of gold and a silver frying pan.'

The third and subsequent players add further items, but anyone who fails to repeat *exactly* what has been said previously is eliminated or 'loses a life'.

The winner is the one who has lost the least number of 'lives' or who is the only one not to have made a mistake.

I Own a Garage (8 plus to 10 plus. Indoors or outdoors)

This game is identical with *The Queen's Kitchen*, but is meant for boys. One player starts by saying, 'I am the owner of a very large garage, and in my garage I have an Austin car.'

From then onwards each player is asked to add the name of another car, anyone failing to do so, or repeating the sequence wrongly, being eliminated.

There are endless variations of this game which can be devised to suit both the age and sex of the players. Some starting sentences might be:

'I collect photographs of film stars and in my collection is a photograph of Jack Hawkins (... and a photograph of ...).'

'I am a great adventurer and on my travels I have been to San Francisco (... and to Timbuctoo ...).'

Story-tellers (Teenagers and upwards)

This is a quieter game (preferably for volunteers) which can nevertheless cause considerable amusement.

The person volunteering to tell a story is given three or four objects, say a ball, a candle, a bus ticket, and a cutting from a magazine of a woman wearing a fashionable hat. He is then asked to make up a story lasting not less than two to three minutes (but not more) bringing in the objects given. When all the volunteers have told their stories, the audience vote for the one they consider to have been the most entertaining and feasible story.

Whenever possible, make the objects given to the story-teller as unrelated as possible. Here are some suggestions from which you can choose:

MARBLES	CIGARETTE HOLDER	RUBBER GLOVE
BUS TICKET	SMALL TIN BOX	CLOTHES PEG
THE ACE OF SPADES	WHISTLE	BANDAGES
TINY DOLL	POTATO	DRIVING LICENCE
NEWSPAPER CUTTINGS	HAIRPIN	BISCUIT
SEASON TICKET	BABY'S NAPKIN	HOT WATER BOTTLE

Impossible Situations (Teenagers and upwards)

This game is similar in principle to *Story-tellers*. Volunteers are asked for and are required to make up a story, the climax or part of which must be the impossible situation which is presented to them, written on a piece of paper, two minutes before they are required to start their story. Here is an example. The first volunteer is given a piece of paper on which is written 'and there I was, at midnight, in the centre of Piccadilly wearing a tall hat, a bathing costume, and football boots'.

The story-teller must then try to make up a story to explain as reasonably as possible how he came to be in such a situation. To explain the situation by saying that the items of clothing were worn to win a bet is not permissible; every effort must be made to make the story as logical as possible so that in the end it will appear quite natural that he should find himself in such a situation.

The listeners vote for the story they consider to be the best or most ingenious explanation of the situation. Here are some more suggestions on situations:

'As I lay under the Prime Minister's dining-room table the door of the room opened and a policeman came in.'

'I realized with horror that I had just shampooed the Bishop's hair with a brilliant green dye.'

'I really had no intention whatsoever of making the Ambassador sit on a plate of ice cream.'

'And there I was standing opposite King Henry VIII in the middle of Madame Tussaud's wearing a bikini.'

'And before I knew what I was doing, I was throwing jelly at the top-table guests at the Lord Mayor's banquet.'

'The President congratulated me on volunteering and shut the door of the rocket behind him.'

The Word Game (10 plus to any age. Indoors or outdoors)

Players sit in a circle or round a table. One person thinks of a word of more than three letters and without saying what the word is calls out the first letter. Let us suppose he thinks of the word 'diver'; he calls out 'd'. The next player thinks perhaps not of 'diver' but 'dynamo', so he says 'y'. The third player not knowing what words the first two had in mind can only think of the word 'dyke' which starts with 'dy' so he says 'k'.

This puts the fourth player in an impossible position, *for the object is to avoid completing a word*. All he can say is 'e' and he loses one 'life'. The fifth player would then start a new word by giving the initial letter. When any player has lost three lives he is eliminated. The game continues until all except one are 'dead'; he is the winner. Certain other simple rules are advisable: (1) Proper names should not be permitted. (2) If a player has any doubts about the word in mind of the preceding player he can challenge him to give his word. If he has a legitimate word in mind, the challenger loses a 'life'; on the other hand, if the one challenged has given a wrong letter or hasn't even thought of a word but is trying to bluff, it is he, and not the challenger, who loses a 'life'. An example of this is given below. The words thought of by each player are given in brackets.

First Player says 'd' (dance)
Second Player says 'i' (dimple)
Third Player says 'n' (dinner)
Fourth Player says 'o' (dinosaur)

Fifth Player cannot for the life of him think of any word starting 'dino'. He keeps a straight face and without hesitation says 'm'.

Sixth Player completely baffled by 'dinom' wonders if dynamometer is spelled with an 'i', decides it isn't, and challenges the fifth player, 'What is your word?' Player No. 5 admits he hadn't been able to think of one, and thus loses a 'life'. The sixth player would then give the first letter of a new word.

CHARADES AND DRAMATIC GAMES

Charades, so popular at parties in the early part of the century, are still popular with younger children (older people can play them as well) and can be introduced as 'quieteners' after a more hectic game.

The essence of the game is as follows. A word of two

or three syllables is chosen which when divided into those syllables makes two (or three) separate words. For instance, the word 'cutlass' is made up of two words 'cut' and 'lass' and the word 'wireless' of 'wire' and 'less'. Having decided upon the word, you act or mime a little sketch to illustrate each syllable in turn and then act or mime the complete word. From your three sketches (in the case of two-syllable words) the audience have to guess what the word is.

Take the word 'wireless'.

For the first syllable 'wire' you could pretend to be walking on a tightrope or pretend you were in a post office. You would then use the word 'wire' in some context.

For the second syllable 'less', if miming, you could first stretch yourself as tall as possible, then gradually make yourself smaller (less) by crouching down. If acting the syllable, you could pretend to be in a restaurant ordering a meal. You could talk to an imaginary waiter serving you with, say, potatoes. You could then use the word 'less' during conversation.

For the complete word in mime, you could pretend to look at the *Radio Times*, select a programme, then switch on an imaginary wireless set, be a little shocked at the volume of sound, and make some remark about 'wireless'.

For a third and more taxing way of playing charades, divide the word into syllables. Then instead of using the syllable (which should, of course, be a word in itself) use a simile. Thus instead of using 'wire' as part of 'wireless', you would use 'telegram'. To illustrate 'less', use 'not so much'. For the complete word 'wireless', use 'radio'.

More than one person, of course, can take part in a charade; in fact, it is better, particularly with younger children, to have at least two. In the example given, two would be excellent; in the first syllable one would be the person sending the wire, the other the post-office clerk; in the second syllable one would be the diner, the other the waiter. Here is a short list of words suitable for miming and acting charades; the syllables are indicated:

address (add-dress)
apartment (apart-meant)
armlet (arm-let)
assent (ass-sent)
authorise (author-rise)
bedridden (bed-ridden)
behind (bee-hind)
bicycle (buy-cycle)
borax (bor-axe)
bowman (bow-man)
butterfly (butter-fly)
cargo (car-go)
carpet (car-pet)
dusty (dust-tea)

impact (imp-act)
jargon (jar-gone)
jigsaw (jig-saw)
justice (just-ice)
kindred (kin-dread)
lapwing (lap-wing)
lipstick (lip-stick)
mandate (man-date)
marrow (mar-row)
mastiff (mast-tiff)
mischief (miss-chief)
nosegay (nose-gay)
patriot (pat-riot)
primrose (prim-rose)

Miming or Acting Proverbs (8 plus to 12 plus. Indoors or outdoors)

The players divide into small groups of three or four. One of the groups then goes out of the room, decides upon a proverb, and then comes back to mime or act it in front of the others, who must try to guess the proverb. Each group in turn does the same. Here are some proverbs from which a selection can be made:

Too many cooks spoil the broth.
A stitch in time saves nine.
Look before you leap.
He who hesitates is lost.
There's many a slip between the cup and the lip.
If at first you don't succeed, try, try again.
Don't put all your eggs in one basket.
A bird in the hand is worth two in the bush.
Never look a gift horse in the mouth.
It's no use shutting the door after the horse has gone.
A rolling stone gathers no moss.

Miming or Acting Nursery Rhymes (8 plus to 12 plus. Indoors or outdoors)

This game is identical in character to *Miming or Acting Proverbs*, except that Nursery Rhymes form the subjects for the mimes or sketches. Here are some suggestions:

Rock-a-bye baby	Ding Dong Bell
Little Boy Blue	Jack Sprat could eat no fat
Sing a song of sixpence	There was a crooked man
Goosey-goosey Gander	Little Tommy Tucker
Polly put the kettle on	The Queen of Hearts
Baa-baa black sheep	Baby-Baby Bunting
Old King Cole	See Saw, Marjorie Daw
Jack and Jill	Mary had a little lamb
Little Jack Horner	Mary, Mary, quite contrary
Georgie Porgie	Hey Diddle-Diddle

Miming or Acting Titles (8 plus to 12 plus. Indoors or outdoors)

This is a variation of *Miming or Acting Nursery Rhymes*, except that songs or well-known book titles are selected by the groups. The performers can either make a little tableau, or mime or play some small scene from the book. Some suggested titles are:

Little Women	Snow White and the Seven Dwarfs
Gulliver's Travels	Ali Baba and the Forty Thieves
Robinson Crusoe	Aladdin
Dick Whittington	Johnny's so long at the fair
Robin Hood	Dashing away with a smoothing iron
Peter Pan	Underneath the spreading chestnut tree

RADIO AND TELEVISION GAMES

Many of the popular radio and television games can be used with advantage at a party. Where necessary they can and should be modified to suit the age of the performers. Here is a reminder selection.

Twenty Questions (Teenagers upwards)

One person, either a volunteer or chosen by lot, thinks of some person, object, or place, such as Charlie Chaplin, a frying pan, or Mount Everest. The remainder of the players then try to find out what has been chosen by asking questions, the answers to which must only be 'Yes' or 'No'. If at the end of twenty questions the answer has not been discovered, the questioners have lost and the same person chooses another object.

Any player who guesses the correct answer becomes the challenger.

My Wildest Dream (Teenagers upwards)

This is similar in principle to *Twenty Questions* except the challenger chooses his 'wildest dream'. This may include such things as 'winning the largest ever Football Pool' or 'being Prime Minister for a week'. The dreamer is questioned by the others present and must answer only 'Yes' or 'No'.

Allow either a specific number of questions or fix a time limit for the questioning. If the questioners do not discover what the dream is about, the 'dreamer' has won. The questioners may make up to three direct guesses – if they fail on these the challenger again wins.

What's My Line? (Teenagers upwards)

Five or six of the guests are chosen to act as challengers, the remainder become the 'panel', or, if so desired, four or five only are selected to act in this capacity. Another person is chosen to act as compere to introduce the challengers.

The challengers decide what job they are supposed to do, for normally it will be little use them selecting their own, as they will probably be well known to the panel. In deciding their jobs, humorous-sounding ones can be chosen, but they must be real ones; one could have such jobs as kipper filleter, gob-stopper maker, and fluffer (a person who keeps tube railway tunnels clean), as well as the more ordinary ones such as receptionist, architect, and so on.

The 'mime' which is meant to be reasonably helpful to the panel must also be decided upon. The first challenger is then introduced and does his mime. The panel members then proceed to question him, each one continuing with his questions until he gets the answer 'no' to any one of them. The compere keeps the score of 'no's', and if the panel have not guessed the occupation before ten negative answers have been given by the challenger, he has won. Small prizes should be given to successful challengers.

Hangman (12 plus upwards. Indoors)

A slate, small blackboard, or large piece of drawing paper is required. Players divide into two teams. One team decides upon a word; one of not less than six or seven letters is preferable. Let us assume that the word chosen is 'FOOTBALL'. The leader of the challenging team then draws upon his board eight dashes to represent the letters making up the word, and at one side of the board he draws a gallows with a rope hanging from it. His board will then look like Fig 46.

The first member of the opposing side then tries to guess a letter in the chosen word. He might, for instance, say, 'Does it have an "e"?' As the word 'FOOTBALL' docs not possess an 'e', no letter is put over any of the dashes, but a head is drawn on the end of the rope. The board will now appear as in Fig 47.

The next person might then say, 'Does it have an "o"?' As the word has two 'o's, these are put in over the appropriate dashes.

The game continues in this fashion. If a wrong letter is called, an addition is made to the hanging body (Fig 48). For each wrong guess, of course, another part of the body is drawn until the completed man has a head, body, two arms, two legs, two eyes, a nose, and a mouth. If the side which is trying to guess the word have a total of ten wrong guesses, the man is hanged and they have lost. The man will then appear as in Fig 49.

At any period of the game, a member of the guessing team, if he thinks he knows the complete word, can call it out when his turn comes. If his guess is a correct one his side wins, but if he is wrong the challenging side completes the hanging man and have another turn.

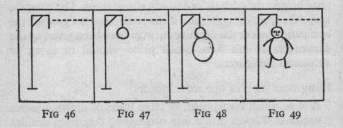

FIG 46   FIG 47   FIG 48   FIG 49

A variation of this game is to have well-known phrases or expressions such as 'HUNGRY AS A HUNTER', 'QUICK AS LIGHT-NING', 'QUIET AS A MOUSE', and so on. If this variation is played, a veiled clue can be given by the challenging side. On the examples given above, for instance, the clue given for the first phrase might be 'A good shot might never be'; for the second 'Certainly not a slow coach' would be appropriate; for the third 'Hobnail boots would be useless' would be a reasonable clue.

Here are some suggested words which might be found a little puzzling to solve:

ABSCESS	BLIZZARD	CAMOMILE	DIURNAL
ABATTOIR	BRACKET	CAPILLARY	DOCILE
ABJURE	BRUSQUE	CASINO	DYNASTY
ABORIGINE	BUZZARD	CAVIARE	EASELS
ABYSMAL	CAJOLE	CHINCHILLA	ECCLESIASTIC
ACETYLENE	CALABASH	CYCLOSTILE	ELIGIBLE
ANCHOVY	CALYPSO	DISSOLUTE	FIZZLES
FRANCHISE	GALAXY	GAMMON	GHERKIN
GNOMES	GYPSIES	HOBGOBLIN	HOOPOE

HOOLIGAN	HYPERBOLA	HYSTERIA	IGLOOS
ILLICIT	INAUGURATE	INTERMIX	JUICES
KNUCKLE	LABURNUM	LATTICE	LEISURE
LENGTHY	LIEUTENANT	LIQUORICE	LLAMAS
LYMPHATIC	MAMMOTH	METAPHOR	METHYLATED
MINIMUM	MOSAIC	MYSTERY	OBNOXIOUS
OOZINESS	OMELETTE	OXYGEN	PAPOOSE
PAPYRUS	PARALYSE	PHONETIC	PHLEGM
PYTHON	QUININE	QUEUES	SANGUINE
SCIMITAR	SCISSORS	SYLLABLE	SYMMETRY
SYNAGOGUE	TYMPANY	TYPHOON	UTILITY
VOODOO	WHINNY	WRITHE	WYANDOTTE

Have a Go (Teenagers and upwards)

A good question master and one who is fairly familiar with this radio game is needed, and he should prepare beforehand a list of simple questions, from which he selects four to ask each guest who is called out. If the guest answers all four correctly he is entitled to compete in the final or 'jack-pot' question, for which a small prize is awarded to the one giving the first correct answer.

Questions similar to, or of the type given below, are suitable ones to ask:

Who wrote *The Dancing Years*? (Ivor Novello)

Who were the four main characters in *The Three Muske-teers*? (D'Artagnan, Athos, Porthos, Aramis)

Who was the Prime Minister in 1939? (Chamberlain)

Who made the song 'Sonny Boy' famous? (Al Jolson)

Tell me the names of four Disney animals (Donald Duck, Pluto, Mickey Mouse, Dumbo, Bambi, etc.)

Who went to Lilliput? (Gulliver)

How many kilometres are there in five miles? (Eight)

Who wrote *Round the World in Eighty Days*? (Verne)

Which two teams were in the 1968 Cup Final? (Everton and West Bromwich Albion)

What is scampi?   (An Italian fish like a large prawn)

What is the capital of America? (Washington)

In which country are the 'outbacks'? (Australia)

Does the camel or the dromedary have two humps? (Camel)

Give me a four-letter word ending in ENY (Deny)

SECTION TWENTY

PROBLEMS, PUZZLES, TRICKS, TESTS, AND TIME-PASSERS

In this chapter there is a selection of problems, puzzles, tricks, tests, and so on which can either be interspersed between more organized games or used as during or after meal activities while tables are being cleared away.

They are also particularly useful for small parties in that they can be done in pairs or small groups.

Some of the individual physical tests should not be attempted, of course, by old people, perchance they strain themselves or stumble and fall down.

Here then is the selection:

(1) A Simple Anagram

Merely ask your guests to write down the word 'CHESTY' and give them five minutes in which to produce from it another simple, common English word. You will be surprised at the number of them that fail completely. The answer is 'scythe'.

Now for a few problems with figures:

(2) Can You Add?

Here is a simple addition sum which will 'catch' nineteen out of twenty people – young or old. Cut a strip of paper about six inches long by an inch wide than fold it concertina-wise as shown in Fig 50. On the folds write the numbers shown.

Display these numbers one at a time to a friend (starting with the 1,000) and ask him to add them up *aloud* as you show them to him.

It looks quite a simple addition, doesn't it? Just try it and see what happens!

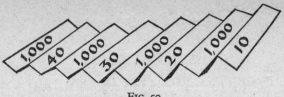

FIG 50

(3) Just Think

Two men set out in a car along a road to a town ten miles away. The first man drives steadily at thirty miles per hour from the tenth milestone from the town to the fifth milestone. The second man then drives from the fifth milestone to the first. Though he too drives steadily at thirty miles per hour he takes less time than did the first man. Why?

Answer: From the tenth milestone to the fifth is five miles; from the fifth milestone to the first is only *four* miles!

(4) A train is half a mile in length. It is travelling at sixty miles per hour. It enters a tunnel which is half a mile in length. How long does it take for the train to pass through and be completely clear of the tunnel? (*Answer:* 1 minute)

(5) Ask a member of the party to write down any number containing three figures but not to let you see what he has written. Suppose the number to be 634.

Ask him then to reverse the number and to subtract whichever is the smaller number from the larger number. In this case the subtraction sum would then be 634–436 which leaves 198.

When he has done this you ask him to tell you the number in the units column. In this case it is 8. You then tell him the complete answer: 198.

The explanation is this: The middle figure is always 9 and the sum of the figures in the units and hundreds columns always totals 9, so that if the unit figure is 8, then that in the hundreds column must be 1, giving the correct answer of 198.

(6) A brick weighs 5 lb and half a brick. How much does a brick and a half weigh? (15 lb)

(7) A farmer bought 100 animals for £100. Pigs cost £5 each, sheep £3 each and rabbits 10s. each. How many of each kind of animal did he get? (10 pigs, 2 sheep, and 88 rabbits)

(8) If you drive a car from home to the seaside at twenty miles per hour and back at forty miles per hour, what is your average speed for the round trip? ($26\frac{2}{3}$ mph)

Progressions

Simple tests of deduction or reasoning which can be made easy or difficult according to the age of the players. Look at the two examples given below:

(1) 3 7 12 18 25 ?
(2) A E I M ?

In example 1, you are required to insert the next number in the progression or sequence. A little study shows that the numbers go in this fashion $3 + 4 = 7, 7 + 5 = 12, 12 + 6 = 18, 18 + 7 = 25$. The next number will therefore be $25 + 8 = 33$. In the second example a somewhat similar method is followed but in this case the gap is constant – there being three letters in alphabetical order between each of the letters given, i.e. 'A' – (B C D) – 'E' – (F G H) – 'I' – (J K L) – 'M'; continuing the sequence will give (N O P) – 'Q'. Therefore 'Q' is the missing letter.

Now try a selection (not more than ten), from the following examples:

(1) 20 30 29 40 38 60 57 ?   (70)
(2) 2 3 7 16 32 ?   (57)
(3) 1 4 9 16 25 36 ?   (49)
(4) 4 8 17 33 58 ?   (94)
(5) 31 28 31 30 31 (30. Days of the month from January.)
(6) $\frac{3}{4}$ $\frac{1}{2}$ 1 $\frac{1}{4}$ $1\frac{1}{4}$?   (0)
(7) 3 pm 3.40 4.10 4.30 4.40 ?   (4.40)
(8) AC BD CE DF EG ?   (FH)

(9) ABC EFG JKL PQR ?   (WXY)
(10) V I B G Y O ?   (R) (Initials of colours of Rainbow.)
(11) C X F U I R L ?   (O)
(12) I L H K G J ?   (F)
(13) A B D G K P ?   (V)
(14) F A H C K F ?   (O)
(15) J F M A M J ?   (J. First letters of the months.)
(16) Aaron Abscess Access Advert Aeroplane ?

(Any word beginning 'Af'.)

Don't Take the Last (8 plus upwards)

This is a game for pairs, requiring fifteen matches, which are laid out side by side on the table. Each player in turn is allowed to pick up one, two, or three matches, but no more. The object of the game is to make your partner pick up the last match. Once you know the secret and are the first player you can win every time – in this manner.

On your first pick up, take *two* matches, leaving *thirteen*. Then whatever number your opponent takes, when it is your second turn reduce the number of matches left to *nine*. (If he takes one, you take three; if he takes two, you take two; if he takes three you take one.) On the next turn, using the same method you reduce the number to *five*. Then no matter how many he takes according to rule, you can reduce the number of matches to *one*, which he must take on his next turn.

Six Fours are Twelve

Present one of your guests with twelve coins or buttons. Then ask him to arrange the coins in such a way that he has six straight lines each containing four coins!

The answer is shown in Fig 51 and is, as you will see, based on two equilateral triangles with their apexes in opposite directions.

Five Fours are Ten

Give your friends ten coins or buttons and ask them to arrange the objects in five straight lines, each line having four

coins in it. It sounds impossible at first. The solution is shown
in Fig 52.

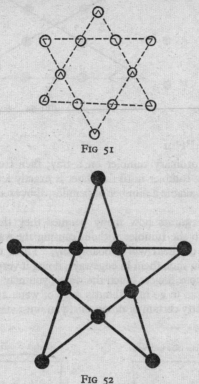

FIG 51

FIG 52

Nine Dots

Ask your guests to draw nine dots in the form of a square as
shown overleaf (Fig 53).

The problem is to draw through the nine dots with *four*
straight lines without taking the pencil off the paper and without retracing a line. Lines can cross each other if necessary.

Again, the answer is a simple one (see Fig 54).

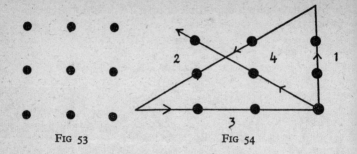

Fig 53

Fig 54

Full to the Brim

Place an ordinary tumbler on a tray, then from a jug of water fill the tumbler until the water is exactly level with the top. Have available a number of pennies, about ten or a dozen will do.

Ask your guests how many pennies they think can be dropped into the tumbler without causing the water to overflow. Most of them will probably say, 'Three or four.' If, however, you slide them in edgeways, doing it very gently and not letting your fingers touch the water, you may get as many as eight or ten to go in without a drop of water spilling over.

To be pretty certain of doing this, you must start off with a

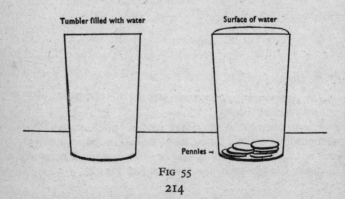

Tumbler filled with water

Surface of water

Pennies

Fig 55

214

dry glass and above all you must ensure that when filling the tumbler, you do not wet the rim.

The Leaning Syphon

This is a little trick which will not only cause some amusement but will interest most people, in that when you have explained how it is done, they will be prepared to spend some time trying to do it. On your table or cocktail cabinet your guests will be surprised to see a soda syphon either full or partially full, apparently leaning over and balanced precariously on a small portion of the rim of the base (Fig 56).

Matchstick →

FIG 56

The syphon is, in fact, kept in this position by half a matchstick which has been carefully slid under the base in the position shown by the arrow.

The syphon is not in as dangerous a position as appears, for if the table is shaken, the syphon invariably topples back safely on its base and does not fall over. If your fingers are a little too bulky to slide the match under the base without difficulty, use a coin to push the matchstick into the required position.

The Puzzle Band

This old, but interesting puzzle can provide both interest and amusement to both children and adults. Prepare a number of strips of paper about twelve to thirteen inches long and an inch or so wide. Now make four or five of them into bands as shown in Fig 57(a) by gumming the ends together. Now take a pair of scissors and ask what will happen to the band if you cut all the way round the middle as indicated by the dotted line.

The answer you will almost certainly get is that you will make two bands, each half as wide as the original. Proceed to do this cutting and everyone will see that the answer given was quite correct. Allow a few members of your audience to cut the other bands you have made up and make half-width bands.

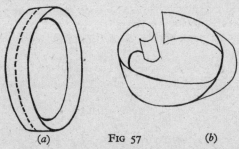

(a) Fig 57 (b)

Next, take one of your strips of paper and *twist it once* before gumming the ends together (Fig 57(b)).

Now ask what will happen if you again cut it in the same way as you did the first band.

You will almost certainly get the answer that you will again finish with two bands as before.

But will you? Why not try it for yourself.

Try also cutting all along the band, not down the centre, but one third of the way from one edge.

And when you have done that, take another strip and twist it *twice* before gumming the ends together and repeating the cutting operations.

RIVER CROSSING PROBLEMS

There are many problems involving people or things crossing a river with limitations on both the means of transport and the order in which the crossing shall be made. The clearest and best way of working out the puzzles is to use matchsticks of various sizes or buttons of different colour or size to represent the various people or objects. Though some of such problems are difficult in that a large number of moves may have to be made, the four given below do not involve many moves and merely require logical reasoning for solution.

Crossing the Ferry (1)

Two boys, Tom and Jack (who each weighed eight stone), along with their father and uncle (who each weighed sixteen stone) wished to cross a river in a rowing boat which would only carry a maximum of sixteen stone. How did they get across?

Answer: Tom and Jack cross first. Jack brings back the boat. The father crosses alone. Tom brings back the boat. Tom and Jack cross again. Jack again brings back the boat. The uncle now crosses alone. Tom brings the boat back and then Tom and Jack cross the river.

Crossing the Ferry (2)

A farmer (for some mysterious reason) wishes to take across a ferry, a fox, a goose, and a sack of corn. The boat will only hold himself and one of the three. If left on their own, the fox will eat the goose or the goose will eat the corn. How does the farmer get them all across intact?

Answer: The farmer takes the goose across the river, leaves it there and crosses back. This time he takes over the fox, but takes back the goose. Next he takes over the corn, leaves it with the fox, then returns to pick up the goose.

Crossing the Ferry (3)

A company of soldiers on an exercise come to a wide river which they wish to cross. There is a small boat containing two small boys. The boat can only carry either one boy and one soldier or two boys. How do they get across?

Answer: Two boys cross. One boy brings the boat back; one soldier and one boy cross, the boy brings the boat back – and so on until all the soldiers are across.

Crossing the Ferry (4)

Three missionaries accompanied by three cannibals are journeying from the jungle to the coast. They come to a river which they must cross. There is a rowing boat which will carry only two people.

The problem is to get them all across the river without *at any time* there being *more* cannibals than missionaries on any side of the river.

The solution is as follows:

First Trip. A missionary and a cannibal go in the boat. The cannibal remains, and the missionary rows back.

Second Trip. Two cannibals row over, one remains, and the other rows back.

Third Trip. Two missionaries row over and a missionary and a cannibal row back.

Fourth Trip. Two missionaries row over and the cannibal already on the bank rows back.

Fifth Trip. A cannibal rows over a cannibal and rows back.

Sixth Trip. The cannibal rows over the last cannibal.

The Jar Problem

You have three stone jars of 8-, 5-, and 3-gallon capacities. The 8-gallon jar is full of water. How can you get exactly 4 gallons of water into the 5-gallon jar?

Answer: The steps are as follows. From the 8-gallon jar fill the 5-gallon jar. Now fill the 3-gallon jar from the 5-gallon one. This leaves 2 gallons. Empty the 3-gallon jar into the 8-gallon one. Now pour the 2 gallons from the 5-gallon jar into the 3-gallon jar. Fill the 5-gallon jar from the 8-gallon jar. Now fill the 3-gallon jar (which is holding 2 gallons) from the 5-gallon jar. This leaves 4 gallons.

Ships that Pass

Two groups of three boats each, A, B, and C, and F, E, and D, are travelling in opposite directions along a canal too narrow for them to pass in the normal manner. There is, however, a small basin (as shown in Fig 58), which will just fit one boat. How do the boats get past each other?

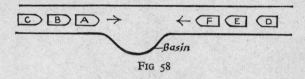

FIG 58

Answer: Boat F enters the basin. Boats A, B, and C sail past the basin until they almost meet boats E and D. Boat F reverses out of the basin and continues on its way. Boats A, B, and C reverse past the basin to allow Boat E to enter. A, B, and C then go forward again to allow E to do exactly as F did. They then reverse again past the basin to allow D to enter. Boats A, B, and C proceed on their way. Boat D reverses out of the basin and goes on its way in turn.

A Shunting Problem

Fig 59 shows a section of railway line with a peculiar double siding and a short extension forming a kind of triangle. On one side of the triangle is a truck A, on the other side is a truck B. The straight section of the siding marked S in the diagram is just large enough to take *one* of the trucks. On the main line is an engine, marked E.

The problem for the engine driver is to change the positions of the two trucks so that A finishes at B and B at A.

Answer: The engine pushes truck A into the space marked S and leaves it there.

The engine then goes back to the main line and goes to truck B which it pushes to truck A. The two trucks are then coupled together and the engine pulls them both on to the main line then proceeds to push them past the left-hand junction. Here truck B is uncoupled from truck A.

B is then pulled along the main line, then pushed up the siding into the space S where it is left. The engine then goes back to the main line, along it, up the left-hand siding and pulls truck B into the spot originally occupied by A and leaves it there.

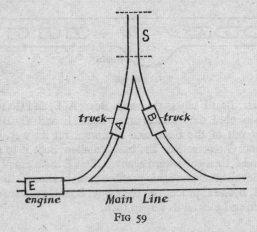

FIG 59

Finally the engine goes back to truck A (on the main line) pulls it past the right-hand junction then pushes it into the place originally occupied by B.

COIN PROBLEMS

Here are problems involving the moving of coins:

Heads and Tails

Hold five pennies stacked neatly in your left hand. With your right hand take the top penny and place it underneath the other four saying as you do so: 'One underneath.' Place the next penny (now the top one) on the table saying: 'One on the table.' Next repeat the first action, i.e. 'One underneath,' then 'One on the table,' then 'One underneath,' and so on until all five pennies are on the table.

Point out to your audience that the pennies on the table are showing alternately 'heads' and 'tails'.

Invite any of them to stack the pennies to produce the same result. Few of them will be able to do it without a lot of thinking and experimenting.

The secret. Stack the pennies with the first three heads (or tails) uppermost and the last two with tails (or heads) uppermost.

Two At A Time

Arrange four shillings and four sixpences (or four black draughts and four white) alternately as shown in Fig 60. Assume there to be two blank spaces at one end. These are numbered 9 and 10 in the diagram.

FIG 60

The problem is to move the shillings and sixpences so that finally you have a group of four shillings and a group of four sixpences next to each other with no intervening space.

Two adjacent coins must be moved every time; they can jump over any number of other coins into any two vacant spaces, including spaces 9 and 10, but not outside this limit.

The aim is to complete the two groups in four moves.

Answer:
(1) Move coins 2 and 3 into spaces 9 and 10.
(2) Move coins 5 and 6 into spaces 2 and 3.
(3) Move coins 8 and 9 into spaces 5 and 6.
(4) Finally move coins 1 and 2 into spaces 8 and 9.

Change-Over

Arrange six coins as shown in Fig 61. First three heads, then a blank space followed by three tails.

The problem is to change the positions of the coins so that the tails occupy positions 1, 2, and 3 and the heads positions 5, 6, and 7. Any coin may move into an adjacent empty space or jump over an adjacent coin (as in draughts) into the next empty space *but* heads can only move to the *right* and tails may only move to the left. Fifteen moves are required.

FIG 61

Answer:

(1) Move 3 to 4	(6) Move 1 to 2	(11) Move 4 to 6
(2) Move 5 to 3	(7) Move 3 to 1	(12) Move 2 to 4
(3) Move 6 to 5	(8) Move 5 to 3	(13) Move 3 to 2
(4) Move 4 to 6	(9) Move 7 to 5	(14) Move 5 to 3
(5) Move 2 to 4	(10) Move 6 to 7	(15) Move 4 to 5

Pairs

Place eight coins (or draughts) in a line (Fig 62). The problem is the apparently simple one of arranging the coins in four pairs of coins with one coin on top of the other. *But* (there is always a 'but') when a coin is moved it must pass over *two* other coins and no coin must be moved more than once.

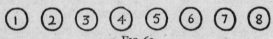

FIG 62

Note also that an empty space does *not* count as a coin but a coin on top of another coin counts as two.

The problem can be solved in four moves:

Answer:

(1) Move 4 on to 7	(3) Move 1 on to 3
(2) Move 6 on to 2	(4) Move 5 on to 8

Problems with Matches

These are always popular and can be introduced at any odd moment any time during the party.

(1) Arrange 15 matches to form 5 squares as shown in Fig 63. Remove 3 matches and leave 3 squares only.

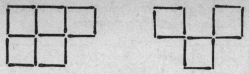

FIG 63

(2) Arrange 17 matches to form 6 squares as in Fig 64. Remove 5 matches to leave 3 squares.

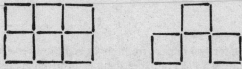

FIG 64

(3) Make 4 squares with 12 matches as shown in Fig 65. By moving and rearranging 4 matches make the figure into 1 of 3 squares of the same size as the original.

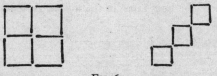

FIG 65

(4) With 16 matches arranged as shown below, add 8 more to divide the figure into 4 parts equal in size and shape.

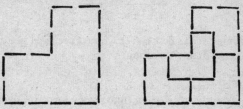

FIG 66

(5) Make the figure shown below with 24 matches, then remove 8 matches to leave only 2 squares.

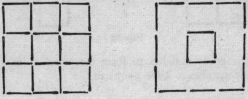

FIG 67

Three in a Row

A game for two players from about eight to twelve years of age, requiring a sheet of paper about eight to ten inches square (which is marked out as shown in Fig 68) and three buttons or counters or draughts for each player. The counters of 'men', etc., should be of a different colour or size for each of the players, to eliminate confusion.

Taking turns, each player places a counter at any spot he wishes where the lines cross in the middle or touch the sides of the paper.

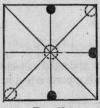

FIG 68

The winner is the first player who succeeds in getting three men in a row in any direction.

Book Cricket

This is another first-class time passer for two boys or girls on wet days either at home or at the seaside.

A book is required (or a newspaper will do) and one sheet of paper and pencil per player.

A scorer's card is made out as below:

SCORING LETTERS	PENALTY LETTERS
A = 2 runs	B = bowled out
E = 2 runs	C = caught out
I = 3 runs	L = leg before wicket
O = 4 runs	X = hit wicket
U = 6 runs	Y = run out
All other letters except penalty letters score one run.	Z = stumped

Each player then writes down the names of his team on the left-hand side of his paper, leaving space to insert the runs made by each as shown in Fig 69. The two players then toss to decide which side is to bat first.

```
┌─────────────────────────────────────────────┐
│              J. BROWN'S XI.                   │
│                                        Score  │
│  Boycott      .    .    .    .    .    .      │
│  Edrich .     .    .    .    .    .    .      │
│  Cowdrey      .    .    .    .    .    .      │
│  Barrington   .    .    .    .    .    .      │
│  Graveney     .    .    .    .    .    .      │
│  D'Oliveira   .    .    .    .    .    .      │
│  Parks .      .    .    .    .    .    .      │
│  Titmus .     .    .    .    .    .    .      │
│  Snow .       .    .    .    .    .    .      │
│  Higgs .      .    .    .    .    .    .      │
│  Jones .      .    .    .    .    .    .      │
└─────────────────────────────────────────────┘
```

Fig 69

A page of the book or newspaper is then opened and the first batsman goes in. Suppose the words to be the same as at the beginning of the description of this game, and suppose Boycott to be batting. His score will be:

1.1.3.1. 3.1. 2.1.4.1.1.2.1. 1.3.1.1.1. Caught out 29

The next batsman now goes in and the scoring continues straight on. As the next letter in the sentence is 'L' poor Edrich is out l.b.w. for a 'duck'.

When all eleven players have batted, another page of the book is chosen at random and the opposing side proceeds to bat. The winning side is, of course, the one that has scored the most runs. More than one innings can be played as desired.

Battleships

This is another old favourite with boys which is easier played than described – however!

Each player has a piece of paper (squared paper if you can get it) on which he draws and numbers and letters two squares each containing one hundred squares as shown in Fig 70.

Each player then draws anywhere in his own Square 'A', two battleships and two destroyers. A battleship consists of three squares with a dot (representing a gun) at each end (see Fig 70) and destroyers of two squares each with one gun. (Notice that ships can be placed either vertically or horizontally.)

Neither player must let the other see where he has placed his ships.

A coin is tossed for the privilege of opening the firing. Let us assume that we are playing and that our opponent wins the toss and starts the battle. He is allowed six shots, one for each gun in his fleet.

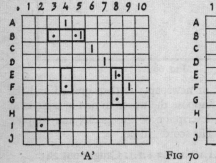 

'A'   FIG 70   'B'

He calls out a square number, say 4 A. We put a small 1 in that square. (This has been done in the diagram.) He does the same on his own Square 'B' as a record of the shots he has fired and to prevent wasting shots by firing them into the same square again.

He then calls 5 B. (This is disaster, for he has eliminated one of our guns.) He calls 6 C. We mark it. His next shot is 7 D. His fifth shot is 8 E. (Disaster again, another gun gone!) And his last shot is 9 F.

Having fired his six shots, he is then entitled to ask, 'Have I hit anything?'

We must give a truthful answer and say, 'Yes, you have hit two battleships and knocked a gun off each.'

It is now our turn to fire, but, as two guns have been eliminated, *we have four shots only*. As we fire them, we mark them, of course, on our own Square 'B' as our record. Let us assume that we are unlucky and do not hit any of his ships.

Our opponent still has six shots, and he knows that two ships are somewhere near to his last line of shots. If he chooses to fire diagonally 5 A, 6 B, 7 C, 8 D, 9 E, and 10 F, we shall get away scot free, but if he were to fire 2 A, 3 B, 4 C, 5 D, 6 E, and 7 F, our top battleship would be completely out of action and, on our next round, we would have three shots only.

And so the game continues, each one firing in turn with the guns at his disposal, until finally all the guns of one side are out of action. The other side wins.

It is suggested that the large squares consist of 100 small squares each and that each side has only four ships, but modifications can be made at will, by having larger or smaller squares with more or less ships.

Variations can be added to by calling the game 'Aeroplanes' or 'Space Ships', and modifying the shape of the craft put in the squares as shown in Fig 71. ('Space Ships' should always be placed diagonally.)

With four or more players a knockout competition can be run – and to keep everyone quiet, the losers can always play each other, or alternatively a small American type tournament

can be organized in which everybody plays everybody else and
the player with the most wins is the winner.

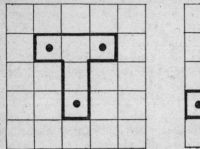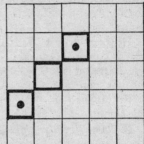

FIG 71

Shove-halfpenny Football (or Hockey)

This game has been popular with boys for years, and is a
wonderful time passer for a wet day at home or at the seaside.

It can be played on a kitchen table, on the linoleum, or
even on a very large tray. *It should not be played on the best
polished table.*

Two goals, two pennies, two flat-edged combs, small rulers,
set squares or protractors, and one halfpenny are required.

The goals, which should be the combined width of two
pennies and a halfpenny, can be marked by matchsticks laid
flat at each end of the table, by thimbles, or where possible
without getting into trouble, by two pins. If none of these
methods is approved, make them out of strips of cardboard as
shown in Fig 72.

The object of the game is to score goals by knocking the
halfpenny through the goals by means of the penny, which in
turn is driven along by the flat-edged comb or ruler, each
player taking it in turn to push or knock his penny (see Fig 73).

The game starts with a centre, one player knocking off; the
opposing penny must be at least three inches away from the
ball (halfpenny).

Other Rules. The game can be played for a given length of

time each way (five to ten minutes) or alternatively can be decided on the best of five or seven goals.

If one player's penny strikes his opponent's penny before

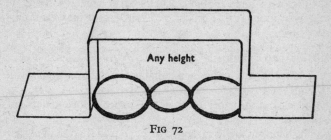

FIG 72

hitting the ball it is a foul, and the one fouled is allowed two knocks from where he was fouled. (The other penny remains where it came to rest after the foul was committed.)

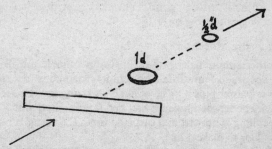

Ruler pushes penny which cannons into the halfpenny driving it forward

FIG 73

If a corner is conceded, two shots are allowed from the corner, i.e. the ball is knocked by the penny and then a second push is taken at the penny from where it came to rest after the first shot.

Other local rules can be devised, but the fewer there are the better.

TESTS OF BALANCE AND PHYSICAL STRENGTH AND DEXTERITY

First of all some simple balancing tests which can be done merely as individual efforts or, if desired, made into team competitions.

Lifting the Pyramid

A simple little competition suitable for children from seven to eight years of age and upwards, teenagers and adults. A number of clean paper serviettes or paper handkerchiefs are required.

The handkerchief is arranged in a pyramid shape and placed on the floor about twelve to eighteen inches away from the feet of the competitor who is then told to stand on one leg, bend down, pick up the handkerchief with his teeth and recover to standing position without losing his balance. The foot on which he is balancing must not move, nor must his hands touch the ground (Fig 74).

Tipping the Matchbox

Another simple balancing competition suitable for all ages from about six upwards. An empty matchbox or empty cigarette packet plus a piece of chalk or string are required.

On a wooden or linoleum-covered floor a short line about two feet long is drawn; in a carpeted room the string is placed on the floor to make a line.

About eighteen inches to two feet in front of this line the matchbox is placed on end on the floor (Fig 75).

Competitors stand behind the line; their toes may be up to but not over the line.

Balancing on one leg they are then required to tip the matchbox over with the toe of the other foot and recover to the balancing position.

Gradually the matchbox is moved farther and farther forwards; the one who tips it over farthest from the line is the winner of the competition.

FIG 74

FIG 75

Balance Marking

Another simple balance competition which can be done indoors on a wooden or linoleum-covered floor or out of doors on a concrete or stone garden path. A piece of chalk is required. Competitors stand behind a line holding the piece of chalk in their hands. Standing on one leg they lean forwards and make a chalk mark on the floor as far forwards as possible then re-cover to standing position (still on one leg) without losing balance. The competitor whose chalk mark is the farthest forwards is the winner.

Inside Out

An activity or test of agility which is definitely for boys and teenagers. It should be done on a carpet or some place where the clothes are not liable to get dusty or dirty. The volunteers lie flat on the stomach with the legs raised behind and the ankles crossed (Fig 76 (*a*) and (*b*)). The feet or the ankles are grasped.

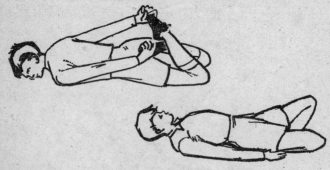

Fig 76 (*a*) and (*b*)

The problem now is to wriggle over on to the back and finally sit in the cross-legged position without releasing the grip on the feet or the ankles.

Alternatively, the volunteer can start by sitting cross-legged grasping the ankles then lowering the back to the ground and turning over to lie flat on the stomach still grasping the feet or ankles.

Horizontal Lift

Here is a simple little competitive activity for male teenagers. Volunteers sit on the floor with their legs stretched forwards in front of them with the feet together. The hands are placed on the floor close to and at each side of the seat. The hands can be flat on the floor, or, if desired, just with the fingers touching.

Each competitor is then merely asked to press on his hands and lift the whole of his body from his seat to his heels completely off the floor and hold the position for, say, two seconds (see Fig 77). This activity is much more difficult to do than

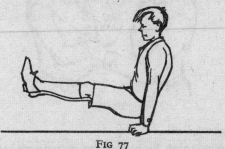

FIG 77

would at first appear. Most people can lift their seats off the ground, but raising the heels is a far different matter.

The four tests or competitions which follow are far more suitable for boys and men than for girls and women.

Arm Lock Wrestle

A fairly strenuous, competitive activity suitable for volunteer boys and male teenagers. Two competitors sit on the floor, feet astride, back to back with their elbows firmly linked. Each then tries to force the other's right (or left) shoulder down to touch the ground. The one who succeeds in so doing is the winner.

Elbow Press

A contest suitable for boys and teenagers. Opponents sit facing each other at a small table or across the corner of a large one. Both rest their upper arms on the table with the forearm vertical and elbows almost touching. They then clasp hands. With a steady sideways and downwards pressure, each tries to force the other's hand down to touch the table.

FIG 78

Finger-press Pull

An activity mainly for boys and male teenagers in pairs. One of the pair stands comfortably astride with the arms bent across

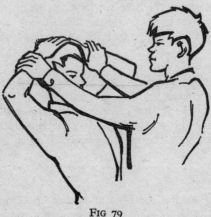

FIG 79

the body at chest height and with the tips of the middle fingers touching.

234

The partner grasps the wrists of his opponent (one with each hand) and then with a *steady*, sideways pull tries to part the touching fingers. Violent jerks or up-and-down pushes are not allowed. This sounds quite a simple thing to do, but in fact, with partners of roughly equal strength it will be found almost impossible to achieve (Fig 78).

Hand-lift from Head

A partner contest similar in nature to *Finger-press Pull*. One of the pair stands with his feet comfortably astride and places his fingertips together flat on the top of his head as shown in Fig 79. The other grasps his wrists and by pushing upwards tries to lift his partner's fingers off his head. As before, there must be no sudden jerks – just a steady push.

SECTION TWENTY-ONE

MIND READING AND FORTUNE TELLING

As an interlude from rushing about or playing games which require lots of thinking and writing, an occasional demonstration of your own, or someone else's, supernatural (!) powers can often afford a few minutes' relaxation for everyone. This sort of activity, however, should not be overdone, for in general most people go to a party to take part in the activities, not to watch for lengthy periods someone showing how much more clever they are than anyone else.

The following few games can be played without any elaborate preparations or memorizing of difficult codes. All you need in most cases is a reliable assistant (who, if possible, should be briefed prior to the party) and a certain flair for being able to talk glibly.

Finding the Right Penny

This is a very simple little 'magic' game which can be played by young children from six years of age upwards.

Place about a dozen pennies in a hat or on a tray. The 'magician' then says that, blindfolded, he will pick from the pennies any one selected by the audience.

He is duly blindfolded. He then asks one of the audience to select any penny he wishes from the hat and to examine it carefully, noting the date, any peculiar distinguishing marks which may be on it, or any peculiarities of colour, so that he will have no difficulty whatsoever in recognizing it again. All the other members of the audience are asked to do likewise with the penny, and when they are all quite satisfied it is dropped into the hat and all the pennies are shaken up to mix them thoroughly.

The magician then gropes about among the coins for a moment or two and produces the correct coin, which, of course, is verified by those who examined it.

The secret? All the pennies in the hat are stone cold except one, the one that has been passed from hand to hand while the audience were examining it!

X-ray Eyes

For this demonstration of your occult powers you need an opaque envelope and a small piece of paper for each guest who wishes to test your powers, which are those of being able to see what is written on a piece of paper sealed in the envelope.

Ask each person to write one or two words, or the name of some person or thing, such as 'Mother Redcap', or 'Tom Finney', or 'Cross-word Puzzle', on their pieces of paper, fold them up, and seal them in the envelopes, making absolutely certain that what they have written cannot possibly be seen through the envelope. You then collect all the envelopes.

Taking one envelope in your hand, you study it intently for some seconds, showing appropriate signs of intense concentration and making remarks such as 'Oh dear, this is a little difficult . . . wait a moment . . . yes, I think . . . I think it's something connected with a sport . . . it's . . . yes, I've got it, I think . . . I can . . . I can see a boxing-ring.' You then look hopefully and eagerly at your audience. 'I think the words are "a technical knock-out". Would anyone have written that?'

To your obvious relief and the surprise of the guest who has written it, he admits that indeed he has written these words on his piece of paper. On which admission, you casually open the envelope, glance at the paper to confirm the words, put it down on the table behind you, and take up the next envelope. Again with appropriate patter you make a correct forecast of what is written in that one – and in all the others as well.

The trick is simplicity itself.

Prior to the game you have agreed with your confederate (who takes no visible or apparent part in the game) that he will write certain words on his piece of paper, in this case, 'a technical knock-out'. When you collect the envelopes, you make absolutely certain that his envelope is put at the bottom of the pile.

When you concentrate on the top or first envelope you really haven't the faintest idea what is written inside, but when you say 'I see "a technical knock-out"' your assistant admits that he has written such a phrase.

The audience (if they don't know the trick) will automatically assume that those words are in the envelope you are holding. When you open it and glance at the paper to make sure, you will, of course, find something completely different, say 'buttercups and daisies'.

Thus, when you concentrate on your second envelope and make your forecast you will ultimately say, 'Yes – it's something to do with flowers – I know, "buttercups and daisies",' which some guest will immediately admit writing.

You go through all the envelopes in a similar manner. The last envelope you glance at for confirmation will contain the first phrase you mentioned, for that is the one written by your assistant.

Naming a Card

This mind reading to select a card chosen by a member of the audience needs a fair degree of concentration both on the part of the magician and his partner. It should not be done at a party without first having had several practices. When, however, it is done well it can be quite baffling.

The trick as it appears to the onlookers is as follows:

The magician says that while he is out of the room anyone in the room can select any card they wish, and on his return, without touching the cards or looking at them in any way, he will, without undue trouble, name the card – which he ultimately does.

There are two steps involving the use of two simple codes to achieve the desired result.

The first thing the magician must determine is the suit in which the card is to be found.

This is determined by the position of the pack of cards on the table.

When the card has been selected by one of the audience and replaced anywhere in the pack, the pack is placed by the assistant on the table very slightly towards one of the four sides of the table.

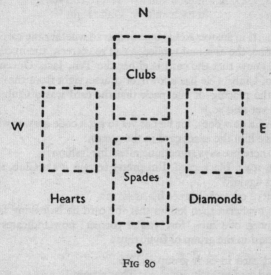

Fig 80

Thus, slightly to the north (as the magician looks at the table) indicates Clubs, slightly to the east, Diamonds, slightly to the south, Spades, and slightly to the west means Hearts (see Fig 80).

Even though the magician knows the suit in which the card is to be found, he does not yet declare this, but merely declares the *colour* of the suit. He then says something such as, 'I think the card is a black one, am I right?'

This is the crucial point where the second code comes in. The assistant must give one of four answers: 'Yes,' 'That's right,' 'You're correct,' or 'Quite right.'

These answers tell the magician in which of four groups in

239

any suit the correct card is to be found. Each suit is divided as below, the code answer to determine the group being shown alongside.

2, 3, 4, 5   in each suit = 'Yes.'
6, 7, 8, 9   in each suit = 'That's right.'
10, J, Q, K   in each suit = 'You're correct.'
Ace   in each suit = 'Quite right.'

Thus, if in answer to his question as to whether the card is a black one, the assistant replied, 'You're correct,' the magician would know that the card is either the Ten, Jack, Queen, or King of Clubs. (He has known, of course, right from the start, from the placing of the pack that the card was a Club, but hasn't yet said so.)

This he now does, for he has yet to get a code answer which will give him the exact card in the group.

He therefore says something after this fashion:

'Oh, it's a black card, I'm pretty certain it's a Club, am I correct again?'

'You're correct,' agrees his assistant.

The magician then knows that the card he is looking for is the Queen of Clubs, for 'you're correct' now indicates the third card in the group of four, thus:

1st card in each group = 'Yes.'
2nd card in each group = 'That's right.'
3rd card in each group = 'You're correct.'
4th card in each group = 'Quite right.'

If the answer 'Quite right' were given to the first query as to the colour of the suit, the magician need have no more worries at all, for 'Quite right' indicates the fourth group, which contains only the Ace. To clarify this system a little more, let us take one more example. Suppose the card selected was the Five of Diamonds.

The assistant would place the pack of cards slightly to the east of the table. The magician would then indicate, or ask if the card were a red one (he already knows it's a Diamond).

The assistant would merely reply, 'Yes,' indicating to the magician that it is either the Two, Three, Four, or Five of Diamonds.

The magician then says, 'It is a Diamond,' to which the assistant replies, 'Quite right,' indicating that the card is the fourth in the group.

The magician then says, 'The card is the Five of Diamonds.'

The code answers can, of course, be varied slightly from those suggested above, but they must sound quite natural and not forced or stilted.

Find the Person

The thought reader leaves the room after announcing that while he is outside the players must select one among themselves to be identified by him when he is called back.

When he is called back he looks at everyone, trying to make it appear that he is in difficulties over deciding who has been selected. Appropriate patter should also be used to add interest. After a few moments' hesitation he finally points to a certain individual, who proves to be the right one.

The answer, of course, is obtained from an assistant, who in this case apparently takes no part in the game. The thought reader, however, takes particular, if somewhat surreptitious, notice of him, because he is sitting (or standing) in an identical manner as the person selected.

It may happen, of course, that the players will select the unknown assistant. This contingency must be covered by a simple code signal such as a yawn or a scratching of the ear, which will automatically mean to the thought reader that his confederate has been chosen. The fact that he yawns or scratches his ear will mean nothing to the remainder of the players, who are unaware of his part in the game.

The Magic Ring

The magician states that he will leave the room, and while he is out, his assistant will shake hands with someone, whom he (the magician) will identify on his return without his assistant saying a word or making any movement whatsoever.

Someone may well say, 'But you know already who it will be; you've arranged it beforehand.'

The magician, however, assures them on his honour that at this moment he has not the faintest idea who it is and, further, that from this moment he will, on his honour, not exchange a word or sign with his assistant.

The magician then goes on to explain that before this trick can be performed, a magic ring must be formed by everyone, including himself, joining hands in a circle, so that the magic power will be transmitted from everyone to himself.

Everyone then joins hands, and the magician mutters magic words and incantations. After a little of his mumbo-jumbo, he quite casually asks if anyone can feel the influence passing round the circle. He is certain to get all kinds of answers, mostly facetious. Finally, he is satisfied that the magic influence has worked and he leaves the room.

While he is out, his assistant – also with some appropriate patter – shakes hands with one of those who made the magic circle.

The magician returns and after a short period of concentration, during which time he can, if he wishes, shake hands with all those who made the circle 'to see from which hand the "influence" is flowing', he decides upon a certain person, and this proves to be correct.

The method, as almost always, is simple; the assistant shakes the hand of the person who first made a remark or gave an answer when the magician asked if anyone could feel the influence passing round the circle.

Variations can be made to this code; it can be the second or third person to answer, or the first one to make a humorous remark; alternatively, it can be the third, fourth, or fifth on the left of the magician when the players formed the circle.

As a quiet interlude in any party a short session of not too serious 'Fortune Telling' can be most entertaining. This is particularly so if someone at the party has done it before and has a flair for telling a story. It should be insisted, however, that the Fortune Telling is being done purely for fun and that no one must take things too seriously (despite all your warnings, someone is bound to do so) or expect things to come true.

Here is a short selection of simple fortune-telling games.

Fortune Dice (Teenagers and upwards)

Two dice are required. The 'fortune teller' prepares a card beforehand on which is put what particular totals or combinations of numbers indicate. If possible the contents of the card should be memorized and the 'fortunes' strung together in a casual, chatty manner, or told dramatically with appropriate looks of pleasure.

The one whose fortune is to be told shakes the dice and throws them on to the table a total of seven times ('Seven is a magic number, you know').

Two things only count as far as the fortune telling is concerned, first the total score shown by the two dice at the last throw (this can be from 2 to 12) and secondly, whether there is a 'pair' or not, i.e. two threes, two fives, and so on. Here is a chart showing the significance of the throws:

Total   *Significance*

(2) You may not be so lucky in the near future. Save as much as you can for a rainy day.

(3) A dark person is going to play an important part in your life in the not too distant future.

(4) You will shortly receive a letter which may be of some financial importance to you.

(5) Your kindliness and generosity may be taken advantage of by someone you know – so do be careful in what you do.

(6) A blonde person regards you with more than indifference. Look out for her (him).

(7) Your future looks quite bright. Even if you have worries now, they will soon disappear.

(8) If a red-headed person has not already entered your life, he (she) soon will and your balance is likely to be a little disturbed.

(9) Be very careful about your health – there is nothing much to worry about – but do look after yourself.

(10) You are going to get some exciting news, and someone you least expect will visit your home very soon.

(11) This means real success in what you desire most. Persevere, use tact and diplomacy and you should gain your objective.

Pairs	*Significance*
Two ones	A period of caution seems necessary in your affairs; step warily.
Two twos	Financial matters are going to play an important part in your life quite soon. Make the most of the situation.
Two threes	Blondes, I see nothing but blondes. They are going to mean a lot to you in one way or another.
Two fours	The sun is shining on your future – step out boldly to meet it.
Two fives	Look after your health – keep yourself as fit as possible, as there may be a testing time not far ahead, and good health will lead to success.
Two sixes	You are indeed in luck – most of your desires will be realized – I envy you.

The fortune teller must be possessed of a quick wit and be able to gloss over apparent contradictions. Local knowledge is, of course, invaluable, and if used tactfully can lead to some humorous 'Fortunes'. The word 'tact' is perhaps the most important thing to remember. You are doing this for fun – not to upset people.

Card Fortune Telling

There are endless ways of telling 'fortunes' by cards. As with *Fortune Dice*, a fertile imagination, a little local knowledge, and an ability to explain away very glibly apparent contradictions is essential if the Fortune Teller is going to be a success.

Here is one simple method; the 'key' should be memorized if possible to add authenticity. Take a single pack of cards and discard all below the eight in each suit. Ace is high. The one who desires to know her fortune shuffles and cuts the remaining cards and hands them to the Fortune Teller, who deals them into two heaps, dealing a card to each pile in turn. The curious one is then given the opportunity of selecting one of the two piles each of which consists of fourteen cards.

The dealer than fans out face downwards the fourteen cards and asks the fortune seeker to take away four cards, leaving ten still in his hands. The four cards which have been removed are then discarded, and the ten remaining cards are laid out on the table in line, face upwards.

It is from these ten cards that the Fortune Teller has to work. A key is given below.

General Indications. The Fortune Teller glances at the cards and notes if there are more of one particular suit than the others, e.g. if there were five Hearts, two Clubs, one Spade, and two Diamonds, Hearts would be the dominant suit, and stress would be laid on this.

The significance of the suits are these:

HEARTS   This is the Love Suit. If this is dominant, then love matters are considered of most importance.

DIAMONDS   These concern domestic and business relations.

SPADES   These concern bad luck. (Don't overstress this.)

CLUBS   The happiness or good luck cards.

Having given a general picture of the future from the whole of the ten cards, each card in turn is considered, and a meaning is attached to each. Here are some notes for guidance and from which a connected and reasonably coherent fortune must be told.

HEARTS

ACE   Marriage affairs, important news, general happiness.

KING   A blond man of some importance to business or love affairs. He can be tall or short, fat or thin – and wealthy.

QUEEN   A blonde woman who is destined to play an important part in the domestic life. Can be young or elderly. (Blonde can also mean 'white-haired'.)

JACK   A Don Juan (to teenagers a 'wolf') who is on the prowl. If handled correctly may be a valuable friend.

TEN   The affairs of the heart or home will flourish even though differences may temporarily upset things.

NINE   New people will be met who will bring about changes in your life. Holidays are involved.

EIGHT   The affection of younger people is going to be of some importance. Patience and tolerance will lead to mutual love and trust.

DIAMONDS

ACE   Financial good fortune, a present, an important letter about money. You are going to be lucky.

KING   A ginger-haired man is due to be of some importance in your life. His influence is almost certain to be good if not at first apparent.

QUEEN   The auburn-haired girl. A good business woman or home manager; she will come into your life with considerable effect.

JACK   A young man of wealth whose basic good character may not at first be apparent.

TEN   This is concerned with rings, holidays, or visits to strange places. You may be concerned in a change of occupation or home. Don't rush about, have second thoughts and then decide.

NINE   You will overcome business or domestic obstacles after a struggle. Keep on persevering.

EIGHT   Watch out for flatterers, particularly in your business. They may ultimately cause trouble if you do not take steps to prevent it.

SPADES

ACE   You are liable to have a short spell of bad luck, but there is always a silver lining. Don't take affairs of the heart too seriously.

KING   A dark man is going to mean quite a lot to you in your private or business life. His 'bark' is much worse than his 'bite'.

QUEEN   The dark-haired woman of good looks and good figure will play an important part in your life after mid-summer. Letters and photographs are involved.

JACK   A young man of stirling worth will be of importance to your career. Don't be put off by first impressions.

TEN   A change of job or residence is involved either for you or for someone you know very well indeed. Your help and advice may be needed.

NINE   Do not be over-concerned with the lighter side of life. Concentrate on your present job in hand or the career you have planned.

EIGHT   Music, art, and literature are going to be of significance to you in the near future. The music may mean romance.

CLUBS

ACE   You are indeed in luck, and things are going to happen very soon. Your great desire will soon be satisfied.

KING   This dark-haired man is connected with music. If you haven't met him yet you soon will and you will fall under his good influence.

QUEEN   Beware of this dark lady. She may cause considerable upset in your life. If you handle her the right way, however, the future may turn out well.

JACK   A good man, a little dull and staid at first sight, but a staunch ally on whom you can place considerable reliance.

TEN   A visit to a hospital or a doctor is possible. Do not worry unduly, things will turn out quite well. There is also some talk about an engagement which will be of interest to you.

NINE   Do not be disturbed by gossip or criticism. If you are convinced your actions are right go ahead as you have planned.

EIGHT   Happiness is your ultimate destiny.

One final essential for a party Fortune Teller. Try to make all your 'clients' feel that you really know a lot more than you have disclosed – but that nevertheless you have told them quite a lot – and in fact you have confirmed what they already feel to be true.

The Wheel of Fortune (Teenagers upwards. Indoors)

This is a simple wheel game which can be constructed with little trouble before the party. Obtain a large sheet of white paper and draw on it in ink a large circle, not less than eighteen to twenty-four inches in diameter. Divide this circle up into a convenient number of segments (thirty-two is a convenient number) and write in each segment forecasts or predictions such as are given above in *Card Fortune Telling*. The circle can now be pinned to a square piece of wood or hardboard and a thin wooden or thick cardboard pointer fixed in position to make *The Wheel of Fortune* ready to use (Fig 81).

The wheel can be used on a table or on the floor with the Fortune Teller squatting cross-legged beside it in eastern fashion. (Some sun-tan make-up and a towel-turban can add to the effect.)

The one seeking to know his fortune is allowed to spin the

pointer five or seven times, and the appropriate remarks are read off the dial.

As an alternative, and to add mystery, the predictions need not be written on the wheel, but numbers only. The Fortune Teller can then have a chart or 'key' from which he can derive the answers.

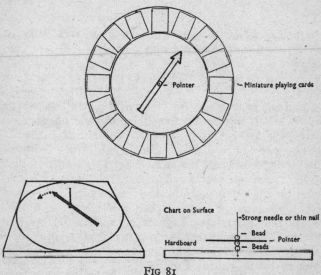

FIG 81

A second alternative is to have playing card symbols drawn in each segment, or even to have a somewhat larger wheel, round the perimeter of which are pasted the miniature playing cards which can be obtained quite cheaply from stationers or multiple stores.

A third alternative is to paint in mock Chinese or Arabic characters – each of which is given on the key with an appropriate prediction. These, however, will be more difficult to memorize.

SECTION TWENTY-TWO

CARD, DICE, AND DART GAMES

In this section the more common games, such as Whist, Bridge, Nap, and Poker, are not included, as they are so well known.

Newmarket

This is a game which can be played by both children and adults and is suitable for from three to eight players. It is extremely useful as a time passer for wet days on holidays.

Two packs of cards are required, though from the second pack only four cards, an Ace, King, Queen, and Jack of different suits are required. These are the 'horses'. In addition, each player requires a supply of counters (say, twenty each), which can be beans, or peas, or matches.

The four horses are placed slightly apart in the centre of the table. Each player then 'backs' a horse by placing a counter on any one of the four cards, and in addition places another counter in the centre of the table. This forms the 'kitty', which is taken by the winner.

The full pack of cards is shuffled and then dealt out with a hand to each of the players plus an additional one, i.e. if there are four players, five hands are dealt. It does not matter that some of the hands contain different numbers of cards. The dealer is permitted to look at the extra hand, and may, if he so wishes, change it for the one he has dealt to himself. If he chooses not to do this, he can 'sell it' to the highest bidder, who then takes the spare hand and discards his own.

The player immediately on the dealer's left then opens the game by placing face upwards on the table a card from any suit, providing it is the lowest of that suit he is holding. Suppose it to be the seven of diamonds. Whoever holds the eight of diamonds then places that card down on the table, face upwards in front of him. This continues until the ace is placed down, when whoever puts it down can then start a new suit by playing the lowest card of that suit that he holds. If during the playing out of a suit a player places down a card which is the same as one of the horses in the centre he takes from the horse any counters which may have been placed on it.

It will happen, however, that some suits are never completed, because one or more of the cards are in the extra hand which has been dealt. In such a case a 'stop' is reached and whoever played the last card must then change suits and play the lowest card of any other suit he chooses from his hand.

If he does not possess cards from another suit the player on his left then has the opportunity of continuing play.

The aims of the game are two-fold, to try to get rid of a horse and collect the counters from the centre card and to get rid of all the cards in your hand. The first one to do so then takes all the counters in the 'kitty', and the game starts again by players rebacking a horse and placing another counter in the kitty. Any horses which have not been played retain the counters on them ready for the next round.

Slap Jack (8 plus onwards)

This is an amusing game, particularly for children between the ages of eight and fourteen. It can be played by any number, but one pack of cards per four or five players is advisable. Where possible it should be played on a round table. When the cards are dealt out each player stacks them in a neat pile, face downwards in front of him but slightly to his left. Each player places his right elbow on the table with his forearm vertical; the elbow should be so placed that when the forearm is dropped the right hand will strike the centre of the table.

Starting with the player next to the dealer, each one in turn takes a card from the top of his pile and places it face upwards in the centre of the table. When a Jack appears, however, everyone in the game slaps his *right* hand down on it.

The one whose hand is actually on the card (i.e. the bottom hand) takes all the cards that are in the centre and adds them to his own pile.

The player who obtains all the cards, or the most after a previously determined time, is the winner.

Old Maid

This is a card game for players of all ages, but very suitable for children. From a full pack of cards one Queen is removed. The remaining fifty-one cards are then dealt out. Some of the hands will be uneven, but this does not matter. Each player then inspects his own hand and places on the table any 'pairs' that he may have, e.g. two Sevens, two Aces, etc. If a player has three cards the same, only two of them are discarded, but if he has four, all are discarded, as they make two pairs.

When this has been done, the dealer holds out his cards (fanned out) face downwards to the next player on his left, who takes one, without, of course, knowing what it is. If it matches one in his hand he is lucky and places another pair down on the table. The third player then draws a card from the second player, the fourth from the third, and so on round and round the table. Ultimately all the cards will have been discarded in pairs, except one Queen, which cannot be made into a pair, because one Queen has been removed from the pack at the beginning of the game.

The unfortunate player holding this odd Queen becomes the 'Old Maid'.

The game is then restarted and continues for as long as desired, the winner being the one who has been the Old Maid the least number of times.

Farmyards (8 plus to any age. Particularly for teenagers)

This game, ideal for four to eight people, can become really hilarious. One pack of cards per four players is advisable. Each player is given the name of an animal with a call reasonably easy to imitate, such as a cat, dog, duck, hen, turkey, cow, horse, donkey, or sheep.

The cards are then dealt out to the players, each one stacking them in a neat pile face downwards without looking at them.

The player on the dealer's left starts the game by lifting the top card from his pile and placing it *face upwards* near to his original pile. Each player in turn does the same. When a card is turned up that 'pairs' any of the other cards showing, each of the two players concerned must immediately make the noise of the animal represented *by the other*. For example, suppose the 'cow' turns up a similar card to the one showing in front of the 'duck', the cow must immediately quack and the duck must moo. Whichever of the two makes the correct call first passes all his face-upward cards to the other. This process continues until one of the players manages to get rid of all his cards. He is then the winner.

During the turning over, when any player has turned all his original pile over, he merely takes the face-upward cards, reverses them, and starts again.

Fish (Any age from 6 upwards)

A memory game sometimes known as '*Concentration*' or '*Pelmanism*'. It is suitable for all ages from six upwards, and can be played by two or more players.

All the cards in a pack are shuffled and then laid out fairly neatly face downwards on the table. The first player then turns face upwards any two cards. If they are a pair, e.g. two Fives or two Queens, he removes them and places them in front of him on the table. He then turns two more over. If they are not a pair he turns them face downwards again.

The other players repeat this process. After the first few players have had a turn the positions of certain cards will be known, and those who remember them are most certain to collect the greatest number of cards.

When all the cards have been picked up the player with the most is the winner.

With larger numbers, two packs of cards can be used.

Cheats (Any age from 8 upwards)

An amusing card game requiring no skill except perhaps the ability to keep a straight face. Suitable for four to eight players. One pack of cards is required for every four players.

The cards are dealt out and the first player to the left of the dealer who holds an Ace places it face downwards on the table, calling out 'One' as he does so. The next player then places a card face downwards, calling out 'Two.' If he does not actually hold a 'two' he still places a card down and still calls out 'Two.' The next player does the same calling out 'Three.' If, however, at any time another player thinks that someone is cheating by calling out a number and placing down a card of a different number he can challenge the player concerned by calling out 'Cheat.' The one who is accused must then turn up his card. If the accusation is true, all the players give him one of their cards; if it is false the accused gives one of his cards to the accuser. The winner of the game is the player who first gets rid of all his cards.

Donkey

This card game is for all ages, but particularly suitable for children at a party as a relief from more hectic chasing-about games. Ideally it is played by thirteen players, as each one has four cards only. If twelve players only are available, then four cards of the same kind, e.g. four 'twos', are removed; for eleven players, all the twos and threes are taken out, and so on. The cards are dealt one at a time to the players until each has four. They then hold these in their hands ready to start. When the dealer says 'go' all the players simultaneously take a card from their hand and pass it face downwards to the next one on their left. This continues quickly and silently, each player discarding cards he doesn't require and retaining those he does *in order to obtain four of the same kind*, i.e. four Kings, four Queens, etc. The moment a player obtains four of a kind, he places them quietly and unobtrusively face downwards on the table and silently folds his arms. As soon as any other player sees this happen, he immediately does likewise. The last player to do this, i.e. the least observant at that moment, is the loser and becomes 'D', the first letter of Donkey. If the same player loses a second time, he becomes 'DO'. The game continues until one person has lost six times, when, of course, he will have become DONKEY. The one who has the least number of letters is the winner.

DICE GAMES

Some simple time-passing games can be played with dice. If actual dice are not available, improvised ones can easily be made by spotting-in sugar lumps from one to six.

Going to Boston (6 plus upwards)

This is an American game requiring three dice which can be played by any number of players, though three or four are most suitable.

The three dice are all rolled at once. (An egg-cup makes a good shaker.) The one with the largest number showing is left on the table. The two remaining dice are then shaken and rolled, and again the one with the larger number is left on the table. The third dice is then rolled and the total of the three dice is taken. That is the score of the first player.

Each player repeats this process, and the one with the highest score is the winner of the round. If two or more players have an equal number they repeat their throws until a winner is found. A given number of rounds are played, and the one who has the most wins is the winner of the whole game.

Vingt-et-un or Twenty-one (Teenagers upwards)

This is a game for any number of players, requiring one dice, and a number of matches or counters for each player.

The game starts by all the players putting one counter into the 'kitty' or pool. Each player in turn shakes and rolls the dice as many times as he wishes, trying to get a total of twenty-one or as near as possible. If he goes above twenty-one he 'busts' and is out of the game.

The player with twenty-one or the nearest to it takes all the counters in the kitty. If two or more players make identical scores they can either play off or share the kitty.

The important thing in the game is deciding when and when not to have another throw. If, for instance, the first four throws resulted in a 6, 3, 4, and 5, giving a total of eighteen, it would probably be better to 'stick' rather than risk another throw, for a 4, 5, or 6 would cause the player to bust. If, on the other hand, the first four throws were 3, 4, 6, and 2, giving a total of fifteen, another throw at least should be taken, for if the maximum of 6 is thrown, a total of twenty-one is reached.

The game can continue for a stated number of rounds or for a given time. The winner of the whole game is obvious; he is the one in possession of the greatest number of counters!

Round the Clock (10 plus upwards)

This is a game for three or four players, requiring two dice. Each player shakes and throws in turn, endeavouring to 'go round the clock' from one to twelve in sequence. Up to six the score on either of the dice can count, or the total showing on the two of them, e.g. if a 1 and a 5 are first thrown, the player can count the 1 only. He then requires a 2. This can be obtained either by throwing a 2 and any other number, or by throwing the two dice, each showing a 1. Similarly, three can be a combination of 2 and 1, four a combination of 2 and 2, or 3 and 1.

From six onwards, the score on both dice must, of course, be used. The player who first reaches twelve is the winner.

DARTBOARD GAMES

As alternatives to the straightforward game of darts try the following little games and competitions. They can be used at a party or to provide amusement on a wet afternoon.

Short Throw Bull's-eye

Each competitor is allowed to throw three darts three times at the 'bull' from a distance of three feet. The throw must be normal in every way. The one who scores the greatest number of 'bulls' is the winner. (No! they don't all get nine!)

As a variation try doing the same thing aiming for double or treble twenty.

Ten-dart Century

This is another simple competition. Each player throws ten darts consecutively and tries to get 100 with the ten (average of ten). Darts which fall out of the board do not score but count as one of the ten.

If a dart goes outside the wire or completely misses the board, whatever number has been scored is automatically wiped out and the player is disqualified for that round.

Ten-dart Low

Ten darts are used again by each player, but the object this time is to score as few as possible with the ten. All other rules are as for *Ten-dart Century*.

Ten-dart High

A similar game to *Ten-dart Low*, except that one tries to get the highest possible score. In this game, darts which go outside the wire or off the board count as a throw but do not disqualify.

Round the Board

Each player has three darts and takes turns in throwing. The object is to throw a dart into each number moving clockwise round the board. One cannot move on until the first number is obtained. A successful throw entitles the player to attempt the next space, e.g. a player starts, aiming for the twenty: his first two darts miss, but with his third he gets it. He is now allowed to go on throwing. If he misses the 'one' with his three darts, the next player begins his throw. If he misses the 'one' with his first dart, gets it with his second, and then misses the next number with his third dart, he is not then allowed to go on but must give way to the next player. The game is won by the player who first goes all round the board and finishes with a 'bull'.

Round the Clock

The rules of this game are similar to those of *Round the Board*, except that each player starts by trying to get the 'one' first and then all the other numbers in sequence, i.e. 2, 3, 4, 5, etc., up to 20, and finally finishing with the 'bull'.

SECTION TWENTY-THREE
GAMES FOR OLD PEOPLE

Though at a party where the guests are of all ages, most of the old people will, quite often, be content to watch the 'carryings on' of the 'youngsters', nevertheless it is an excellent thing to include in your programme some games in which everyone can join so that the old people can feel that they are actually *in* the party and not merely spectators on the sideline.

One has sometimes to be tactfully firm to prevent old people joining in games which are not really suitable for them, such as energetic races and competitions. Inevitably, there is the old gentleman who, in the excitement of the occasion, imagines that he is still as fit and agile as he was twenty years or more ago, and in attempting to do some activity which is too strenuous injures himself or even collapses.

If there is any desire or demand for it, a short whist drive, a game of bridge, or a card game such as *Newmarket* can always be organized in another room while the young people play more energetic games or dance.

On the following pages are given details of a few games of the types particularly suitable for old people.

Finally, at the end of this chapter are listed the titles of thirty-six further suitable games to be found in other chapters of this book. Page references are given.

Bingo or Housey-Housey or Lotto

This game is now too well known to merit description. Sets, complete with rules, can be bought over a wide range of prices from local toyshops. The 'caller' should regulate his speed of calling to suit the slowest of his players.

Dice Derby

A simple but effective race game for the floor or table which can be made quite cheaply from a strip of American cloth or even white cartridge paper.

For the table game your 'Race Course' should be slightly less than the length of the table and from twelve to eighteen inches wide.

Having cut your strip of cloth (or paper) mark it out as shown in Fig 82 below. Only five lanes are shown, but these

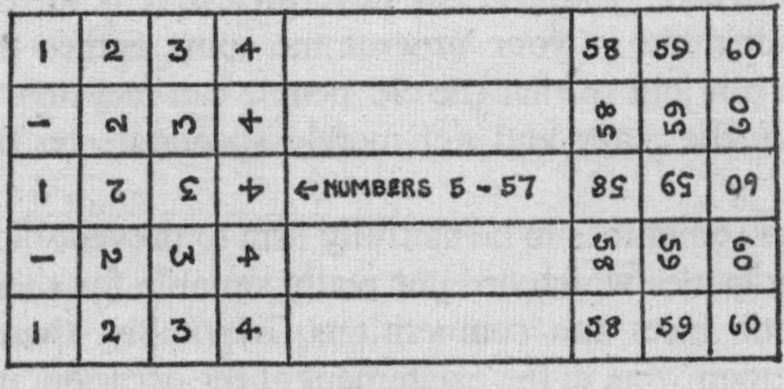

1	2	3	4				58	59	60
1	2	3	4				58	59	60
1	2	3	4	← NUMBERS 5 – 57			58	59	60
1	2	3	4				58	59	60
1	2	3	4				58	59	60

FIG 82

can be as many as desired. Similarly, though only sixty spaces are indicated, these also can be increased to any convenient number. Note that the numbers are marked in such a way that all the people sitting round a table or in a circle round a 'course' on the floor will be able to see the numbered squares without any difficulty.

A course to be used on the floor can and should be larger than one for table use.

'Horses', small plastic ones from toyshops, then race down the course, each one moving forward according to the number thrown on a dice, either by an independent 'Clerk of the Course' or by the 'owner'. If desired, 'penalties' and 'obstacles' can be introduced and rules such as 'No horse can start until a six has been thrown', and so on.

An improvised game such as this can give considerable pleasure. Though I have called it 'Dice Derby', it can be designated 'Silverwood', 'Brands Hatch', 'T.T. Race',

'Boat Race', 'Yacht Race', or 'Marathon', etc., according to the figures or symbols used on the course.

Tiddleywink Golf

A game for pairs or foursomes of any age from about eight years of age and upwards. It is particularly suitable for small numbers of older people. Each player requires a large tiddleywink and a small one. A suitable 'course' is laid out on the floor, 'holes' consisting of receptacles of varying sizes such as an egg-cup, a pudding basin, a bowler hat, a saucer, an empty ice-cream carton, and so on. Not only should the diameters of the holes be of varying sizes but also their heights from the ground. The distances between each hole should also be of various lengths. Obstacles to represent 'bunkers' can also be placed along the 'fairways'; these can be devised from books, dusters, and even a shallow plate containing water. (If such a hazard is introduced, place it on a waterproof sheet.)

The game can be played between pairs on a 'stroke' or 'hole' basis and even a championship can be arranged on a knock-out basis.

Cats Out of the Bag

A team game particularly suitable for small numbers of old people, though it can well be played by guests of any age. Let us assume that there are twelve players divided into two teams of six.

In a cloth bag, small sack, or even a strong brown-paper bag, put twelve pairs of identical objects. Such objects might well be: two buttons, two safety-pins (fastened), two rubbers, two corks, two empty matchboxes, a pair of cuff links, two large paper-clips, two unsharpened pencils, two thimbles, two table-tennis balls, two toothbrushes and two old torch batteries. (No pointed or sharp objects should be used.)

On the word 'Go', the first players from each team go to the bag and try to find by 'feel' alone (they must not look into the bag) two identical objects. As soon as he or she has acquired two such objects, he goes back to his team, touches the second

261

player who goes to the bag and tries in turn to find a pair of objects.

The winning team is the one, all of whose members have got a pair of objects first.

Find the Girls

A singing game which is also quite suitable for younger people. Two sides are picked and a coin is tossed to decide which one starts. The first team starts by singing a song, old or new, the title of which contains the name of a girl, e.g. 'Sweet Rosie O'Grady'. While they are singing, the second side decide what they are going to sing, say, 'Lily of Laguna'. The moment the first side have completed their song, the second side must begin.

The contest goes on until one of the sides cannot think of a song which has not already been sung.

It is useful, if one member of the side acts as a leader, for him to decide which song his side will sing from the suggestions whispered to him or her by his members.

Here are some suggested songs – both old and new:

Sweet Rosie O'Grady	Mary of Argyle
Lily of Laguna	Alice Blue Gown
Ramona	Don't Bring Lulu
Daisy	I Want to Cling to Ivy
Louise	Charlie Girl
Margie	Jeannie
Dinah	Fanlight Fanny
Who is Sylvia?	Clementine
Come into the Garden, Maud	Sally
Ida	Violetta
Georgie Girl	Second-hand Rose
Pamela	Polly Perkins
A girl like Nina	Sweet Adeline

Pile of Matches

A time-passer for groups of four or five players requiring one small-necked empty bottle and ten (or less) matches per player.

Each player in turn places a match on the mouth of the bottle. If, in trying to add a match, any player knocks off any matches he pays a penny (or a counter) into a jackpot on the table and adds the matches to those he already has.

The player who first successfully gets rid of all his matches wins the contest and takes the jackpot.

If a number of groups are playing, the winners of each group make a final pool to decide the overall winner of the game.

Games for Old People

SECTION TWENTY-FOUR

GAMES FOR MOTOR-CAR JOURNEYS

———————

Long car journeys can be boring to adults and absolute purgatory for children. When the children have exhausted their reading and drawing material, or in between times, try some of the following time-passers.

Sentence Making

Each player in turn notes the first two car registration letters seen and tries to make up a sentence using the letters as the initial letters of the words, e.g. suppose the first two cars seen were 101CMP and ASQ392. A sentence has to be made with words commencing with C, M, P, A, S, and Q, such as 'Charlie meets Pat and salutes quickly.' It doesn't matter how stupid or silly the sentence is, so long as it is a sentence, e.g. with the registration letters AMX and ABV, one could say, 'A magic xylophone almost bashed Violet.'

Allow one or two minutes for a sentence to be made. If one is made in the time, one point is scored. The first player to get eleven or fifteen points is the winner.

Collecting Places

A car handbook is required and a piece of paper and a pencil for each player. Players take passing cars in turn and write down the registration letters. These are looked up in the handbook, and the name of the town or county is written alongside them.

The first player to collect ten, fifteen, or twenty different towns or counties is the winner.

Collecting Colours

Any colour (except black and white) is chosen. The players then look out for cars of the chosen colour, and immediately they see one, they call out. The first one to call out scores a point; if the calls are made simultaneously no point at all is scored. The first player to score twenty wins the game. It is better to name colours which are neither common nor rare, for in the first case a game will finish too soon, and in the second case it might never finish at all, or the children will get bored. Two colours, such as cream and blue, or cream and salmon can be used as alternatives to single colours.

Collecting Animals

Two players or more, each with a pencil and paper, are required for this game. If two are playing, one takes the near side of the road, the other the off side. If more than two are playing, divide into two teams.

The object is to spot animals which score points of the value shown below:

Ordinary cats 1 point each	Black sheep 5 points each
Black cats 5 points each	Ordinary cows 1 point each
Ordinary dogs 1 point each	Black cows 5 points each
Black dogs 5 points each	Ordinary horses 1 point each
Ordinary sheep 1 point each	Black horses 5 points each

All other animals 1 point each except monkeys 10 points, elephants 20 points, giraffes 30 points, lions 50 points, and tigers 60 points.

On ninety-nine car trips out of a hundred no one will score more than 10 points at any one time – but on the hundredth trip you *may* pass a circus!

The first player or team to score 100 points wins the game.

Collecting Cars

This game is similar to *Collecting Colours*, except that the players try to spot cars of a named make, e.g. ten Ford Consuls, ten Austins, ten Morris Minors, and so on.

Car Guessing

As a car approaches along the road, each player tries to guess its make. If two players guess the same, the one who speaks first collects a point (if the guess is correct). If they call out simultaneously no point is scored. No points are scored if the guess is made as or after the car actually passes.

Round the Clock

Players take turns in looking at car numbers on the road, i.e. the first player takes the first car that passes, the second takes the second car, and so on. The object is to collect numbers from one to twelve in the correct order. Suppose the first car that passes has a number, 3179. The first player then counts '1' because the number 3179 has a '1' in it.

The second player then has to wait for a car which passes, when it is his turn, which also has a '1' in it. The game continues until someone has got to '12' – around the clock.

A car number 1307 would not count as a '10', but 1037, or 3510 would. Similarly, 2113 would count as '11' but not 1213 because the two '1's are separated.

Score Fifty Thousand

Each player requires a pencil and a piece of paper. Again, players take cars in turn as they pass. The numbers on the registration plates are written on the papers, and the first player to reach a score of fifty thousand or more is the winner.

The number to be scored can be changed, if so desired, but should not be less than twenty thousand, as three older cars with four-figure numbers could easily end the game too soon.

Guess the Distance

An object, such as a hill, or church, or village, on the road ahead is selected, and immediately those playing try to guess the distance. This is checked from the speedometer, and the one with the nearest guess is the winner.

Blind Man's Guess

Again some object on the road ahead is selected. Players then close their eyes, and when they think the object has been reached they call 'now' and open their eyes. The one nearest the object scores a point. The player who first gets five points is the winner.

Make the Alphabet

This time-passer is similar in principle to *Round the Clock*, except that instead of trying to get numbers in order, players, taking cars in turn, try to obtain the letters of the alphabet in their correct order.

More than one letter, providing they are in correct alphabetical order on the registration plate, can be scored by a player, e.g. suppose a car had registration letters AMY, then 'A' only would be scored. If the next car had BYC, 'B' only would be counted, but if the letters were BCY, then 'B' and 'C' would both be added to the 'A'.

Activities for Older Children and Adults

As an occasional relief to the monotony of a long journey, older children can be given time-passing tasks such as:

(1) Working out the average speed of the car at the end of each hour.

(2) Making a route mileage chart. As each place on the journey is reached, it is written down along with the number of miles from the previous place.

(3) Naming from a map each river that is crossed on certain sections of the journey.

Small sweepstakes can also be organized on such things as estimating the mileage that will be covered in the next hour, or estimating the time at which a certain town or village will be reached. In events such as these, the driver is, of course, excluded.

Licence Plate Words (Any age)

With the advent of three-letter registration marks a number of three-letter words have now been made such as EMU, FAR, POT, COW, GUM, and so on. The children take a car in turn, either approaching or passing, and score one point for every word found. If desired, further interest can be added by scoring double points for animals' names.

Another alternative is to score points if the registration letters of two successive cars can be made into a word, such as JUM and PER to give JUMPER, or COW and BOY to make COWBOY. The words need not be all six-letter ones, of course, HU and MP would give HUMP or MA and NY would give MANY. Similarly, a single-letter plus a two- or three-letter registration can give a variety of words. Some examples are T and EA to give TEA, P and AT giving PAT or L and AMP for LAMP.

These games can be competitive over a short period of, say, half an hour or can be played on the length-of-the-journey basis, the words being written down in small notebooks or on postcards and the points totalled at the journey's end.

SECTION TWENTY-FIVE
BEACH AND PICNIC GAMES

———

While one normally associates parties with houses, many of the most successful 'get-togethers' occur during our limited summer days on the beach. Here are some suggestions for games which can be played immediately after a swim (to get warm), when the sun goes in or when that cold breeze ('you always get it about this time, my dear') whistles across the beach or when the children have started to throw sand at each other and it is dropping mainly in the tea and sandwiches.

AFTER-SWIM GAMES (FOR PAIRS)

In spite of their belligerent titles these games are quite suitable for both sexes.

Knee Boxing

Skip about lightly and try to tap your partner's knees with your flat hands. He, of course, is trying to do exactly the same to you.

Chinese Boxing

Partners face each other holding up both arms. Each then grasps the other's *left wrist* with his own *right hand*. This leaves the *left hand* free. With this free hand each tries to tap the other on top of the head without having his own tapped in a similar manner.

Advantage Wrestle

All you have to do in this game is to try to get *behind* your partner, grasp him round his waist, and lift him off the ground

– making certain that he does not succeed in doing exactly the same to you.

Danish Wrestling

Opponents stand facing each other, right foot touching right foot, each grasping the other's right hand. Now, by pulling, pushing, or twisting, each one tries to make the other move his right foot from position. The left foot can be moved about quite freely. After a little while, change hands and feet – left foot to left foot, left hand grasping left hand.

Foot Fencing

Again partners stand facing each other. Moving about very lightly each one tries to touch the other's feet with his toes. The touch must be as light as possible; stamping, hacking, and kicking should *definitely* be discouraged.

Sawing Wood

Partners stand close to each other with the left leg forwards, hands clasped, one arm straight, the other bent. A sawing-like action is then done. It is advisable to start slowly and work up to a good fast rhythm with the trunk twisting round as much as possible.

Duck Fighting

Short doses of this activity are recommended, otherwise the knees will ache too much. Face your partner in the knees-full-bend position with the arms forward. Now by hopping about quite freely on both feet try to make your partner fall over or touch the sand with his hands. You can do this by slapping his hands with your own, or making him miss when he tries to do the same to you.

Elbow Tug-of-war (Any age)

Draw three straight lines on the sand about ten to fifteen feet apart. Partners stand on the centre line and link their right or left arms at the elbows. Each then tries to tug the other backwards to his rear line. Change elbows and repeat.

Coffee Grinding (Any age)

Partners face each other, both with arms raised midway upwards. They grasp each other's hands. Keeping their hands firmly clasped, they turn under their hands until standing back to back. They continue the turning movement until they are back to their starting position.

They then try to do this complete movement for as long as, and as fast as, they possibly can.

Hopping Tug-of-war (6 and upwards)

Partners face each other grasping hands and standing on one foot. They then try to tug each other backwards over a pre-arranged distance. Draw three lines as in *Elbow Tug-of-war*.

Hopping Neck Wrestle (8 and upwards)

More suitable for boys. Partners stand on one foot and clasp each other round the neck with both hands. By pulling, pushing, tugging, and twisting, each tries to make the other put his raised foot to the ground. Change feet and repeat the activity.

Lift the Jelly Fish (6 and upwards)

Partners should preferably be about the same size and weight. One lies on the dry sand completely relaxed. His partner then tries to pick him up and carry him a short distance of, say, ten yards. If the lying partner remains perfectly limp and does not assist in any way, the standing partner will find that lifting him is a most difficult operation indeed.

Lifting the Sack or Weighing Salt (8 and upwards)

Partners of about equal size and weight stand back to back and link elbows tightly. First one and then the other bends forward and lifts his partner off the ground. The movement must be made rhythmical to get the most benefit from it.

Obstinate Calf (6 and upwards)

Partners stand facing each other. One half-crouches, half-kneels, facing the other and looking up, i.e. the head must be kept well pressed back. The standing partner clasps the kneeling one round the back of the neck with both hands then tries to pull him forwards. The 'calf' resists and tries to move backwards.

Obstinate Wheelbarrow (6 and upwards)

Partners take up a 'wheelbarrow' position. The standing partner tries to push the wheelbarrow forwards; the wheelbarrow, however, is prepared to go in any direction but forwards, and avoids this by turning, twisting, and wriggling.

Bull Fight (8 and upwards)

Definitely a boy's activity. Partners face each other on hands and knees. Each then tucks his head under the other's left shoulder and tries to push his opponent backwards along the sand.

ACTIVITIES FOR THREES AND FOURS

Break-out (6 and upwards)

This is an energetic game for four or more. Three players join hands to make a circle, the fourth stands inside the circle. On the word 'Go', the centre player tries to break out of the circle, the other three doing their utmost to prevent this happening. Each player should have a turn inside the circle.

One Against Three (6 and upwards)

Four players. Three join hands to make a circle. The fourth stands outside the circle and indicates one of the circle players that he will try to touch. The circle players try to prevent this happening by spinning round. The outside player must run round the circle to try to make his touch. Each player should have a turn outside the circle to save anyone becoming too exhausted.

Poison (6 and upwards)

Four or more players. A circle of about three feet diameter is drawn, or a towel is placed on the sand. The players join hands in a circle round it. Then by pulling, pushing, and tugging, each player tries to make someone else step into the circle or on to the towel without doing so himself.

King of the Ring (8 and upwards)

This game is more suitable for boys and men, though, no doubt, tomboys would more than hold their own.

A fairly large circle is drawn on the sand, inside which all the players stand. Then by pulling, pushing, dragging, heaving, and charging, each player tries to get someone to step outside the ring without doing so himself. The last person to remain in the circle becomes 'King of the Ring'.

Races and Relays (Any age)

There is an almost infinite variety of races and relays that can be devised for the beach. A number of such races are given in Sections 12, 16 and 17. Use these as they are, or adapt them to suit the occasion and location.

Immediately after a swim, 'all-in' races are more suitable than Relays, where players wait for a turn to perform. A simple race of the all-in type is:

Racing Against a Ball

Two lines are drawn about thirty to forty yards apart. The leader and all the players stand on one of the two lines. The leader then throws or rolls a small ball towards the other line, and all the players try to race it to the line. A fair amount of judgement is required on the part of the thrower, so that it is 'touch and go' as to whether the ball or one of the players wins the race.

Other suggestions for 'all-in' races are Hopping, Running

Backwards, Running on all Fours (Monkey Race), Wheel-barrow Races (Partners), Jumping off both Feet (Kangaroos).

GAMES FOR LARGER NUMBERS

The nine games given in this section require a minimum of marking and equipment; nothing more complicated than a large rubber ball and spades are required for any of them. Obvious and well-known games such as football and cricket have been omitted, the stress being placed on games which are suitable for both sexes and whose rules are so extremely simple that even young children can learn them in a few minutes.

Three Passes (8 to any age, boys or girls)

One ball, of any size, only is required; suitable for four to twelve players. Each player has a partner. The object of the game is for each pair to make three consecutive good passes between each other, e.g. Jack to Jill, Jill to Jack, Jack to Jill. Other players, of course, are trying to intercept the passes and get hold of the ball to make their own passes. The passes are made from hand to hand, but with boys only, foot passing can be substituted if desired.

The leader starts the game by throwing up the ball, and after any pair have made three passes the game stops for a moment. The leader restarts the game by again throwing up the ball. The first pair to make three passes five times are the winners.

In order to prevent the players scattering all over the beach, it is advisable to draw a rectangle on the sand about twenty yards long by ten yards wide and confine the game to that area.

Spade Ball (8 to any age)

This team game is for sides of five to eleven players, more if needs be, requiring one ball (a large rubber one if possible), and two spades or sticks.

A simple court about twenty yards by ten yards is marked

out as shown in Fig 83. Two circles, one at each end, are drawn; these should be about six feet in diameter. In the centre of each circle is stuck the spade or stick.

Note. If there are only five-a-side, the size of the court can be reduced to, say, fifteen yards by eight yards.

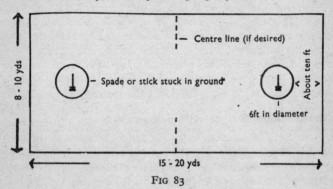

FIG 83

The object of the game is for each side to hit or knock down with the ball, the spade or stick in their opponents' circle.

Rules

(1) The game is started by the referee throwing up the ball between two players from opposing sides, standing in the centre of the court.

(2) All passes must be made by hand.

(3) There must be no running with the ball (as in Rugby). It must be passed immediately it is received.

(4) There is no kicking, tackling, pushing, or charging allowed. Rough play of any kind is forbidden.

(5) In each circle a goalkeeper stands. He is not allowed to leave this circle.

(6) No one except the goalkeeper is allowed to enter the circles.

(7) If a goalkeeper knocks down his own spade it counts as one point to the opposing side. All other goals, i.e. hits on the spade, count as two points.

(8) The game is played for an equal length of time each way.

(9) Play can take place behind as well as in front of the circles.

(10) Throw-ins, corners, etc., are as in Football or Hockey.

Any other rules can be made, if desired, but the fewer there are consistent with the safety of the players, the easier and more enjoyable will be the game for everyone.

Circular Rounders (8 to any age)

A simple form of rounders requiring either a small ball or an inflated beach ball. The court is marked out as shown in Fig 84.

Two equal teams are formed, and a coin is tossed to decide the fielding and striking sides. Each striking side then endeavours to score runs, the one making the greater number being the winner.

The fielding side Pitcher throws the ball between waist and shoulder height to the Striker, who hits it with his hand as far

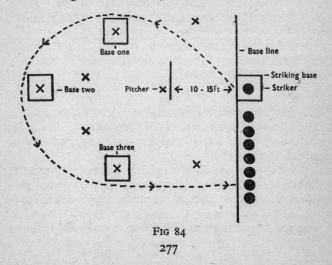

FIG 84

as possible. He then tries to run all round the bases and back to behind the base line (course shown by dotted line) before the fielding side have passed the ball to Base One, Base Two, Base Three, and back to the Pitcher.

If, when the Striker hits the ball, it is caught by a fielder, the Striker is out.

In this version of rounders no intermediate waiting at bases is allowed; once a ball has been struck by the Striker he must try to make a complete run.

The distances between bases will vary according to the age and capabilities of the players, but twenty-five to thirty feet is an average distance.

Arch-ball Rounders (8 to any age)

This game is a variation of *Circular Rounders*. The field of play is marked out in exactly the same way and the method of pitching, striking, and running is identical. The difference is in the method of fielding. Instead of the ball being thrown round the bases, it is returned immediately to the Pitcher. At the same time all the fielders rush to form a line behind him, and the ball is passed backwards, overhead, down the line.

If it is received by the last man in the team before the Striker reaches the safety of the Base Line, he is out.

An alternative method of passing the ball down the line is underneath the legs. In such a case the game would then become *Tunnel-ball Rounders*.

Ring the Stick (8 to any age)

Two sticks and one rubber or rope quoit are required. This team game, suitable for both boys and girls, is a variation of *Spade Ball* (see page 275).

A quoit is used instead of a ball, the object being to score points by throwing the quoit on to a stick held by a side's own goalkeeper, who is situated in the circle drawn in the opponents' half of the field.

The goalkeeper can assist by trying to catch the quoit on

his own stick; he does not merely have to stand there holding the stick rigid.

All the other rules are as for *Spade Ball*.

Bucket Ball (8 to any age)

Two small pails or buckets (the kind normally used on the beach) and a tennis ball or small rubber ball are required for this second variation of *Spade Ball*.

The object is to score goals by throwing the ball into a bucket held by your own goalkeeper, who is situated in the circle in your opponents' half of the field. As in *Ring the Stick*, the goalkeeper is allowed to take an active part in the game by trying to catch the ball in his bucket; he does not just have to stand passively holding the bucket, hoping that someone on his own side is an excellent shot. Again, all other rules are as for *Spade Ball*.

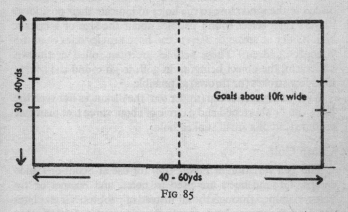

FIG 85

Hurly Burly (8 to any age)

A team game for from five to eleven players a side. One ball of any size and a simple court marked as shown in Fig 85 are all that is required. The goals can be marked with pebbles, sticks, or spades.

279

Equal sides are picked and a coin is tossed for 'ends'. The object of the game is to score goals. The ball can be propelled by any method; it can be thrown, kicked, dribbled, run with as in Rugby, or headed. If a person who is carrying the ball is touched by a player from the opposing side he must pass the ball immediately. There must be no rough play; charging, pushing, shoving, and tackling are not allowed.

Play should continue for about ten minutes each way.

In scoring, the ball can be thrown or kicked through the goals or it can be carried through in the hands of a player.

Pebble Golf

A pleasant 'after the meal' or 'before the swim' game which doesn't involve father in too much energy is *Pebble Golf*. A number of holes, say nine, about six inches across and six inches deep are dug on the beach at varying distances apart from thirty to one hundred yards. Small sandcastle flags are placed in the sand close to the holes to indicate their positions. Players then select round pebbles about the size of a cricket ball. (Older or stronger players can have heavier ones than the younger children.) These pebbles are then rolled or thrown underarm, the object being, as in golf, to go round the course in as few strokes (or throws) as possible.

With younger children (under ten) the distances between the holes can be shortened and a circle of about three feet diameter used instead of a small sunken hole.

Camp Golf

This is a variation of *Pebble Golf* for use at Scout or Guide camps. Groundsheets are used as holes, and enamel or tin plates skimmed through the air instead of pebbles. When plates are used the course immediately ahead must be clear of other players, and the missiles must be kept at below waist height.

Picnic Occupations

Most of the outdoor games mentioned in this book can be played on picnics both on the beach and in the country. In between these more strenuous activities, to give you a rest and the children a change, it is often a good thing to organize simple competitions in which the children go off and work on their own or with a partner.

A small prize, be it only a bar of chocolate or an extra bottle of lemonade, makes an additional incentive far beyond the actual value of the reward. Here are some suggestions for the beach and the country. A time and space limit should be set, otherwise you are liable to spend the rest of the day looking for wandering children.

BEACH COMPETITIONS

(1) Collect as many different kinds of seaweed as you can in half an hour.

(2) Collect as many different kinds of shells as you can.

(3) Collect as many different kinds of pebbles as you can.

(4) See who can find a pebble that looks most like a golf ball or a tennis ball.

(5) See who can collect three pebbles that look most like birds' eggs.

(6) See who can collect the most curious-looking pebble.

(7) See who can find the largest piece of wood.

(8) See who can collect the largest number of corks.

(9) See who can collect the largest number of limpet shells (or the biggest limpet shell).

(10) See which pair can make the biggest castle in half an hour.

(11) Build a sandcastle that looks like a real castle.

(12) Build a circular sand wall at the edge of the sea (when the tide is coming in) and see whose wall lasts the longest.

(13) Work in pairs or threes. Build a castle near the water's edge and stick a small flag on top of it. The one whose flag is the last to be knocked down by the sea is the winner. (This is sometimes known as 'Tide Fight'.)

(14) See who can build the best motor boat or motor car out of sand.

(15) See who can make the longest line of pebbles in fifteen minutes. Each pebble must touch the next.

(16) See who can make the largest number of sand pies in ten minutes.

(17) See who can dig the deepest hole in a quarter of an hour. (Work in pairs or threes.)

(18) See who can collect the largest number of crabs, shrimps, small fish, etc., in thirty minutes. This can be varied according to location, e.g. the biggest crab, the largest shrimp, the most starfish, etc.

(19) Collect as many feathers as you can in twenty minutes.

(20) Collect as many different kinds of flowers or grasses (where there are sandhills) as you can in half an hour.

COUNTRYSIDE OCCUPATIONS

(1) Collect as many different kinds of flowers as you can.

(2) See who can find the biggest leaf.

(3) Collect as many different kinds of leaves (or grasses) as you can in half an hour.

(4) Collect as many different blue (pink, red, yellow) flowers as you can.

(5) See how many birds' nests you can find. (Don't touch them.)

(6) Collect the biggest bunch of buttercups or daisies.

(7) Gather as many different kinds of berries as you can. (Warn them not to try to eat any of them – particularly Deadly Nightshade.)

(8) For young girls. See who can make the longest daisy chain in twenty minutes.

(9) See who can make the longest and neatest plait from rushes.

(10) Stalking and tracking games and competitions can also be organized; e.g. the 'scout' sits in the centre of an open space, the remainder disappear out of sight and then try to get as near to him as possible without being seen. Anyone who is spotted joins the scout and helps him to spot the others. At the end

of a specified time (quarter to half an hour) the scout shouts 'Time up' or blows a whistle. All those remaining unseen then stand up, or disclose themselves; the one who is nearest to the scout is the winner and becomes the scout for the next turn. Some of the more enthusiastic ones will try to camouflage themselves with grasses and leaves. This can be suggested at the beginning of the game.

SECTION TWENTY-SIX

BARBECUES

Though games are not normally played at barbecues, this type of party has become so popular in recent years that it was considered not inappropriate to include some suggestions on the running of such an occasion in a book of this nature.

Barbecues, which are American in origin, are basically outdoor picnics where the food is cooked on a special type of charcoal fire on the spot.

Obviously, the success or failure of a barbecue is largely dependent upon the weather and for this reason the period from June to September is the one most favoured. Even so, in a climate so fickle as that experienced in our islands, the organizer must be prepared to cancel or switch dates at almost a moment's notice. For similar reasons, barbecues may also have to be arranged at short notice. Perhaps one of the safest ways of going about arranging a barbecue is to fix a period of time, say a week during which you feel it will be domestically convenient to run such a function. Having settled on this period, then a close attention to the weather forecasts is indicated and if these show a reasonable chance of some fairly settled weather over a period of two or three days, then select the actual day and telephone your invitations.

It is realized, of course, that such a procedure is not always possible and that you may well have to plan several weeks ahead, and just hope that the day you have chosen will be the one fine one of an English summer!

The organization of a barbecue can be divided into two distinct parts: (1) The preparation of the barbecue – i.e. the actual cooking facility selection, and (2) the selection, preparation and cooking of the foods for and/or by the guests.

Preparation of the Barbecue

Cooking at a barbecue is generally done over a charcoal fire (which eliminates smoke and smuts) on a grill, but variations of this may be necessitated by individual conditions or circumstances.

A simple barbecue can be improvised from one or two biscuit tins (which have had holes punched in the sides for ventilation) with a cooker grid placed over the top of them for a grill. Even a hole in the ground (for the fire) with a grid supported over the top on bricks can serve as an efficient barbecue. On the other hand, if you intend to hold two or three such parties a year, it may well be worth your while to purchase a commercially-produced barbecue from one of the big stores. These can be obtained at prices suitable for every pocket. Many of them have the advantage of being easily portable.

Charcoal, which is essential for the fire, can be obtained from most large ironmongers' shops and many coal merchants in 14-lb bags. At the time of writing such a bag costs approximately 12s.

The lighting of charcoal is not quite so simple as lighting a coal fire, and it does not get really hot quite so quickly, so adequate time must be allowed for this on the evening of the barbecue. If you have, or can borrow, some bellows for creating a strong, concentrated draught, your task will be made both easier and quicker. A pump such as is used for inflating air-beds can also be used as bellows.

Though the charcoal can be ignited by pouring a little methylated spirit or lighter fuel on a few pieces and then placing more on top, this can be potentially dangerous. A far safer and more effective method is to use a few bars of solid methylated fuel, 'Meta', such as is commonly used for starting-off primus stoves. Break up three or four of the Meta bars in the bottom of the biscuit tin and loosely stack some of the charcoal over them. Ignite the bars and then as the charcoal begins to glow or get hot, gradually build up the fire. By night the fire will glow red, by day this will not be evident and the charcoal, when hot, will have a grey ashy appearance. Dependent on the amount of draught available will be the time for the fire to get hot enough for fairly quick grilling; a judicious use of the bellows at intervals will be found most effective. One of your guests will no doubt be delighted to act as the chief stoker and keep the fire going while you supervise the actual cooking arrangements.

For a fairly large charcoal fire to become hot enough for reasonably quick and effective cooking, three-quarters of an hour to an hour should be allowed on your time-table; on the other hand, a biscuit-tin fire can be got to the right heat in about fifteen to twenty minutes, so it might well be worth while to build up your fire to the size you require from biscuit-tin units, thus saving time, for with help, three units will still take only twenty minutes to reach cooking heat.

Before you actually start cooking, ensure that you have available items such as paper serviettes and your cooking implements. Long-handled toasting forks and large tongs are invaluable to save your hands from getting scorched or burned. A thick gardening glove or oven glove will also help to avoid discomfort.

Foods for Barbecues

The following items are suitable for barbecues: steaks, chops and cutlets, bacon, slices of gammon, hamburgers, large and small sausages, and chicken joints.

Kebabs which consist of small pieces of various foods such as sausages, onions, etc, cooked on long metal skewers are also popular.

Potatoes can be cooked in their jackets or alternatively they can be peeled and a hole scooped out in which a knob of butter and a small piece of cheese is placed. Each potato is then wrapped in metal foil and placed on the grill for cooking; onions can be treated in a similar manner.

Other popular items are corn-on-the-cob (wrapped in foil as above) and fruits such as apples and bananas; tomatoes, however, tend to go soft, drop through the grill and cause spluttering.

Fish can be expensive and need a fair amount of preparation; herrings, mackerel, and kippers will cause the least trouble.

Popular barbecue drinks are beer, cider, fruit juices, and fizzy orange and lemonade. Cardboard cups and beakers will save breakages and washing up, and can be burned after use.

CARD GAME SKILLS